T0385770

FIGURING
IT OUT

FIGURING IT OUT

SIXTY YEARS OF ANSWERING INVESTORS' MOST IMPORTANT QUESTIONS

CHARLES D. ELLIS

WILEY

Published by John Wiley & Sons, Inc., Hoboken, New Jersey.
Published simultaneously in Canada.

For general information on our other products and services or for technical support, please contact our Customer Care Department within the United States at (800) 762-2974, outside the United States at (317) 572-3993 or fax (317) 572-4002.

Wiley also publishes its books in a variety of electronic formats. Some content that appears in print may not be available in electronic formats. For more information about Wiley products, visit our web site at www.wiley.com.

Library of Congress Cataloging-in-Publication Data:

Names: Ellis, Charles D., author. | John Wiley & Sons, publisher.
Title: Figuring it out : sixty years of answering investors' most important
    questions / Charles D. Ellis.
Description: Hoboken, New Jersey : Wiley, [2022] | Includes index.
Identifiers: LCCN 2022015212 (print) | LCCN 2022015213 (ebook) | ISBN
    9781119898955 (cloth) | ISBN 9781119898979 (adobe pdf) | ISBN
    9781119898962 (epub)
Subjects: LCSH: Investments. | Portfolio management.
Classification: LCC HG4529.5 .E445 2022 (print) | LCC HG4529.5 (ebook) |
    DDC 332.6—dc23/eng/20220414
LC record available at https://lccn.loc.gov/2022015212
LC ebook record available at https://lccn.loc.gov/2022015213

Cover image(s): © GETTY IMAGES | CASSP
Cover design: PAUL McCARTHY

Printed and bound by CPI Group (UK) Ltd, Croydon, CR0 4YY
C9781119898955_120123

To Burt Malkiel, dear friend over many wonderful years as co-author,[1] co-director,[2] co-board member,[3] co-teacher,[4] co-advisor,[5] Dean,[6] and delightful source of understanding and wisdom. No one could be a better companion in striving to figure out the dynamic world of investing.

---

[1]*Elements of Investing.*
[2]Vanguard.
[3]Rebalance and Wealthfront.
[4]CFA workshop at Princeton.
[5]Pew Charitable Trusts.
[6]Yale School of Management.

Contents

Foreword   ix
Note on the Text   xi
Introduction   xiii

  1   The Changing Game   1
  2   The Loser's Game   35
  3   The Winners' Game   47
  4   The Winner's Game II   61
  5   The Rise and Fall of Performance Investing   73
  6   Seven Rules for More Innovative Portfolio Management
         in an Age of Discontinuity   89
  7   Will Success Spoil Performance Investing?   93
  8   To Get Performance, You Have to Be Organized for It   99
  9   Investing Success in Two Easy Lessons   107
 10   The End of Active Investing?   111
 11   In Defense of Active Investing   119
 12   Murder on the Orient Express: The Mystery
         of Underperformance   127
 13   Best Practice Investment Committees   141
 14   Levels of the Game   157
 15   An Invitation to Winning   163
 16   Small Slam!   167
 17   A Lesson from Seaside Cemetery   171
 18   Tommy Armour on Investing   173
 19   Ted Williams' Great Lessons for Investors   177
 20   Symptoms and Signs   181
 21   Lessons from the Warwick and Château Chambord   191

22	Investment Management Fees Are Higher Than We Think	199
23	Computer People May Be Planning a Revolution	203
24	Characteristics of Successful Investment Firms	207
25	A New Paradigm of Investment Management	215
26	Lessons on Grand Strategy	221
27	Pension Funds Need MORE Management MANAGEMENT	227
28	The Significance of 65	233
29	Where Were We?	237
30	Hard Choices: Where Are We Now?	243
31	Bonds for Long-Term Investors?	251
32	What Role Should Bonds Play?	261
33	Too Much Liquidity Will Cost You	265
34	Letter to My Grandkids: 12 Essential Investing Guidelines	269
35	Miss Sally's Attic	277
36	Ben Graham: Ideas as Mementos	281
37	The Corporate Tax Cut	291
38	Repurchase Stock to Revitalize Equity	295
39	Anti-Trust, Bank Mergers, and the PNB Decision	315
Index		325

Foreword

To invest well is not easy. At least that's what the data suggests—just look at the well-documented consistently poor performance of most portfolios, whether individual or institutional. But it doesn't need to be as hard as we have made it, says this book. If we focus on what really matters over the long term, we can each help ourselves and our clients figure out what's most important for eventual success. We tend to allow short-term influences to occupy far too large a share of mind, to the detriment of focusing on actions that will improve long-term outcomes.

That central message is what this book is about, and embedded in it is a timeless roadmap that investors and investment practitioners can and should follow. It is a set of principles derived from the many front-row seats that Charley Ellis has occupied over the last six decades—a period that encompasses the most profound transformations that have taken place in the investment industry.

Charley's keen observations and writings over these years elucidate what has changed—and also what has been enduring. The essays of this book represent (1) his foundational principles for succeeding in the business of investment management; and (2) his unambiguous insights and guidance that make investment stewardship much less daunting—for the sophisticated as well as the lay investor.

The power of Charley's insights comes from their validation in history. He teaches us that "figuring it out" in investing is being able to see in current and future developments what matters and what does not, which in turn needs to be anchored in a well-developed understanding of the past and the nature of the forces that have brought us to the present. That's why wise people study history and seek out the original documents. That's why we read biographies of great leaders. And that's why historians say the best way to understand the present is to understand the past and the best way to understand the past is to study what came before and caused it. And that's why we ask new friends, "Please tell me your personal story." This book provides just such narratives through a documentary history of this period of great industry change.

Each essay yields enduring insights and lessons, among them:

- For clients of investing organizations, individuals and institutions will both benefit from behind-the-scene insights into the degree of change in the very nature of the daunting challenges faced by all active managers. As Dorothy said to Toto: "We're not in Kansas any more"— again!
- For those who are aiming to make their careers in this remarkably well-paid field of endeavor or are early in their careers as practitioners, here is an opportunity to appreciate how change is itself a powerful constant in the investment space, and how critical it is to anticipate and embrace innovation and evolution.
- For practitioners near the completion of their careers, there are provocative reminders of past developments we underestimated (to our regret) or recognized only slowly. And they keep coming!
- For those who seek metaphorical investing advice that will remain ingrained, "The Loser's Game," "Murder on the Orient Express," and "Investing Success in Two Easy Lessons" are must reads.
- For those who wonder where and how fees can so adversely affect investors' long-term welfare, several essays make it all quite clear.
- For those who still harbor hopes that indexing may have had its day, the negative case is clearly presented.
- For those who are looking to succeed as a client, "The Winners' Game" and "Best Practice Investment Committees" provide must-read guidance.
- For those who worry that business profitability all too often encroaches on professional values, there are several appeals from an ultimate insider for a re-orientation of the industry.

Investing and investment stewardship are a journey. Through beautifully written and colorful prose, this book brings to life the pitfalls we will face time and again, and it provides a clear roadmap for making that journey less hazardous and ultimately one of great success.

André Perold
Partner and CIO of HighVista Strategies
George Gund Professor of Finance and Banking, Emeritus,
Harvard Business School
Boston, Massachusetts

Note on the Text

These essays were originally written decades ago, and, at that time, investment managers were male, so "he/him/his" are the form used in the book.

Introduction

One of the great joys of a professional life, as physicist Richard Feynman once explained, is the joy of "figuring it out." Of course, figuring out investing questions is not as important and certainly not as enduring as figuring out the basic laws of physics, but it certainly is, has been, and likely will be as fascinating—and more fun.

Readers leafing through this collection of pieces will, I hope, enjoy being reminded of some of the great controversies that have animated the world of professional investing over the past 60 years. For me, the privilege of engaging in those controversies in various ways—depending on my role as teacher at, lucky me, Harvard, Yale, and at Princeton, or as a speaker at conferences all over North America, Europe, and Asia, or as a participant in a 30-year series of seminars for senior investment managers (sponsored by a leading Wall Street research firm) or in a seemingly infinite number of lunches and dinners—gave me a wonderful way to learn from others and to learn how best to express my own thoughts.

Within the enormous world of the economy, the world of investing always was and is relatively small, but that reality has also offered great advantages. Within our community, we know each other and are friends, often dear friends. We like to share our best ideas and insights and are always learning from each other. And almost always, we have fun. Do you know of any other field in which age differentiates so little? Is there any other field in which practitioners continue well into their eighties? Any other so replete with new learning? Any so well paid? Any in which each individual would be good friends with at least 100 peers and often with over 300 all over the world? Of course, the number of friendly acquaintances might be 10 times greater.

When I left Harvard Business School 60 years ago with an MBA and headed to Wall Street in 1963 and a happy career in investing, the School offered no courses in investing, there were no CFAs, and almost nobody was interested in the stock or bond markets. Worldwide employment in the securities and investment fields was less than 5,000. Half a century later, employment was well over 500,000 and likely one million and HBS offered three dozen courses on all sorts of investing, and almost everyone seemed interested in the securities markets. At least as important, the average talent of the men and women engaged in all aspects of investing had steadily increased to make the field known today for having many of the most talented, best-informed, hardest-working, and best-paid people in the world.

Over the years, many, many forces have combined to change—and change again and again—the realities of the field of investing. It has been my great privilege to be an active observer of the forces driving those changes.

Changes in beliefs have come far more slowly. Among those "slow to change beliefs" have been the belief that identifying first-rate managers is the client investor's main priority, that fees are low ("only one percent"), and bonds should be used in substantial amounts to create "balanced" portfolios. Meanwhile, a few other beliefs *have* changed. Market timing is now viewed negatively. International investing is viewed positively— and "active" investing continues to give way to indexing.

Performance measurement firms have shown that identifying superb managers is not easy and SPIVA data shows grimly that, over the longer term, fewer and fewer active managers have been able to achieve market-beating results. Worse, identifying the favored few *in advance* is nearly impossible and those who fall short fail by much larger amounts than the slim benefit of "success." Gradually, but slowly, more and more investors have taken note and now, at an accelerating rate, indexing is gaining greater and greater acceptance as the rational way to invest in today's stock markets because, over the long term, indexing *assures* "Top Quartile" results.

Fees are increasingly recognized as large—particularly relative to lower returns—and investment managers increasingly compete for business by advertising their lower fees. (But recognition has still been moderate, most likely for two reasons: First, nobody actually writes a check to pay for a manager's service: fees are quietly deducted from the assets managed. Second, fees are almost always described as a percent of assets. If fees were described as a percent of returns—or worse for active managers, as a percent of risk-adjusted incremental returns—surely, the pressure would be far greater.)

Belief in bonds as the way to damp down changes in the stock market continues among investors and their advisers. This will likely continue. The "opportunity cost" of owning bonds vs. owning stocks is hard to compare to the "anxiety cost" of being exposed to stock market fluctuations. Canards like "Invest your age in bonds" are easy to remember and somehow sound like experience-based wisdom. And, of course, few investors see their securities portfolios correctly as only one component of their Total Financial Portfolio which, for most of us, has large stable value components like our homes, the net present value of our future incomes or savings, and our Social Security benefits.

Psychologists tell us that beliefs, whether political or social or financial, are very hard to get believers to change, particularly if those beliefs are long held or part of a system. Attempting to cause change in beliefs by using logic or evidence typically leads to increasing resistance or "digging in." That's why Darwin lamented that his scientific friends would have to die off before his carefully documented theories would be accepted—and he was right!

Many unusual realities contributed to my life of learning: studying for my PhD when the academic community was super-charged with the exciting discovery of efficient markets and MPT; teaching advanced courses on investing multiple times at both Yale and Harvard; teaching for 15 years in week-long programs for experienced professionals at Princeton, leading a 30-year series of twice-a-year three-day seminars with the "best and brightest" fund managers; many years of service to the CFA Institute; service on over a dozen investment committees around the world, consulting repeatedly with well over 100 of the world's best investment managers; writing several books on investing; and, best of all, having the privilege of many great personal/professional friendships around the world with leading practitioners, so I was, time and again, able to see the process of change. These 39 articles, like reports from the field, tell my story of learning about important aspects of investing.

While many investors focus their attention on finding a really good investment manager, my unusually wide exposure—largely through three decades of consulting for Greenwich Associates with many investment managers and securities firms around the world, particularly in the US, Japan, and the UK (but also Germany, Switzerland, Canada, Singapore, and Australia) gave me a special insight. I realized that it was almost *easy* to find excellent investment managers but that was not the right question; the right question was whether it was realistic to search for a manager who was sufficiently *better* than the many really good investment managers so that he or she would achieve "better than the market" results *after* costs and fees and, for individual investors, taxes. That is a very different question. And the grim reality is that the answer to that question is almost always, No!

So, while some part of these articles can be claimed to be original ideas, most are reports by an observer who was fortunate to have learned from others and was able to join the pieces into a hopefully useful whole. For me, the experience of writing and figuring things out has been great fun and a chance to learn from others. Sometimes my learning came before the particular pieces came together and sometimes came afterwards because some pieces seemed controversial when they first appeared and led to great discussions—and clearer explanation. One happy surprise for me: While some of these pieces may have become outdated because things changed, none have proven to be wrong. As always, my hopes are two: First, that readers will enjoy them and, second, that any disagreements will be shared with me so I can keep learning.

Charles D. Ellis
New Haven, CT
March, 2022

1

The Changing Game

Examples of major changes in the whole system of a major industry are few and far between, except in technology. Virtually every aspect of investment management—fees, competitors, technology, regulators—and information have changed over the last half-century. Even the speed of change has changed.

C harles Darwin lamented that his innovative theory of evolution would not be accepted by the scientific community until his friends and colleagues had died or retired. His peers would have to be replaced by others whose careers were not so invested in or based on and devoted to pre-Darwinian concepts that they had become unwitting captives of their prior work and stature as traditional biologists.[1]

The stock market itself is Darwinian—always evolving. And as increasing numbers of investment professionals with more training and better tools and more access to more information *and* as investors move money toward more capable managers *and* as managers compete to attract more business, fund executives promote their best performing portfolio managers and analysts, it cannot be surprising that the effectiveness of active investors as a group continues to increase. That's why we say, "Markets are always learning." And that's why securities markets have been unrelenting in their increasing efficiency—and harder and harder to beat or even match—particularly after covering the higher

---

[1]This included Professor Louis Agassiz, Harvard's and America's leading biologist, who became famous in history as the man who stubbornly refused to accept Darwin's theory of evolution.

fees now being charged. The fees may well have been justified in the early or middle years of a 50-year transformation, but a rich variety of charges have combined to bring to an end the era of successful active management.

In his classic book, *Scientific Revolutions*, Thomas Kuhn explained why the problem Darwin faced was not confined to biology or science: It is universal. Those who have succeeded greatly and have risen to the top positions in their fields naturally resist—often quite imaginatively and often quite stubbornly—any new, "revolutionary" or disruptive concept. There are two main reasons for resistance: First, most of the new hypotheses, when rigorously tested, will not prove valid. So, over time, leading members of the Establishment can get over-confident and dismissive of *all* new ideas. Second, the members of the Establishment in any field have too much to lose in institutional stature, their carefully developed reputations as experts, the value of their many years of past work, and their earning power—all dependent on the status quo—*their* status quo. So they defend against the "new." Usually, they are proven right—so they win. But not always.

Dynamics of Innovation

There is a remarkably consistent iterative process by which the best innovations overcome resistance and eventually gain acceptance. The *process* of change follows a repeating pattern although the *pace* of change can differ markedly from one innovation to another.[2] Two kinds of actors play key roles: Innovators and Influentials. *Innovators* tinker and experiment all the time, looking for the next new thing. Unlike most people, they are so keen to find and use the latest innovation and they enjoy being first so much that they do not mind the costs in time, energy, or expense of most innovations not proving out, so they continue experimenting with what's new. Figure 1.1 shows how Innovators are the first to try things out.

Influentials are different. While they like finding new and better ways, they dislike the cost, bother, and frustrations of "new way" failures. So their strategy is to watch the Innovators and their experiments closely and, when the Innovators' experiments work, selectively adopt the most promising successes. As a result, Influentials learn about successes early

---

[2]The use of penicillin and hybrid-seed corn illustrates the process. Farmers converted to hybrid seed over 10 long *years*; doctors adopted penicillin in less than 10 *months*.

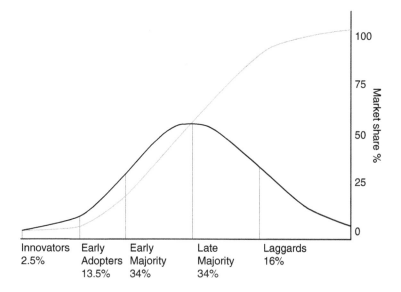

Figure 1.1 Incremental and Cumulative Acceptance

and develop considerable skill at evaluating which Innovators have the best innovation records and are most repeatedly successful. And this is why they become Influentials.

While Influentials are monitoring the Innovators for successful innovations, many Followers are monitoring the Influentials. When Influentials adopt a new way, the Followers[3] will then—in increasing numbers and with increasing commitment—follow their lead. (Of course, that's why they are called Influentials.)

In his scholarly book, *Diffusion of Innovations,* Everett Rogers established the classic paradigm by which innovation reaches a "tipping point" and then spreads exponentially through a large social group. Most members of a social system rely on observing the decisions of others when making their own decisions.[4] Decisions to adopt a new way repeatedly follow a five-step process:

1. Awareness of the new way.
2. Evaluation: forming a favorable (or unfavorable) opinion.

---

[3]Followers can be divided into two groups, sometimes called "Early Majority" and "Late Majority" and even later "Laggards" follow. Acceptance by "Early Majority" produces the "tipping point" phenomenon.

[4]In institutional investing, a "dependency" exists when an influential "selection consultant" drives all or most of his clients to add (or terminate) a particular manager, but otherwise most institutions and most individuals appear to make manager selection decisions rather independently on their own terms and schedule—*not* "I'll have what she's having."

3. Deciding whether or not to change to the innovation.
4. Action: Adopting (or rejecting) the innovation.
5. Confirmation: evaluating the results of the innovation.

Deciding, the third step, depends on the decider's confidence in the benefits, the decision's compatibility with current habits and norms, and how the decider anticipates others will perceive the decision and whether they will approve.

The speed with which new and better ways of doing things are adopted is a function of several contributing factors: how large and how visible are the benefits; the speed with which benefits become visible; the ease and low cost of experimentation; the ease and low cost of reversing a mistaken decision; and the quality of the channels or networks by which information and social influences get communicated and expressed. Resistance to change, on the other hand, is a function of uncertainty about the benefits of the innovation or the ease of adoption; the risk of social approbation the new adopter may experience; the risk tolerance of the prospective adopter; the speed with which rewards and benefits will be received; etc.

Diffusion is the social process by which individual adopters influence others to adopt. Opinion leaders are important in any social movement, so diffusion will be retarded by any stigma attached to adoption. As an example of social stigma, Rogers cites the failure of a public heath campaign in Peru because local culture held that only "unwell" people would drink boiled water. So healthy people refused to boil theirs. Significantly, index investing was attacked, several years ago, as a haven for "wimps without skill," just "settling for just average," and even dismissed as "unAmerican."

Combining Kuhn's and Rogers' theories on innovation together provides a way of understanding how and why the inevitable triumph of indexing is steadily advancing *and* how and why its advance is still being resisted or even ignored by many practitioners devoted to active management. The distribution of an innovation and its adoption works through the interaction of a social system[5] and its opinion leaders. The speed of distribution varies with the strength of the social system.

---

[5]There are two types of social systems: homophilous and heterophilous. Heterophilous social systems are populated by many different types of participants from different backgrounds who are more likely to be interested in new ideas and innovations. Homophilous systems are more consistent and conservative—and more attentive to conforming to pre-existing norms. For example, the QWERTY keyboard is still used despite the fact that another keyboard allows most people to type much faster.

The informal social system for the selection of investment managers is remarkably weak. For individual investors, three inhibiting characteristic factors dominate: the all-too human desire among individuals to "do better" by trying harder; the "yes, you can" encouragements of investment advisors, consultants, and other perceived experts who make their living as advocates of trying harder to do better; and the media advertising, articles, and program content that focus on and celebrate winning.[6] You will, or course, hear little about the numbing consistency with which a majority of active managers fall short of the index or how seldom past years' "winners" are winners *again* over the next few years or longer.

The iterative process of social acceptance and resistance can seem glacially slow as they work their way through many layers and kinds of social resistance—particularly the resistance by those with a lot to lose if substantial acceptance develops. But impatient observers might consider the difficult pathway of, for example, the theory of evolution. Texas *still* requires public schools to treat evolution and creationism as equally serious alternatives. Persuading Americans to use seat belts—even when the historical data was powerful—took years and lots of public service advertisements, deliberately annoying noises, and local police enforcement.[7]

Early "Performance Investing"

In his *General Theory*, J. M. Keynes wrote: "The game of professional investment is intolerably boring and over-exacting to anyone who is entirely exempt from the gambling instinct; whilst he who has it must pay to this propensity the appropriate toll." Note the word "game" as coined for all time in 'Adam Smith's[8] mid-1960s best seller, *The Money Game*,

---

[6]If you watch stock market reports on TV, note how much the newscasters sound like sportscasters.

[7]Other examples include reduced cigarette smoking and use of seat belts in automobiles. Other changes have faced strong resistance: like desegregation in the 1960s, control over assault weapons or reducing obesity, which leads to adult onset diabetes with all its anguish. Persuading smokers to quit smoking needed a bold and costly "confrontational" campaign working on 14 different dimensions and took years of hard data on early deaths from cancer plus heavy taxation, smoking bans on planes, in buildings and by individual companies. So we know the process of changing behavior is often slow, particularly to those who expect prompt, rational action based on objective evidence.

[8]*Nom de plume* of George J.W. Goodman.

where he chronicled and explained with delightfully sardonic humor the amazing new world of "performance" investing. It was, as he said, "an exercise in mass psychology, in trying to guess better than the crowd how the crowd would behave."[9] The author went on to explain, "The true professionals in the Game—the professional portfolio managers—grow more skilled all the time. They are human and they make mistakes, but if you have your money managed by a truly alert mutual fund or even by one of the better banks, you will have a better job done for you than probably at any time in the past."

'Adam Smith' then turned appropriately to the grand old man of performance mutual funds, Fidelity's Edwin C. Johnson, as his ultimate source of profound thought:

'The market,' said Mister Johnson, 'is like a beautiful woman—endlessly fascinating, endlessly complex, always changing, always mystifying.[10] I have been absorbed and immersed since 1924 and I know this is no science. It is an art. Now we have computers and all sorts of statistics, but the market is still the same and understanding the market is still no easier. It is personal intuition, sensing patterns of behavior. There is always something unknown, undiscerned.'[11]

'Adam Smith' then led his readers through a charming review of Gustave Le Bon's *The Crowd,* linked that with Sigmund Freud, reflected on Chester Bernard's *The Functions of the Executive,* and then returned to Keynes. ". . . Americans are apt to be unduly interested in discovering what average opinion believes average opinion to be; and this national weakness finds its nemesis in the stock market . . . Investment based on genuine long-term expectation is so difficult today as to be scarcely practicable."

Turning next to Ben Graham, 'Adam Smith' quoted from the Dean of Analysts' great book, *The Intelligent Investor,*

Mathematics is ordinarily considered as producing precise and dependable results; but in the stock market, the more elaborate and abstruse the mathematics, the more uncertain and speculative are the conclusions

[9]Adam Smith, *The Money Game* (New York: Vintage Books, 1976), p. 18.
[10]There goes Ben Graham's Mr. Market again, cleverly "protecting" us from seeing the truth and enticing us with hopes of being the lucky one who, despite the adverse odds, will be the winners.
[11]Ibid., p. 25.

we draw therefrom. In 44 years of Wall Street experience and study, I have never seen dependable calculations made about common stock values or related investment policies, that went beyond simple arithmetic or the most elementary algebra. Whenever calculus is brought in, or higher algebra, you could take it as a warning signal that the operator was trying to substitute theory for experience.[12]

'Adam Smith' also popularized the question that seemed to capture the imagination of investors in the 1960s: "Do you sincerely want to be rich?" as in, "Do you really want to detach yourself from reality?" He provided his readers with an attention-getting bit of history:

You can also see the point in time when 'performance' surfaced. In February, 1966, Gerry Tsai, born in Shanghai and tutored at Fidelity, came to New York. He had been running Fidelity Capital. He had a reputation as a shrewd trader, and he was doing well, but, as he told Mister Johnson, 'I want to have a little fund of my own.' Gerry thought maybe he could raise $25 million and so did the underwriters, Bache & Co. But the spirit was abroad in the land. The orders went over $50 million to $100 million, finally to $247 million on the first day, and within a year to more than $400 million. Gerry Tsai was not the first 'performance' manager; Mister Johnson and Jack Dreyfus had pioneered that well. But he was the first real 'star.'[13]

The early 1960s practitioners of "performance" investing experienced early-stage difficulties that would be unfamiliar to later participants. Block trading was just beginning; brokerage commissions were fixed—at an average per share of over 40 cents; in-depth research from Wall Street was new; computers were confined to the "cage" or back office; Quotron machines that could show current prices were new; and trading volume was 1/10 of 1% of today's volume. "Performance" investing was costly and overcoming the costs was not easy.

Those who succeeded attained "hero" status—particularly among the managers of the major mutual funds. Understandably, these heroes attracted lots of business to their mutual funds.

As demand for "performance" built up, supply expanded in both the number of mutual fund providers and the variety of fund offerings:

[12]Ibid., p. 135.
[13]Ibid., p. 181.

open-ended, closed-ended, no-load, balanced, growth, value, small cap, bonds, high-yield bonds, international, emerging markets, and even frontier markets. Today, mutual funds serve over 52 million American households[14] and manage $26 trillion world-wide.

Another example of change came with the surge in corporate pension assets in the 1950s and 1960s—beginning with the GM-UAW labor settlement in 1952. With Federal wage and price controls firmly prohibiting a large pay increase, the parties solved their conflict by agreeing to fund "fringe benefit" for the auto workers, primarily pensions. Uncomfortable with the 5% limit on equities imposed on *insured* pensions, General Motors and other corporations turned to their major banks' trust departments—they had had traditional investment experience caring for the personal trusts of wealthy customers—for 50:50 stock and bond portfolios. Accepted as a "customer accommodation" at little or no fee,[15] corporate pension assets accumulated rapidly. Soon, the larger money center banks became enormous investment managers, as well as the major consumers of brokers' research and big customers for Wall Street's emerging capabilities in block trading.

Change led to further change as new investment firms organized to compete for the burgeoning pension business—some as dedicated subsidiaries of mutual fund organizations, but most as independent firms. Their main proposition: active management by the most talented young analyst/portfolio managers—who would be first to find and act on investment opportunity—could meet or beat the same results that "performance" mutual funds were achieving *and* would work directly with your corporation's pension fund. The "new breed" and their proposition were compelling, particularly in comparison to the committee-centric, conservative, even stodgy trust administrators at the banks.

As mutual funds advertised "performance" and performance investing, a new service[16] was created that measured the performance of the banks and insurance companies that were managing most major pension funds and compared their results to the new breed of investment firms. The data on the money-center banks' performance was often disconcertingly disappointing to the banks' customers. Adding insult to injury,

---

[14]Versus 23.4 million in 1990.
[15]Doubting they could charge much in fees and interested in protecting their important corporate customer relationships, the banks found a novel backdoor way to make money as investment managers. They directed the trust department's commission business to those brokers who agreed to keep large balances on deposit—balances that the bank could profitably lend out. (The terms of reciprocity were agreed at, typically, $5 in commissions for every $100 of balances and were closely monitored by both sides.)
[16]A. G. Becker & Co.

these new firms were often populated with the "best and brightest" young men and women who were leaving the banks whose formal trust department procedures they found stultifying and financially unrewarding. Increasingly, the money that was accumulating in pension funds began pouring out of the bank trust departments and into the new investment counsel firms that promised superior performance.

Significantly, the terms of competition had changed in ways that continued to surprise the banks and insurers. With their long experience in institutional financial services, such as bank loans or cash management or commercial insurance, the banks *knew* to expect tough price competition and bargaining by major corporate customers. So, the banks and insurers competed on low price. But pension management had been converted by performance investing from a *cost*-driven market into a *value*-driven market—with value determined by perceptions and expectations of future investment performance.

Pricing of investment management services has had an interesting history *and* a single direction: higher. Before the thirties, conventional fees for separate account clients were charged as a percent of the income received in dividends and interest. During the 1930s, Scudder, Stevens & Clark shifted the base for fee calculation to a 50:50 split—half based on incomes and half based on assets. Still, the level of fees charged was low. So investment counseling might be a fine *profession*, but it certainly was not a great *business*. Those going into investment management typically hoped only to cover their costs of operation with client fees and then make some decent money by investing their own family fortunes. If the investment profession was interesting, the investment business certainly was not.

"Performance" investment management was different. The new investment managers were pricing their services on the basis of expected or perceived *value*. While all fees were seen as quite low—"only 1%"— the new managers found they could easily charge fees much higher than the banks and insurance companies had ever charged. Happily for investment managers, higher fees became a confirmation of the higher value expected to be delivered and "quibbling" about fees was increasingly dismissed. ("You wouldn't choose your child's brain surgeon on the basis of price, would you?") Over the 1960s, 1970s, and 1980s, assets of mutual funds, pension funds, and endowments ballooned at the same time fees for investment management rose steadily higher and higher. So the *business* became increasingly profitable—eventually, one of the world's most profitable businesses. And this profitability flowered into higher and higher compensation to successful analysts and portfolio managers and higher profits for investment firms. High pay—and interesting work—attracted more aspiring analysts and portfolio managers—meaning more competition for each other—which developed into the dynamics that would inevitably make it increasingly difficult to achieve sufficiently superior performance, to justify the increased fees being charged—a reality we will return to later.

Soon, a new kind of corporate middle management role emerged: the internal management of external investment managers of pension funds. Supervising 10, 20, or even 30 investment managers and meeting each year with 25 to 50 investment firms hoping to be selected and then selecting the best of breed—and doing all three well—required the expertise of full-time specialists—typically aided by external investment consultants.[17] At most corporations, pension fund executives—often on a few years' rotation through differing jobs in financial management—report to an investment committee. Most committee members are internal finance people who are understandably preoccupied by their own daunting responsibilities in capital budgeting, controllership, capital raising, etc. and usually have not studied investing or investment management extensively. So internal executives often hired external investment consultants who wielded increasingly great influence, particularly on selecting and monitoring numerous active managers.

In the early 1970s, investment consultants began providing a specialist service for an annual fee that was less than the all-in cost of another junior fund executive. Based on regular in-depth interviews and careful assessment of past investment performance, these consultants offered to provide independent evaluations of dozens of investment managers and bring the "best of the best" for a final evaluation by the fund executive and his investment committee. (It cannot be surprising that indexing was seldom recommended.) By the mid-1980s, over half of the larger pension funds were using one or more investment consultants. With dozens of these consultants[18] scouring the nation for promising new investment managers and recommending the use of dozens of specialist

---

[17]Many of these specialists enjoyed the work and the travel to meet with current and prospective managers and decided to make careers as fund executives.

[18]In the long run, their results also proved disappointing. (Being in business, they naturally presented themselves in the most favorable light. In particular, this meant that when they stopped recommending a manager—usually for failing to perform—they deleted that manager from their records. After all, why continue to track a manager who had failed? How many go back to see—let alone go inside—a house they moved out of some time ago? One important result: By deleting "failed" managers from their selection results—and adding new "winners"—the consultants, however unwittingly, substantially enhanced their own records.)

managers, getting into business became easier and faster for promising new investment firms. Increasing numbers of energetic investment managers formed new firms—or new pension divisions for established investment organizations—to pursue the burgeoning demand.

Because securities markets always have more noise than information, observers relying on available data—individual investors, institutional fund executives, investment consultants, and even the managers themselves—will be unable to sort out sufficient information from the noise when evaluating active managers to make good estimates of which managers will achieve superior future results. This difficulty traces back, layer after layer, to the well-known prediction troubles in stock selection and portfolio management: Success in a securities market is not determined by whether you are right, but by whether you are *more* right than other buyers and sellers who are acting on their beliefs that they are more right than you are. In his wonderful book, *The Signal and the Noise,* Nate Silver[19] explains why we mistake more confident predictions for more accurate ones. He reminds us: ". . . it is not so much how good your predictions are in an absolute sense that matters, but how good they are *relative to the competition.* In poker, you can make 95 percent of your predictions correctly and still lose your shirt at a table full of players who are making the right move 99 percent of the time." As Silver says, "That's why poker is a hard way to make an easy living."[20]

Vanguard examined reported mutual fund performance over time and found no significant pattern. The Vanguard study concluded:

Results do not appear to be significantly different from random, aside from the bottom quintile. Taking this analysis to its logical next step, one might rightly assume that funds that fall to the bottom quintile might be the next to fall into the liquidated/merged bin. Indeed, when we [studied] funds that fell into the bottom quintile as of December 31, 2006, we found that fully 50% were liquidated or closed by year-end 2011, and that 10% remained in the bottom quintile, while only 21% managed to right the ship and rebound to either of the top two quintiles.

As Vanguard explained its research:

---

[19]Founder of the *New York Times* political blog, FiveThirtyEight.com.
[20]Nate Silver, *The Signal and the Noise* (New York: Penguin, 2012), p. 313.

To analyze consistency within the actively managed fund space, we ranked all U.S. equity funds in terms of risk-adjusted return for the five years ended 2006. We then selected the top 20% of funds and tracked their risk-adjusted returns over the next five years (through December 31, 2011) to see how consistently they performed. If those top funds displayed consistently superior risk-adjusted returns, we would expect a significant majority to remain in the top 20%. A random outcome, however, would result in approximately 17% of returns dispersed evenly across the six categories.

The results, as shown in Figure 1.2, were disconcertingly close to completely random.

Changes in supply and demand and the role of intermediaries interact repeatedly in the dynamic investment management marketplace to create new forms of change. One early example of change centers on mutual funds. Beginning with Massachusetts Investors Trust and State Street Fund in the late 1920s, mutual funds provided individual investors—who typically invested in only a few stocks and had been using expensive retail stockbrokers—with a better product that incorporated diversification, convenience, and professional supervision by experienced investment professionals overseen by distinguished boards of directors—all delivered reliably and regularly for a moderate fee. As experience proved out the advantages, demand for mutual funds increased and as demand increased, supply, of course also increased. More and more mutual funds were organized, distribution channels developed, and funds got increasingly advertised. Initially, mutual funds were sold

Figure 1.2 Fund Leadership Is Quick to Change: Performance Ranking as of December 31, 2011

primarily to small, "uneconomic" customers that the investment counselors didn't want to service (such as large clients' grandchildren) but the funds gradually carved out a wider and deeper market, eventually attracting even large individual investors and smaller institutions.

Innovation in investment "products" continued and accelerated. Rare before the 1980s,[21] hedge funds gained favor with wealthy individuals in the 1990s and then, after the millennium, with institutions. In 2000, an estimated 3,335 hedge funds and 583 "funds of funds" had assets of $500 billion (Figure 1.3). By 2012, the numbers had more than doubled to 7,768 hedge funds and 1,932 funds of funds. (The latter figure was down from 2,682 in 2007.) Currently, in a "normal" year, 1,000 new hedge funds are launched and 750 old funds are liquidated.[22] Total hedge fund assets have been estimated at $2 trillion with at least one fund being over $50 billion.[23]

Hedge funds are different from other institutions. Fees are typically "2 and 20," substantial leverage is used, portfolio turnover is high, and every aspect of their operations is intensive as they all strive in various

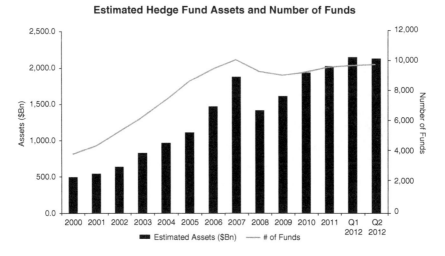

Figure 1.3 Estimated Hedge Funds' Assets and Number of Funds, 2000–2012

---

[21]Graham-Newman, led by Ben Graham in the 1920s, was one of the earlier hedge funds. After WWII, Alfred W. Jones started his eponymous fund and in 1955, *Fortune* reported it had out-performed even the best mutual funds.
[22]Deloitte Development LLC., 2012.
[23]Bridgewater had $51 billion in June, 2011.

ways to "get an edge"—to find and exploit market opportunities. As highly efficient "money machines," hedge funds have become Wall Street's largest accounts, so they routinely get "the first call." Spawning enormous compensation—one manager was allegedly paid $4 billion for a single year—hedge funds attract "the best and brightest" and the most intensively competitive.[24] And as they scour the market for anomalies, the hedge funds increase the market's efficiency.

Index Funds' Growth

Change begets change and one important long-term change began back in 1971. Wells Fargo Bank created an index fund for a $6 million portfolio of Samsonite Corporation's pension fund. Originally an equal weighted fund, the fixed brokerage commissions created serious cost problems, so the fund was switched in 1976 to the market-weighted S+P 500 index. In 1974, Batterymarch and the American National Bank also launched index funds.[25] In 1976, Vanguard launched the first index mutual fund. It is now the largest mutual fund in the world and Vanguard has become one of the nation's largest and most respected investment managers. (Worldwide, there are over 100 index funds matching one or another market index.) After adjusting for survivorship bias, over the past 25 years Vanguard's index fund has beaten 85% of the nation's actively managed mutual funds.

Index funds have increased rapidly. In the 15 years from 1997 to 2011, the number of index mutual funds nearly tripled from 132 to 383. In assets, index funds grew twice as rapidly, up *six* times from $170 billion to $1.1 trillion. (While nearly 80% of index funds are *equity* funds, index *bond* funds grew *twenty-five* times—from $10 billion to $222 billion.)

The growth of indexing cannot have been helped by a major "branding blunder" by indexers when accepting confinement to a culturally pejorative name: passive. In our active, can-do, competitive culture, who is such a timid soul that he or she would rather be known as "passive" than "active"? Fairly or not, names *do* matter. Consider the following pairs and decide, which would you prefer?

---

[24]It cannot be surprising that most of the prosecutions for insider trading involve hedge funds.
[25]Wells Fargo's unit went through several owners and is now a major part of BlackRock. Key people at American National Bank, frustrated by institutional rigidities, left to create Dimensional Fund Advisors in 1988.

Total Net Assets and Number of ETFs¹

Billions of dollars, year-end, 2001–2011

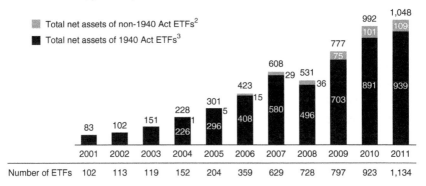

Number of ETFs	102	113	119	152	204	359	629	728	797	923	1,134
	2001	2002	2003	2004	2005	2006	2007	2008	2009	2010	2011

¹ Data for ETFs that invest primarily in other ETFs are excluded from the totals.

² The funds in this category are not registered under the Investment Company Act of 1940 and invest primarily in commodities, currencies, and futures.

³ The funds in this category are registered under the Investment Company Act of 1940.
Note: Components may not add to the total because of rounding.

Figure 1.4 Total Net Assets and Number of ETFs, 2000–2011.

- Tony Curtis vs. Bernard Schwartz
- Rita Hayworth vs. Margarite Cansino
- Ralph Lauren vs. Ralph Lifshitz

In recent years, ETFs (Exchange Traded Funds)[26] that match indexes have also proliferated and attracted many investors. ETFs got off to a slow start but were soon surging in volume and proliferating in variety.[27] Assets of ETFs have increased from $83 billion in 2001 to over $1 trillion in 2011 and now to nearly $3 trillion (Figure 1.4).[28] There are now over 4,700 ETFs and trading in ETFs represents over 15% of total NYSE trading volume.

---

[26]Low costs (because they are not actively managed and have no 12b-1 fees) and tax efficiency due to low turnover and transparency are important attractions.

[27]In 1989, Index Participation Shares, an S+P 500 proxy, were traded in modest volume on the American and Philadelphia Exchanges but were stopped by a Chicago Mercantile Exchange lawsuit. A similar product began trading on the Toronto Stock Exchange and was so well received that AmEx executives decided to design a product that fit the SEC's requirements. Introduced as SPDR: (Standard + Poor's Depositary Receipts) or "Spiders."

[28]*The Economist,* January 26, 2013.

Accumulating Evidence

Long before the build-up in index fund investing, academic research was providing increasingly powerful theoretical and documentary support for a shift away from active investing over to passive or index investing. (Practitioners—busy ringing the cash registers—paid little or no attention.) In 1952, a 14-page paper by 25-year-old Harry Markowitz clarified that risk and return are both separate and correlated and that a rational investor should strive to minimize risk *and* maximize returns at the portfolio level.[29]

In the 1960s, Bill Sharpe showed how to separate market or systemic risk from manager-determined non-market risk, a different kind of risk that could be minimized through diversification and why investors should always diversify as much as practicable. In 1967, Michael Jensen published in *The Journal of Finance* a study of mutual funds from 1945 to 1964 and reported that despite taking more risk, the average fund lagged the market index by 1.1% per annum.

Years later, Sharpe explained what all investors need to know and understand in his short *Financial Analysts Journal* article, "The Arithmetic of Active Management."[30] Sharpe stated two simple propositions:

- Before costs, the return on the average actively managed dollar will equal the return on the average passively invested dollar.
- After costs, the return on the average actively invested dollar will be less than the return on the average passively invested dollar.

Sharpe went on to explain that for any active manager to recover all his costs *and* produce a net return above the market index, other investors "must be foolish enough to pay"—via inferior performance—all the costs incurred by the institutions *and* an attractive incremental profit that would compensate adequately for the risks of falling short.

Eugene Fama led in the formulation of the efficient market hypothesis in the 1960s and tested it by examining the performance of all domestic mutual funds with 10 years or more of recorded performance. His conclusion: "superior investment has escaped detection." (His conclusion would have been even more negative had he used a capitalization-weighted index such as the S&P 500.) As Fama recently summarized his research:

---

[29]Markowitz published *Portfolio Selection: Efficient Diversification of Investments* (Hoboken, NJ: John Wiley & Sons, 1959) to develop his thesis more fully.
[30]Vol. 47, No. 1, January/February, 1991, pp. 7–9.

Active management in aggregate is a zero-sum game—before costs. Good (or more likely just lucky) active managers can win only at the expense of bad (or unlucky) managers. This principle holds even at the level of individual stocks. Any time an active manager makes money by overweighting a stock, he wins because other active investors react by underweighting the stock. The two sides always net out *before* the costs of active management. *After* costs, active management is a negative-sum game by the amount of the costs (fees and expenses) borne by investors. After costs, only the top 3% of managers produce a return that indicates they have sufficient skill to just cover their costs. This means that going forward, and despite extraordinary past returns, even the top performers are expected to be only about as good as a low-cost passive index fund. The other 97% can be expected to do worse.[31]

Quantitative observers will surely be forgiven if they point out that only 3% of active managers beating their chosen markets is not far from what would be expected from a purely random distribution. Meanwhile, *qualitative* observers will caution that odds of 97 to 3 are terrible—particularly when risking real money that will be sorely needed by millions of people in retirement or to help finance our society's most treasured educational, cultural, and philanthropic institutions.

In 1973, Burt Malkiel's ever-popular *A Random Walk Down Wall Street*—destined to sell over 2 million copies—provided an easy-to-read compendium of the proliferation of academic studies of investing. Diversification, as Malkiel notes, is "investing's only free lunch." Malkiel reported the daunting data that even without adjusting for survivorship bias, more than 60% of large cap equity funds underperform the market over 5 years; more than 70% underperform over 10 years, and over 80% underperform over 20 years![32] The funds' "slugging average" is even worse because those that underperform do so by over 1½ times as much as out-performers' margin of market superiority.

In 1974, Nobel Laureate Paul Samuelson's article "Challenge to Judgment" in the *Journal of Portfolio Management* concluded, "the best of money managers cannot be demonstrated to be able to deliver the goods of superior . . . performance." Over the next 35 years, study after study

---

[31]Paper presented at the 65th Annual CFA Conference in Chicago in May, 2012, and published in *FAJ* Vol. 68, November 6, as "An Experienced View on Markets and Investing" by Eugene F. Fama and Robert Litterman.
[32]Burton Malkiel, *A Random Walk Down Wall Street* (New York: W.W. Norton, 2007), p. 263.

continued to document the same grim overall results. Model-based estimates and market reality have come into dauntingly close alignment.

More recently, Allen Roth estimated the percent of actively managed funds that would be expected—if all results were perfectly *random*—to outperform a broad market index fund over various intervals at 43% over one year, 30% over five years, 23% over 10 years and only 12% over 25 years. (For a portfolio of five funds, expected outperformance would drop to 11% over 10 years and only 3% over 25 years.)[33]

Studying actual results, Richard Ferris found the same small 12% of actively managed funds had actually outperformed the S&P 500. Similar results have been found with "small cap" funds and for funds in Japan, Asia ex-Japan, the UK, Canada, and in emerging markets and for REITs. For bond funds, success is even less frequent: only 20% achieve superior results and once again, past performance does not predict future results.

Curiously, academics, who have objectively studied the most extensive data, have had little impact on the thinking or actions of practical decision-makers. MBAs may study efficient markets while in school, but apparently leave "all that theory" behind when they go into investing or financial management at corporations. As C.P. Snow would have recognized, practitioners and academics live in different worlds, hold different sets of beliefs, and speak separate languages, and have no great respect for each other.

Meanwhile, back in the "real world" of actual investing, the self-chosen task of the investment consulting firms proved far more difficult than expected. They were not able to identify winning firms consistently. (This cannot be entirely surprising. If, for example, a consulting firm were able to select superior managers consistently, we would soon know it—probably with help from that masterful firm. But "the dog isn't barking" because there's no one there.) Of course, investment consultants do deliver other kinds of value to their clients: data on performance of the client's managers versus many other managers; advice on asset mix, rate of return assumptions, spending rules, or new investment ideas; and steadying advice when temptations are strongest at market highs or lows.

The challenge investors accept when selecting an active manager is *not* to find a talented, hard-working, and highly disciplined manager. That would be easy because there are so many of them. The challenge is

---

[33]Theoretically, active managers can move into cash to minimize the adverse impact of a bear market, but in practice, over the past 40 years, the average mutual fund did not outperform its benchmark in four out of seven bear markets (Vanguard).

to select a manager sufficiently *more* hard-working, *more* highly disciplined, and *more* creative than the other managers equally aspirational investors have chosen—*more* by at least enough to cover the manager's fees. This has become exceedingly difficult to do for one major ironic reason: increasingly consistent excellence among investment managers has been increasing market efficiency.

As a result of combining all these powerful change forces, market activity has been transformed from the activities of amateur "market *outsiders*" making only occasional one-stock decisions over to dominance by professional "market *insiders*" continuously comparison shopping the market. The result is that the securities markets have become increasingly efficient. And this means that deviations from the equilibrium prices based on informed experts' expected returns—in turn, based on analyzing all accessible information—are only increasingly unpredictable and random "noise."

Given the "noise" in the data on managers' investment performance records, Fama went on to conclude: "An investor doesn't have a prayer of picking a manager that can deliver true alpha. Even over a 20-year period, the past performance of an actively managed fund has a ton of random noise that makes it difficult, if not impossible, to distinguish luck from skill." (What he did not say, but we know is important, is this: behind any long-term record are many, many internal organizational changes in the important factors: markets change, portfolio managers change, assets managed by a firm change, managers age, families, incomes, and interests change, organizations change, etc. etc. All that means any long-term performance record must be interpreted with great care.)

Bayesians think in two importantly powerful ways: continuously using new data to come closer and closer to approximating reality *and* thinking about and estimating the future in probabilistic terms. Despite the specificity of prices, the stock market is an extraordinary aggregation of complex forces and variables. Unfortunately for our investment performance, we humans are notoriously biased in our evaluations. We favor the stocks of companies we have studied and even more strongly favor the prospects of stocks we already own in our portfolio. Each corporation is a complexity of many changing economic conditions, changing demand in each of many market segments, changing competition, changing technologies, changing internal leadership, and, importantly, both bad and good luck. Some variables are reinforcing, some self-correcting, some conflicting, some self-canceling, some brief, some enduring. The flutter of statistical uncertainty is inherent and persistent. Even the causes of changes are uncertain and often hidden. The variety of changing factors, their varying significance, and their many complex interactive dynamics of leading and lagging causation are dazzling. Estimating and forecasting the future of any variable are difficult; forecasting the interacting futures of many changing variables is extraordinarily difficult.[34]

Changing Markets

Fifty years ago, when institutions did only 10% of total NYSE trading and amateurs—averaging less than one trade a year—did the other 90%, beating the market (i.e. beating the part-time amateur competition) was not just possible, it was probable for a well-informed active professional. Individual investors were not only amateurs without access to research, they also made their decisions primarily for *outside* the market reasons: an inheritance or bonus received or a down-payment on a home or college tuition to pay. Today, the markets are overwhelmingly dominated by expert professionals armed with extensive research and a continuous flood of extensive market information, economic analyses, industry studies, and company reports *and* they are constantly comparison shopping *inside* the market for any comparative advantage.

Over the past 50 years, as well-educated, experienced, full-time, dedicated and highly motivated professionals have displaced the amateur individual investors, the stock markets have become increasingly efficient. Trading by professional investors has surged from a small minority of all trading to an overwhelming majority, over 95% of all listed trading in stocks and nearly 100% of off-board trading in listed stocks; *plus* 100% of algorithmic trading *plus* nearly 100% of trading in derivatives (which may now equal or exceed the value of shares traded in the "cash" market).

In 1961—for the first time since 1929—annual trading volume on the New York Stock Exchange was over 1 billion shares. By 1972, volume was 4.1 billion—and that was just the beginning. Volume multiplied 8-fold over the next 20 years and then, another 12-fold from there over the *next* decade. Turnover rose from 15% in 1961 to 23% in 1972 to 105% in 2002 and even higher in 2012 and over those 40 years, trading volume surged upward nearly 90 times! Table 1.1 shows the rise in shares traded from 1973 to 2011.

---

[34]Most market "technicians" are gone or have faded into the background and insignificance.

Table 1.1 Rise in Shares Traded, 1973–2011

Year	Shares traded
	(billions)
1973	4.1
1982	16.5
1992	31.6
2002	363.1
2011	533.5

Professional investors that dominate today's markets have steadily become more and more consistently advantaged in education, analytical skills, industry and company expertise, access to information, and organizational resources—computers, Internet, and teams of analysts. MBAs and PhDs from leading universities are now "a dime a dozen" normal. Bloombergs and CFAs are ubiquitous. CFA Charters are one indicator of the world-wide persistent change toward professionalism. With the deliberately low entry threshold of a single not-very-difficult exam in 1963, 267 CFA Charters were awarded in that first year. Interest among analysts increased and in 1966, 564 won Charters, even though the exams were now three in annual sequence and substantially more demanding and the preparatory study of the "body of knowledge" more daunting. With the sharp market drop, new Charters fell to 214 in 1971.

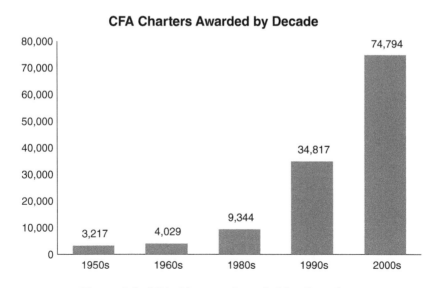

Figure 1.5 CFA Charters Awarded by Decade

Then, with only occasional relapses,[35] Charters rose to over 11,000 in 2012. The total number of Chartered Financial Analysts is now over 130,000 and another 220,000 have registered as candidates—worldwide (see Figure 1.5).[36]

Research reports of all sorts on industries, companies, economies, demographics, politics, etc. flood the Internet, fax machines, and mailbags every day. Everybody has access to more market information than they can possibly use. And with Regulation FD to "level the playing field," the SEC is assuring that all information is always disclosed to all investors at the same time.

Each of the individual changes noted below may have been important. The compound change has been astounding. Over the past 50 years,

- NYSE trading volume has risen from 2½ million shares a day to 5 *billion*—a 2,000 times increase.
- Equity derivatives trading has gone from zero to more in value than the NYSE cash market.
- Bloomberg machine placements have gone from 0 to over 300—and were rising rapidly.
- In absolute terms, the capabilities of the first and second quartile investment professionals have been steadily rising.

The unsurprising result: the stock market got harder and harder to beat because the competition got better and better and harder to beat or keep up with, particularly after the substantial fees.

Significantly, no method has been found to identify in advance which actively managed funds would prove to be the winners and once again, the losing funds lost more (1.7%) than the winners won (1%) *before* taxes.[37] Table 1.2 shows the large majority of actively managed funds—of all types and sizes—that underperform.

For all investors, the quality of competition has again and again raised the standard of excellence to a higher and higher level of speed,[38] expertise, and skill required to keep up with the competition or to be a

[35]Particularly after a peak of 10,045 to 4,618 in 2008 with the Global Financial Crisis.
[36]Pass rates indicate the rigor of the three sequential examinations: 38% for Level I, 47% for Level II, and 52% for Level III.
[37]Taxes cost the typical actively managed fund's shareholders about 1% of assets more than an index fund's shareholders, according to Morningstar.
[38]Douglas MacArthur asserted—with his usual confidence—that the history of warfare could be summarized in just *nine* letters: NOT IN TIME.

Table 1.2 Percentage of Funds Underperforming Benchmarks, Adjusted for Survivorship Bias: 15 Years to December 31, 2011

Size	Value funds	Blended funds	Growth funds
Large	57	84	75
Medium	100	96	97
Small	70	95	78

Top Quartile or Top Decile manager.[39] The market has been changing in many ways that collectively raise the standards of capability required just to keep up with the average competitor, let alone significantly outperform. And more and more rational, educated, informed, and competitive participants continue to join in the search for pricing errors and that all have ready access to almost all the same information. So the probabilities continue to rise that any mispricing will be discovered—and swiftly arbitraged away into insignificance.

Importantly, given the many collectively transformative ways in which the gathering, processing, and distribution of investment information have increased in breadth, depth, speed, and accuracy, a rational observer would accept that securities market prices—determined by the consensus of thousands of experts committing substantial real money in virulent competition with all other experts—are more efficient than ever. And the levels of skill needed to be "competitive" are now higher than ever. So, the core question is not whether the markets are *perfectly* efficient, but only whether markets are sufficiently "efficient" that active managers burdened with the handicaps of operating costs and fees—correctly understood—are unlikely to be able to keep up with and very unlikely to get much ahead of the market—the trading-weighted consensus of experts. The important question is whether investors have sufficient reason to accept the risks and uncertainties of active management, given the difficulty of successful manager selection and the poor prospects for superior net returns.

Of course, realization of the ever-increasing difficulty will not come quickly or easily—particularly from active managers. We cannot reasonably expect them to say, "We, the emperors, have no clothes," and give up

---

[39]One change is not widely recognized but appears to be important. With some of the most capable and best-informed managers (e.g. hedge funds) trading far more intensively, investment managers would be wise to evaluate themselves according to the competitive excellence of their *transactions*—not just their portfolio performance. Studied this way, chances are great that the Top Decile *managers,* as measured by capability, execute most of the Top Quartile *transactions.*

active management when they are so well paid for continuously striving. In addition, Kahneman recommends recognizing the socializing power of a culture like the one that pervades investment management:

> We know that people can maintain an unshakeable faith in any proposition, however absurd, when they are sustained by a community of like-minded believers. Given the professional culture of the financial community, it is not surprising that large numbers of individuals in that world believe themselves to be among the chosen few who can do what they believe others cannot.

The most potent psychological cause of the illusion is certainly that the people who pick stocks are exercising high-level skills. They consult economic data and forecasts, they examine income statements and balance sheets, they evaluate the quality of top management, and they assess the competition. All this is serious work that requires extensive training, and the people who do it have the immediate (and valid) experience of using these skills.[40] Unfortunately for advocates of active investing, Kahneman is also familiar with the extensive research over the past 50 years that shows conclusively that "for a large majority of fund managers, the selection of stocks is more like rolling dice than playing poker. Typically, at least two out of three mutual funds underperform . . . in any given year."

> More important, the year-to-year correlation between the outcomes of mutual funds is very small, barely higher than zero. The successful funds in any given year are mostly lucky; they have had a good roll of the dice. There is general agreement among researchers that nearly all stock pickers, whether they know it or not—and few of them do—are playing a game of chance. The subjective experience of traders is that they are making sensible, educated guesses in a situation of great uncertainty. In highly efficient markets, however, educated guesses are no more than blind guesses.[41]

Kahneman, relying on objective data, shows little mercy as he rounds on to his conclusion:

> A major industry appears to be built largely on an *illusion of skill*. Billions of shares are traded every day, with many people buying each

---

[40]Daniel Kahneman, *Thinking, Fast and Slow* (New York: Penguin, 2012), p. 217.
[41]Ibid., p. 215.

stock and others selling it to them. Most of the buyers and sellers know [or, being well-informed, *should* know] that they have [mostly] the same information; they exchange the stocks primarily because they have different opinions. The buyers think the price is too low and likely to rise, while the sellers think the price is high and likely to drop. The puzzle is why buyers and sellers alike think that the current price is *wrong*. What make them believe they know more about what the price should be than the market does? For most of them, that belief is an illusion.

And, as the market has become increasingly dominated by increasingly skillful and well-informed competitors, the importance of the illusion has increased asymptotically toward no longer credible.[42]

Kahneman is even-handed in his balloon pricking. Reviewing the popular business literature on how superior managerial practices can supposedly be identified and somehow put to work with favorable results, he says, "Both messages are overstated. The comparison of firms that have been more or less successful is to a significant extent a comparison between firms that have been more or less lucky."

Because luck plays a large role, the quality of leadership and management practices cannot be inferred reliably from observations of success. And even if you had perfect foreknowledge that a CEO has brilliant vision and extraordinary competence, you still would be unable to predict how the company will perform with much better accuracy than the flip of a coin. On average, the gap in corporate profitability and stock returns between the outstanding firms and the less successful firms studied in *Built to Last* shrank to almost nothing in the period following the study. The average profitability of the companies identified in the famous *In Search of Excellence* dropped sharply as well within a short time. A study of *Fortune*'s Most Admired Companies finds that over a twenty-year period, the firms with the worst rating went on to earn much higher stock returns that the most admired firms.

You are probably tempted to think of causal explanations for these observations: perhaps the successful firms became complacent, the less successful firms tried harder. But this is the wrong way to think about what happened. The average gap must shrink, because the original gap was due in good part to luck, which contributed both to the success

---

[42]Ibid., pp. 212, 213.

of the top firms and to the lagging performance of the rest. We have already encountered this statistical fact of life: regression to the mean.[43, 44]

Kahneman uses a specific example to explain his thesis:

Some years ago I had an unusual opportunity to examine the illusion of financial skill up close. I had been invited to speak to a group of investment advisers in a firm that provided financial advice and other services to very wealthy clients. I asked for some data to prepare my presentation and was granted a small treasure: a spreadsheet summarizing the investment outcomes of some twenty-five anonymous wealth advisers for each of eight consecutive years. Each adviser's score for each year was his (most of them were men) main determinant of his year-end bonus. It was a simple matter to rank the advisers by their performance in each year and to determine whether there were persistent differences in skill among them and whether the same advisers consistently achieved better returns for their clients year after year.

To answer the question, I computed correlation coefficients between the rankings in each pair of years: year 1 with year 2, year 1 with year 3, and so on up through year 7 with year 8. That yielded 28 correlation coefficients, one for each pair of years. I knew the theory and was prepared to find weak evidence of persistence of skill. Still, I was surprised to find that the average of the 28 correlations was .01. In other words, zero. The consistent correlations that would indicate differences in skill were not to be found. The results resembled what you would expect from a dice-rolling contest, not a game of skill. *No one in the firm seemed to be aware of the nature of the game that its stock pickers were playing.*[45]

---

[43]Ibid., p. 207.

[44]Kahneman's favorite equations—because they explain so much so well—are:

1. Success = Talent + Luck
2. Great Success = A Little More Talent + A Lot More Luck

   Or, as Robert Burns taught in a favorite poem,

   O wad some Pow'r the giftie gie us

   To See Oursels as others see us

   It wad frae monie a blunder free us

   An' foolish notion.

[45]Ibid., p. 215.

A client selecting active managers has to answer two different and increasingly difficult questions:

- Will Manager A be one of the best managers over the next several years?
- Will Manager A be *enough* better, in today's expert market—after adjusting for risk—to justify the fees?

Despite all the extensive accumulating evidence that active managers have not, and by the iron logic of competition, will not, outperform the market they themselves dominate, clients somehow continue to believe *their* managers can and will outperform. (The triumph of hope over experience is not confined to repetitive matrimony. The average US institutional client expects its managers to outperform by a cool 100 basis points.)[46] Of course, the difficulty of selecting significantly superior managers increases as the number of managers used by an institution or by an individual increases, and most institutions use multiple managers.

Consider the many factors that have encouraged investors to pursue active management: media advertising is extensive and notoriously concentrates on "superior" performance; media coverage centers on reporting the "winners" who cheerfully provide *ex post* explanations of how they believe they achieved their successes; investment committees focus on selecting only the best manager from a group of pre-selected "winners;" and investment consultants are retained to search the world to find the best of the best. Given the reality that their firm economics depend on clients continuing to use their services, why would they be expected to tell their fee-paying clients that they are on a "mission improbable"? Another possible explanation is that fund executives believe they can easily and successfully switch from manager to manager. As one fund executive recently declared to a large audience, "We don't marry our managers; we date them through Match.com."[47] Unfortunately, in the years *after* the decision to change, the fired manager typically out-performs the newly hired manager.[48]

---

[46]Corporate and public pension funds are only slightly less optimistic while endowments and unions are somewhat more optimistic. Among pension fund executives, the elusive magic of outperformance is now the most favored way to close the current funding gaps.

[47]Panelist at Institutional Investor's Endowment and Foundation Conference in Boston, June 4–6, 2012.

[48]See "Murder on the Orient Express," *FAJ*, Vol. 60, No. 4, July–August 2012.

The persistent drumbeat of disappointing underperformance by active managers was for many years deniable because there were no clear alternatives to trying harder and hoping for the best. Blessed in most situations with the benefit of optimism, clients continued to see the fault as theirs and gamely continued to try to find Mr. Right, convinced there were no valid alternatives. But now, with the proliferation of low-cost index funds and ETFs, there are clear-cut alternatives. And clients are increasingly recognizing that reality and even taking action. The real question now is "Why are clients *not* changing from active to indexing?" The answer lies with deeply rooted human optimism.

Behavioral Economics

Many puzzling examples of less-than-rational human behavior can be explained by turning to behavioral economics—and many clues can be found to help explain why the pace of change to indexing has been so slow *and* why the pace is likely to continue gradually accelerating. Behavioral "tilt" affects the way we form our perceptions and beliefs, how we behave, and how we make decisions. Many well-documented "tilts" help to explain why the pace of shifting has been so slow, including the following:

- **Ambiguity effect**: since future performance data is unknown, that uncertainty makes it easier to say, "Well, let's wait and see. This manager still looks like a winner."
- **Base rate fallacy**: Basing beliefs or decisions on specific exceptions and ignoring the normal experience. "We only consider Top Quartile managers—and then we pick the best of them, so we should get superior performance."
- **Choice-supportive bias**: "Well, we haven't taken a lot of time studying our own past experience, but I'm pretty sure that overall, we've done things pretty well."
- **Confirmation bias**: "We know there are superior managers and we've seen lots of data from our consultant on the managers they recommend, so we're confident our process will bring us a superior group of managers."
- **Past-purchase rationalizing**: "We wouldn't have chosen these managers if we weren't confident, they would eventually out-perform."

As Kahneman warns:

The planning fallacy is only one of the manifestations of a pervasive optimistic bias. Most of us view the world as more benign than it really is, our own attributes as more favorable than they truly are, and the goals we adopt as more achievable than they are likely to be. We also tend to exaggerate our ability to forecast the future, which fosters optimistic overconfidence. In terms of its consequences for decisions, the optimistic bias may well be the most significant of the cognitive biases. Because an optimistic bias can be both a blessing and a risk, you should be both happy and wary if you are temperamentally optimistic.[49]

Kahneman goes on to explain that errors of prediction are inevitable because the world we live in is itself highly unpredictable and that a high level of confidence is not to be trusted as an indicator of accuracy. He then asks: "Why do investors, both amateur and professional, stubbornly believe that they can do better than the market, contrary to an economic theory that most of them accept, and contrary to what they could learn from a dispassionate evaluation of their personal experience?"

He then laments, "Unfortunately, skill in evaluating the business prospects of a firm is not sufficient for successful stock trading, where the key question is whether the information is already incorporated in the price of its stock."[50] As we now know, most of the relevant and attainable information about the economy, the industry, the company, and the stock is already known or anticipated and so is incorporated in each stock's price almost all of the time.

Behavioral economists' studies show, with remarkable consistency, that Pareto's 80:20 Law applies to most groups of people when asked to rate themselves on whether they are above average or below average. As we see ourselves, we hail from America's favorite hometown: Lake Wobegon. Over and over again, about 80% of us rate ourselves "above average"[51] on each of these parameters:

- Being a good listener.
- Having a good sense of humor.

---

[49]Kahneman, *Thinking, Fast and Slow*, p. 251.
[50]Ibid., p. 217.
[51]A recent survey found 87% of respondents confided they would deserve to go to heaven—well above their estimates of heaven for Mother Teresa and Martin Luther King.

- Being a good conversationalist.
- Being a good friend to others.
- Being a good driver.
- Being a good dancer

  and . . .

- Being a good investor.

The last rating—with 80% of us rating ourselves as "above average" as investors—may be the key to explaining why indexing has not been pursued more boldly. Institutional fund executives—despite all the extensive and consistently contradictory data from *past* years—are remarkably confident that in the *future,* their active managers will somehow achieve significantly superior results. Year after year, research by Greenwich Associates reports that institutional investors expect their managers to beat their benchmarks by one hundred basis points annually. With this degree of confidence in active management—no matter how sternly contradicted by extensive past data—there's little wonder that demand for active management continues strong.

In *The Right Stuff,* Tom Wolfe showed his readers what the outstanding test pilots he wrote about could not see: The cause of deadly accidents was not "pilot error"; the accidents were predictable and inevitable. In work so exceedingly difficult in an environment so fraught with inherent variability, even the world's best test pilots could not always be in control. Similarly, the young white women in the (2011) film, *The Help*, could not see the social wrong that we now see all too clearly from a different perspective. As Burt Malkiel says, "It's hard for people to accept [indexing] because it's like telling someone there is no Santa Claus. People don't like to give up believing."

Fees Are Not Low

Meanwhile, investors continue to look right past one factor—fees— because almost everyone assumes that fees are *not* important. But seen correctly—compared to results actually achieved—fees are very important. Let's contrast conventional perceptions with reality. Conventionally, fees for equity management are typically described with one four-letter word and a single number. The four-letter word is "only," as in "only 1%"

for mutual funds or "only ½ of 1%" for institutions. If you accept 1%,[52] you'll easily accept the "only." But isn't that a self-deception?[53]

"Only 1%" *is* the ratio of fees to *assets,* but is that in any way the right way to define and calculate fees? The investor already *has* the assets, so active investment managers must be offering to deliver something else—*returns.* If annual future equity returns are, as the consensus now holds, 7%, then that 1% of assets quickly balloons to nearly 15% of returns—a much higher and much more realistic charge. But that's not the end of it.

A more informed and rigorous definition of fees for active management would begin with recognizing the wide availability of a market-matching "commodity" alternative at a very low fee: indexing. Since indexing consistently delivers the full market return at no more than the market level of risk, the correct definition of fees for active management that informed realists would use, *after* adjusting for market risk, is the *incremental* or marginal fee as a percent of *incremental* or marginal returns.

Among mutual funds, fees vary significantly from fund to fund and by type of fund—and even between comparable index funds. In America, actively managed funds average more than 1% as shown in Table 1.3. Note that mutual fund fees in America are significantly lower than funds in other countries.

In addition to expense ratios, another charge of, typically, 25 basis points has been levied as 12b-1 or "distribution fee."[54] These fees are

---

[52]The impact of "only 1%" can accumulate over time into a very large number. In one example, two investors each start with $100,000 and add $14,000 each year for 25 years. One investor selects a manager charging 1.25% while the other pays only 0.25%—a difference of "only 1%." After 25 years, both have over $1 million, but the difference between them is stunning: $255,423—over a quarter of a million dollars ($1,400,666 vs. $1,145,243). For bond funds, fees—as a percent of incremental returns above index bond funds—have been enormous:

Taxable bond	103	175
Municipal bond	99	160

[53]Of course, with 12b-1 charges, total mutual fees in the US are over 1% of assets (and 15% of expected returns *and* over 100% of expected incremental returns) and in Canada, the UK, and many other countries, mutual fund fees are over 2%.

[54]Their primary stated purpose is to pay brokers not to "churn" customers' mutual fund investments, which hurts long-term investors because the funds would have to keep extra cash balances to cover redemptions.

Table 1.3 Fees for Mutual Funds in US in Basis Points, 2011

	Average fees	90th percentile fee
Equity funds	**144**	**220**
Aggressive growth	149	221
Growth	137	209
Sector	154	237
Growth income	121	195
Income equity	124	193
International equity	157	232

either paid directly to brokers for "shelf space" or pay for advertising and other marketing expenses. These fees add significantly to investors' total costs—particularly when correctly calculated versus incremental returns.[55, 56]

So now the crucial question is clear: What marginal benefit do active managers offer at what marginal cost? Fees of 50 basis points (½ of 1% of assets) for institutions are an incremental 45 basis points higher than institutional index fund fees of, say, 5 basis points (or less). That 45 basis point charge is the correct incremental fee to compare to incremental returns.

Very few of the most successful active managers outperform by an average of 100 basis points over the long run, but even for these heroes, the true fee—marginal fee as a percent of incremental return—would be 45%. For an active manager consistently out-performing by ½%—surely a compelling Top Decile performance—the true or marginal fee would be 90%.

Objectively, the incremental fees for incremental risk-adjusted returns from active management are *not* low. They are *high*—very high. Fama's research says only 3% of active managers cover the cost of their fees. Since a majority of managers underperform the market, the true fee for the *average* active manager is actually well in excess of 100% of incremental returns. This grim reality has gone largely unnoticed by clients—so far. But "not yet being caught" is certainly not the strong protective moat that Warren Buffett wants around a business.

---

[55]Another 5.4% fee or "load" is often deducted from the mutual fund investor's assets at the date of purchase. Load funds have lost shares of assets in recent years. From 2001 to 2011, "load" funds increased assets by only $500 billion while "no-load" fund assets increased by over $3 trillion—six times as much.
[56]Over a 15-year period—1995 to 2010—the "high cost" quartile of mutual funds substantially out-performed the "low cost" quartile by 7.4% vs. 5.6%. In a period with a market return of 7%, the 1.6% difference would be over 40% of the expected market return.

Ironically, the active managers' inability to "beat the market" is most certainly *not* a slam on them as investment experts, but rather a tribute to the extraordinary skill, hard work, and persistent striving for excellence shown every day by the many remarkable people attracted to investment research and management over the past 50 years. In brief, the professionals are so "good at the game" that only a very few can be capable of both covering their costs *and* out-performing the expert consensus.

For our profession, for each individual and for each firm in active investment management, the question is: When will we recognize that the skills of other market participants have increased so much that we can no longer expect to outperform by enough to cover the costs of trading *and* management fees *and* offer—after fees and costs—a good value to our clients? Another central question is: When will our clients decide that continuing to strive to beat the market is not a good deal for them? These questions are crucial because to continue selling the service after passing that tipping point would clearly raise the kinds of ethical questions that separate a profession from a business.

As a business, investment management is a booming success, but as a profession, investment management has been repeatedly failing. Understandably, practitioners want both a great business and an admired profession, but our collective decisions and behaviors—far more than insiders yet recognize—show that in what we *do* versus what we *say*, we put "great business" far ahead of "admired profession."

Part of the reason we are able to put business first is that most clients are part-timers who don't realize what's really going on and part of the reason is that we insiders don't see reality all that clearly either—so we see no particular reason to worry or take action. If the "emperor has no clothes," why do these beliefs persist? One way to test our thinking is to ask the question in reverse: If your manager consistently and reliably delivered the full market return with no more than market risk for 1/10 of 1%, would you switch to one of a group of managers who charge well over 1% *and* produce unpredictably varying results that fall short nearly twice as often as they out-do the market, and when they fall short lose, on average, $1.65 versus gaining $1.00 when they do out-perform? The question answers itself.

For those who are willing to move forward from the Loser's Game of trying to beat the market consensus of informed, skillful, determined professionals, the good news is that they can re-frame their client relationships into a Winners' Game,[57] in which both clients and managers

---

[57]The Winners' Game.

can be successful. The "secret" is to put the interests of clients first and integrate investment product with the all-important service of investment counselling: guiding each client toward an explicit and well-reasoned specification of that particular client's realistic investment objectives *and* the specific investment program most likely to achieve those objectives within that client's interim risk tolerance *and* helping each client stay on course through market extremes—both highs and lows.

Of course, the Winners' Game may not be as financially rewarding to investment managers as a business, but as a profession it would be fulfilling *and* it is the only admirable way forward that will inspire client and customer loyalty—with all the attendant economic benefits—and provide practitioners with deep professional satisfaction.

Source: Conference paper given at Oxford University in 2012.

2

The Loser's Game

As the percentage of trading by expert professionals surged upward from 10% to 30% to 70%, expert investors increasingly equally informed and equally well-armed with technology had a harder and harder time overcoming the costs of operations and fees. This made active "performance" investing increasingly a loser's game in which the outcome is determined by the errors of the loser. That such a dour conclusion could be so well received by the severely challenged players is a compliment to the sportsmanship of professional investors. By 2020, the percent of NYSE trading done by institutional experts was over 90% and actively managed funds failing to keep up with their chosen benchmarks had risen over the long term of 15 years to a deeply daunting 89%.

Disagreeable data are streaming out of the computers of Becker Securities and Merrill Lynch and all the other performance measurement firms. Over and over and over again, these facts and figures inform us that investment managers are failing to perform. Not only are the nation's leading portfolio managers failing to produce positive absolute rates of return (after all, it's been a long, long bear market) but they are also failing to produce positive relative rates of return. Contrary to their oft articulated goal of outperforming the market averages, investment managers are not beating the market: The market is beating them.

Faced with information that contradicts what they believe, human beings tend to respond in one of two ways. Some will assimilate the information, changing it—as oysters cover an obnoxious grain of silica with nacre—so they can ignore the new knowledge and hold on to their former beliefs; and others will accept the validity of the new information. Instead of changing the meaning of the new data to fit their old concept of reality, they adjust their perception of reality to accommodate the information and then they put it to use.

Psychologists advise us that the more important the old concept of reality is to a person—the more important it is to his sense of self-esteem and sense of inner worth—the more tenaciously he will hold on to the old concept and the more insistently he will assimilate, ignore, or reject new evidence that conflicts with his old and familiar concept of the world. This self-harmful behavior is found among very bright people because they can so easily develop and articulate self-persuasive logic.

For example, most institutional investment managers continue to believe, or at least say they believe, that they can and soon will again "outperform the market." They won't and they can't. And the purpose of this article is to explain why not.

My experience with very bright and articulate investment managers is that their skills at analysis and logical extrapolation are very good, often superb, but that their brilliance in extending logical extrapolation draws their own attention far away from the sometimes erroneous basic assumptions upon which their schemes are based. Major errors in reasoning and exposition are rarely found in the logical development of this analysis, but instead lie within the premise itself. This is what worried Martin Luther. It's what *The Best and The Brightest* was all about. It's what lifted LTV above $100; why the Emperor went for days without clothes; and why comedians and science fiction writers are so careful first to establish the "premise" and then quickly divert our attention from it so they can elaborate the persuasive details of a developing "logic."

The investment management business (it should be a profession but is not) is built upon a simple and basic belief: Professional money managers can beat the market. That premise appears to be false.

If the premise that it is feasible to outperform the market were accepted, deciding how to go about achieving success would be a matter of straightforward logic. First, the market can be represented by an index, such as the S&P 500. Since this is a passive and public listing, the successful manager need only rearrange his bets differently from the S&P "shill." He can be activist in either stock selection or market timing, or both. Since the manager will want his "bets" to be right most of the time, he will assemble a group of bright, well-educated, highly motivated, hardworking young people, and their collective purpose will be to beat the market by "betting against the house" with a "good batting average."

The belief that active managers can beat the market is based on two assumptions: (l) liquidity offered in the stock market is an advantage, and (2) active investing is a Winner's Game.

The unhappy thesis of this article can be briefly stated: Owing to important changes in the past ten years, these basic assumptions are no longer true. On the contrary, market liquidity is a liability rather than an asset, and institutional investors will, over the long term, underperform the market because money management has become a Loser's Game.

Before demonstrating with mathematical evidence why money management has become a Loser's Game, we should close off the one path of escape for those who will try to assimilate the facts. They may argue that this analysis is unfair because so much of the data on performance comes from bear market experience, giving an adverse bias to an evaluation of the long-term capabilities of managers who have portfolio betas above 1.0. "Of course," they will concede with dripping innuendo, "these interesting analyses may have less to say about dynamic fund managers operating in a decent market." Perhaps, but can they present us with evidence to support their hopes? Can they shoulder the burden of proof? After many hours of discussion with protesting money managers all over America and in Canada and Europe, I have heard no new evidence or persuasive appeal from the hard judgment that follows the evidence presented below. In brief, the "problem" is not a cyclical aberration; it is a long-term secular trend.

The basic characteristics of the environment within which institutional investors must operate have changed greatly in the past decade. The most significant change is that institutional investors have become, and will continue to be, the dominant feature of their own environment. This change has impacted greatly upon all the major features of the investment field. In particular, institutional dominance has converted market liquidity from a source of profits to a source of costs, and this is the main reason behind the transformation of money management from a Winner's Game to a Loser's Game.

Before analyzing what happened to convert institutional investing from a Winner's Game to a Loser's Game, we should explore the profound difference between these two kinds of "games." In making the conceptual distinction, I will use the writings of an eminent scientist, a distinguished historian, and a renowned educator. They are, respectively, Dr. Simon Ramo of TRW; naval historian, Admiral Samuel Elliot Morrison; and professional golf instructor, Tommy Armour.

Simon Ramo identified the crucial difference between a Winner's Game and a Loser's Game in his excellent book on playing strategy,

Extraordinary Tennis for the Ordinary Tennis Player. Over a period of many years, he observed that tennis was not one game but two. One game of tennis is played by professionals and a very few gifted amateurs; the other is played by all the rest of us.

For the ten years ending December 31, 1974, the funds in the Becker Securities sample had a median rate of return of 0.0%. The S&P total rate of return over the same period was 1.2% per annum. (Within the Becker sample, the high fund's annual rate of return was 4.5%, the first quartiles fund's return was 1.1%, the median 0.0%, the third quartile 1.1% and the low fund's annual rate of return −5.6%.)

Unfortunately, the relative performance of institutionally managed portfolios appears to be getting worse. Measuring returns from trough to trough in the market, the institutionally managed funds in the Becker sample are falling farther and farther behind the market, as represented by the S&P 500 Average. It appears that the costs of active management are going up and that the rewards from active management are going down.

Although players in both games use the same equipment, dress, rules, and scoring, and conform to the same etiquette and customs, the basic natures of their two games are almost entirely different. After extensive scientific and statistical analysis, Dr. Ramo summed it up this way: Professionals *win* points; amateurs *lose* points. Professional tennis players stroke the ball with strong, well-aimed shots, through long and often exciting rallies, until one player is able to drive the ball just beyond the reach of his opponent. Errors are seldom made by these splendid players.

Expert tennis is what I call a Winner's Game because the ultimate outcome is determined by the actions of the winner. Victory is due to winning more points than the opponent wins—not, as we shall see in a moment, simply to getting a higher score than the opponent, but getting that higher score by winning points.

Amateur tennis, Ramo found, is almost entirely different. Brilliant shots, long and exciting rallies, and seemingly miraculous recoveries are few and far between. On the other hand, the ball is fairly often hit into the net or out of bounds, and double faults at service are not uncommon. The amateur duffer seldom beats his opponent, but he beats himself all the time. The victor in this game of tennis gets a higher score than the opponent, but he gets that higher score because his opponent is losing even more points.

As a scientist and statistician, Dr. Ramo gathered data to test his hypothesis. And he did it in a very clever way. Instead of keeping conventional game—"15 All," "30–15," etc.—Ramo simply counted points *won* versus points *lost*. And here is what he found. In expert tennis, about 80% of the strategy for winning outcome is determined by the activities of the *winner*. Amateur tennis is a Loser's Game—the final outcome is determined by the activities of the *loser*. The two games are, in their fundamental characteristic, not at all the same. They are opposites.

From this discovery of the two kinds of tennis, Dr. Ramo builds a complete strategy by which ordinary tennis players can win games, sets, and matches again and again by following the simple stratagem of losing less, and letting the opponent defeat himself. Dr. Ramo explains that if you choose to win at tennis—as opposed to having a good time—the strategy for winning is to avoid mistakes. The way to avoid mistakes is to be conservative and keep the ball in play, letting the other fellow have plenty of room in which to blunder his way to defeat, because he, being an amateur (and probably not having read Ramo's book) will play a losing game and not know it.

He will make errors. He will make too many errors. Once in a while he may hit a serve you cannot possibly handle, but much more frequently he will double fault. Occasionally, he may volley balls past you at the net, but more often than not they will sail far out of bounds. He will slam balls into the net from the front court and from the back court. His game will be a routine catalogue of gaffs, goofs, and grief.

He will try to beat you by winning, but he is not good enough to overcome the many inherent adversities of the game itself. The situation does not allow him to win with an activist strategy and he will instead lose. His efforts to win more points will, unfortunately for him, only increase his error rate. As Ramo instructs us in his book, the strategy for winning in a loser's game is to lose less. Avoid trying too hard. By keeping the ball in play, give the opponent as many opportunities as possible to make mistakes and blunder his way to defeat. In brief, by losing less become the victor.

In his thoughtful treatise on military science, *Strategy and Compromise*, Admiral Morrison makes the following point: "In warfare, mistakes are inevitable. Military decisions are based on estimates of the enemy's strengths and intentions that are usually faulty, and on intelligence that is never complete and often misleading." (This sounds a great deal like the investment business.) "Other things being equal," concludes Morrison, "the side that makes the fewest strategic errors wins the war."

War, as we all know, is the ultimate Loser's Game. As General Patton said: "Let the other dumb bastard lose *his* life for his country." Golf is another Loser's Game. Tommy Armour, in his great book *How to Play Your Best Golf All the Time*, says: "The way to win is by making fewer bad shots."

Gambling in a casino where the house takes at least 20% of every pot is obviously a Loser's Game. Stud poker is a Loser's Game, but Night Baseball with deuces, trays, and one-eyed Jacks "wild" is a Winner's Game.

Campaigning for elected office is a Loser's Game: The electorate seldom votes for one of the candidates but rather against the other candidate. Professional politicians advise their candidates: "Help the voters find a way to vote *against* the other guy, and you'll get elected."

Recent studies of professional football have found that the most effective defensive platoon members play an open, ad hoc, enterprising, risk-taking style—the proper strategy for a Winner's Game—while the best offensive players play a careful, "by the book" style that concentrates on avoiding errors and eliminating uncertainty, which is the requisite game plan for a Loser's Game. "Keep it simple," said Vincent Lombardi.

There are many other Loser's Games. Some, like institutional investing, used to be Winner's Games in the past, but have changed with the passage of time into *Loser's Games*. For example, 50 years ago, only brave, athletic, strong-willed young people with good eyesight had the nerve to try flying an airplane. In those glorious days, flying was a Winner's Game. But times have changed and so has flying. If you got into a 747 today, and the pilot came aboard wearing a 50-mission hat with a long, white silk scarf around his neck, you'd get off. Those people do not belong in airplanes any longer because flying an airplane today is a Loser's Game. Today, there's only one way to fly an airplane. It's simple: Don't make any mistakes.

Prize fighting starts out as a Winner's Game and becomes a Loser's Game as the fight progresses. In the first three or four rounds, a really strong puncher tries for a knockout. Thereafter, prize fighting is a grueling contest of endurance to see who can survive the most punishment, while the other fellow gets so worn out that he literally drops to defeat.

Expert card players know that after several rounds of play, games like Gin Rummy go through a "phase change" after which discards no longer improve the relative position of the discarding player. During this latter phase, discards tend to add more strength to the opponent's hand than they remove weakness from the hand of the discarder. This changes long hands of Gin Rummy into a Loser's Game, and the correct strategy in the latter phase of the game is to evaluate discards not in terms of how much good they will do for your hand to get rid of them, but rather how much good they may do for your opponent.

Many other examples could be given, but these will suffice to make the distinction between Winner's Games and Loser's Games, to explain why the requisite player strategy is very different for the two kinds of games, and to show that the fundamental nature of a game can change and that Winner's Games can and sometimes do become Loser's Games. And that's what has happened to the Money Game.

The Money Game was a phenomenal Winner's Game in the mid-1920s when John J. Raskob, a prominent business executive, could write an article for a popular magazine with the encouraging title "Everybody Ought to Be Rich." The article gave a cookbook recipe that anybody could, theoretically, follow to riches beyond the dreams of avarice. The Great Crash abruptly reversed the situation and made investing a Loser's Game for nearly two decades.

It was during these decades of the 1930s and 1940s that preservation of capital, emphasis on the safety of bonds, and sober-sided conventional wisdom came to dominance and the foundation was laid for the renaissance of the Winner's Game. The bull market of the 1950s gave dramatic and compelling evidence that the situation had changed, that big money could be made in the market. And this news attracted people who like to make big money—people who like to win.

The people who came to Wall Street in the 1960s had always been—and expected always to be—winners. They had been presidents of their high school classes, varsity team captains, and honor students. They were bright, attractive, outgoing, and ambitious. They were willing to work hard and take chances because our society had given them many and frequent rewards for such behavior. They had gone to Yale and the Marines and Harvard Business School. And they were quick to recognize that the big Winner's Game was being played in Wall Street.

It was a glorious, wonderful, euphoric time. It was a time when almost anybody who was smart and willing to work hard could win. And almost all of us did.

The trouble with Winner's Games is that they tend to self-destruct because they attract too much attention and too many players—all of whom want to win. (That's why gold rushes finish ugly.) But in the short run, the rushing in of more and more players seeking to win expands the apparent reward. And that's what happened in Wall Street during the 1960s. Riding the tide of a bull market, institutional investors obtained such splendid rates of return in equities that more and more money was turned over to them—particularly in mutual funds and pension funds—which fueled the continuation of their own bull market. Institutional investing was a Winner's Game and the winners knew that by playing it faster, they would increase the rate of winnings. But in the process, a basic change occurred in the investment environment; the market came to be dominated by the institutions.

In just ten years, the market activities of the investing institutions have gone from only 30% of total public transactions to a whopping 70%. And that has made all the difference. No longer are the "New Breed on Wall Street" in the minority; they are now the majority. The professional money manager isn't competing any longer with amateurs who are out of touch with the market; now he competes with other experts.

It's an impressive group of competitors. There are 150 major institutional investors and another 600 small and medium-sized institutions operating in the market all day, every day, in the most intensely competitive way. And in the past decade, these institutions have become more active, have developed larger in-house research staffs, and have tapped into the central source of market information and fundamental research provided by institutional brokers. Ten years ago, many institutions were still far out of the mainstream of intensive management; today such an institution, if any exists, would be a rare collector's item.

Competitively active institutional investing has resulted in sharply higher portfolio turnover. The typical equity portfolio turnover has gone from 10 to 30%. As we've already seen, this acceleration in portfolio activity plus the growth in institutional assets and the shift of pension funds toward equities have increased the proportion of market transactions of institutions from 30 to 70% which has, in turn, produced the basic "phase change" that has transformed portfolio activity from a source of incremental profits to a major cost, and that transformation has switched institutional investing from a Winner's Game to a Loser's Game.

The new "rules of the game" can be set out in a simple but distressing equation. The elements are these:

1. Assume equities will return an average 9% rate of return.
2. Assume average turnover of 30% per annum.
3. Assume average costs—dealer spreads plus commission of 3%.
4. Assume management and custody fees total 0.20%.
5. Assume the goal of the manager is to outperform the averages by 20%.

Solve for "X": $(X.9) - [30.(3+3)] - (0.20) = (120 \cdot 9)$

$$X = \frac{[30 \cdot (3+3)] = (0.20) + (120 \cdot 9)}{9}$$

$$X = \frac{1.8 + 0.20 + 10.8)}{9}$$

$$X = \frac{12.8}{9}$$

$$X = 142\%$$

In plain language, the manager who intends to deliver net returns 20% better than the market must earn a gross return before fees and transactions costs (liquidity tolls) that is more than 40% better than the market. If this sounds absurd, the same equation can be solved to show that the active manager must beat the market *gross* by 22% just to come out even with the market *net*.

In other words, for the institutional investor to perform as well as, *but no better than*, the S&P 500, he must be sufficiently astute and skillful to "outdo" the market considerably by 22%. But how can institutional investors hope to outperform the market by such a magnitude when, in effect, they are the market today? Which managers are so well staffed and organized in their operations, or so prescient in their investment policies that they can honestly expect to beat the other professionals by so much on a sustained basis?

The disagreeable numbers from the performance measurement firms say there are *no* managers whose past performance promises that they will outperform the market in the future. Looking backward, the evidence is deeply disturbing: 85% of professionally managed funds underperformed the S&P 500 during the past 10 years. And the median fund's rate of return was only 5.4%—about 10% *below* the S&P 500.

Most money managers have been losing the Money Game. And they know it, even if they cannot admit it publicly. Expectations and promises have come down substantially since the mid-1960s. Almost nobody still talks in terms of beating the market by 20% compounded annually. And nobody listens to those who do.

In times like these, the burden of proof is on the person who says, "I am a winner. I can win the Money Game." Because only a sucker backs a "winner" in a Loser's Game, we have a right to expect him to explain exactly what he is going to do and why it is going to work so very well. This is not very often done in the investment management business.

Does the evidence necessarily lead to an entirely passive or index portfolio? No, it doesn't necessarily lead in that direction. Not quite. But the "null" hypothesis is hard to beat in a situation like this. At the risk of over-simplifying, the null hypothesis says there is nothing there if you cannot find statistically significant evidence of its presence. This would suggest to investment managers, "Don't do anything because when you try to do something, it is on average a mistake." And if you can't beat the market, you certainly should consider joining it. An index fund is one way. The data from the performance measurement firms show that an index fund would have outperformed most money managers.

For those who are determined to try to win the Loser's Game, however, here are a few specific things they might consider.

First, be sure you are playing your own game. Know your policies very well and play according to them all the time. Admiral Morrison, citing the *Concise Oxford Dictionary*, says: "Impose upon the enemy the time and place and conditions for fighting preferred by oneself." Simon Ramo suggests: "Give the other fellow as many opportunities as possible to make mistakes, and he will do so."

Second, keep it simple. Tommy Armour, talking about golf, says: "Play the shot you've got the greatest chance of playing well." Ramo says: "Every game boils down to doing the things you do best and doing them over and over again." Armour again: "Simplicity, concentration, and economy of time and effort have been the distinguishing features of the great players' methods, while others lost their way to glory by wandering in a maze of details." Mies Van der Rohe, the architect, suggests, "Less is more." Why not bring turnover down as a deliberate, conscientious practice? Make fewer and perhaps better investment decisions. Simplify the professional investment management problem. Try to do a few things unusually well.

Third, concentrate on your defenses. Almost all of the information in the investment management business is oriented toward purchase decisions. The competition in making purchase decisions is too good. It's too hard to outperform the other fellow in buying. Concentrate on selling instead. In a Winner's Game, 90% of all research effort should be spent on making purchase decisions; in a Loser's Game, most researchers should spend most of their time making sell decisions. Almost all of the really big trouble that you're going to experience in the next year is in your portfolio right now; if you could reduce some of those really big problems, you might come out the winner in the Loser's Game.

Fourth, don't take it personally. Most of the people in the investment business are "winners" who have won all their lives by being bright, articulate, disciplined, and willing to work hard. They are so accustomed to succeeding by trying harder and are so used to believing that failure to succeed is the failure's own fault that they may take it personally when they see that the average professionally managed fund cannot keep pace with the market any more than John Henry could beat the steam drill.

There is a class of diseases which are called "iatrogenic," meaning they are doctor-caused. The Chinese finger cage and the modern strait-jacket most tightly grip the person who struggles to break free. Ironically, the reason institutional investing has become the Loser's Game is that in the complex problem each manager is trying to solve, his efforts to find a solution—and the efforts of his many urgent competitors—have become the dominant variables. And their efforts to beat the market are no longer the most important part of the solution; they are the most important part of the problem.

Source: Charles D. Ellis (1975) The Loser's Game, *Financial Analysts Journal*, 31:4, 19–26, copyright © CFA Institute reprinted by permission of Taylor & Francis Ltd, http://www.tandfonline.com on behalf of CFA Institute.

3

The Winners' Game

*"If you come to me with a problem," Dad told us, "Come with a solution."
So, here is one way to provide an effective solution to the problem described
in Chapter 2, "The Loser's Game:" Use low-cost index funds for all investment operations. With years of experience with markets and long-term understanding of different types of investments and the behavioral mistakes of
investors, as professionals, we should concentrate on guiding each of our clients
to their optimal investment plan and help them to stay on plan even as wily
old Mr. Market tries to get us to change our investments in one way or
another and more often.*

Everyone likes to succeed in investing. Millions of investors
depend on investment success to assure their security in retirement, to provide for their children's education, or to enjoy better lives. Schools, hospitals, museums, and colleges depend on successful
investing to fulfill their important missions. As investment professionals,
when the services we offer help investors achieve their realistic long-
term objectives, ours can be a noble profession.

The accumulating evidence, however, compels recognition that
investors are suffering serious shortfalls. Part of the problem is that investors make mistakes. But they are not alone. As investment professionals, we need to recognize that much of the real fault lies not with our
clients but with ourselves—the unhappy consequence of three major
systemic errors. Fortunately, we can—and so should—make changes to
make sure investing is, both for our client investors and for ourselves,
truly a winner's game.

For all its amazing complexity, the field of investment management really has only two major parts. One is the *profession*: doing what is best for investment clients. The other is the *business*: doing what is best for investment managers. As in other professions, such as law, medicine, architecture, and management consulting, there is a continuing struggle to get the right balance between the *values* of the profession and the *economics* of the business.

We must be successful at both to retain the trust of our clients and to maintain a viable business and in the long run, the latter depends on the former. Today, investment management differs from many other professions in one most unfortunate way: We are losing the struggle to put our professional values and responsibilities first and our business objectives second.

We can stop losing the struggle if we redefine our mission to emphasize the investment counseling values of our profession—and our understanding of investors and investing—to help clients focus on playing the investment game that they can win and that is worth winning. Fortunately, what is good for our professional fulfillment can, in the long run, also be good for business.

While the investment profession, like all learned professions, has many unusually difficult aspects that require great skill and is getting more complex almost daily, it too has just two major parts. One part is the increasingly difficult task of somehow combining imaginative research and astute portfolio management to achieve superior investment results by outsmarting the increasingly numerous professional investors who now dominate the markets and collectively set the prices of securities. Always interesting, often fascinating, and sometimes exhilarating, the work of competing to "beat the market" has been getting harder and harder and has now become extraordinarily difficult. Most investors are not beating the market; the market is beating them.

Difficulty is not always proportional to importance. In medicine, simply washing hands has proven to be second only to penicillin in saving lives. Fortunately, the most valuable part of what investment professionals do is the least difficult: investment counseling. As experienced professionals, we can help each client think through and determine the sensible investment program most likely to achieve his or her own realistic long-term objectives within his or her own tolerance for various risks given variations in income, changes in the market value of assets, or constraints on liquidity. Then, we can help each client stay with that sensible investment program, particularly when markets seem full of exciting, "this time it's different" opportunities or fraught with disconcerting threats of doom. As kids familiar with the realities of sailing, we terrified our landlubber cousins by going out on a windy day and deliberately tacking close to the wind to cause our small sailboat to heel far over, knowing when the boat seemed most certainly about to capsize that the "righting arm" of the keel was actually even more certain to prevent its tipping any farther.

Success in this investment consulting work is not simple or easy but is much easier than success in "beat the market" investment management. And with the new tools available to investment professionals, it is getting easier even as performance investing is getting steadily harder.

Three Errors

With remarkable irony, those of us devoting our careers to investment management have unintentionally created for ourselves three problems. Two are errors of commission with increasingly serious consequences. The third is an even graver error of omission. Unless we change our ways, this troika of errors will harm the profession that has been so intellectually and financially rewarding to so many of us. Let me first explain each error in turn and then propose the best solution.

Error 1. Falsely Defining Our Mission

The first error is that we have falsely defined our professional mission to our clients and prospective clients as "beating the market." Fifty years ago, those taking up that definition of mission had reasonable prospects of success. But those years are long gone. In today's intensively competitive securities markets, few active managers outperform the market by even 1% over the long term, most managers fall short, and in terms of magnitude, underperformance substantially exceeds outperformance. In addition, identifying the few managers who will be the future "winners" is notoriously difficult, and the rate of subsequent failure among one-time "market leaders" is high.

Truly massive changes have transformed the markets and investment management so greatly that for most investors, beating the market is no longer a realistic objective, as more and more of us are recognizing. Here are some of the changes that over 50 years have compounded to convert active investing into a loser's game:

- NYSE trading volume is up over 2,000 times—from about 3 million shares a day to over 6 billion. Other major exchanges around the world have seen comparable changes in volume.
- The mix of investors has flipped 180° from 90% of total NYSE listed trading being done by individuals to 90% being done by institutions. And anyone with a long memory will tell you that today's institutions are far bigger, smarter, tougher, and faster than those of yore. Derivatives have gone in value traded from nil to larger than the cash market.
- Nearly 100,000 analysts—up from zero 50 years ago—have earned CFA charters and another 200,000 are candidates, led by those in North America, China, and India.
- Concentration is extraordinary: The 50 most active institutions do 50% of all NYSE listed stock trading, and the smallest of these 50 giants spends $100 million annually in fees and commissions buying services from the global securities industry. Naturally, these institutions always get the "first call."
- Regulation Fair Disclosure, commonly known as Reg FD, has "commoditized" most investment information now coming from corporations. Everybody gets it at the same time.
- Algorithmic trading, computer models, and numerous inventive quants are all powerful market participants.
- Globalization, hedge funds, and private equity funds have all become major forces for change in the securities markets' competitive intensity. Bloomberg, the Internet, e-mail, and so forth have created a technological revolution in global communications. We really are "all in this together."
- Investment research reports from major securities firms in all the major markets around the world produce an enormous volume of useful information that gets distributed almost instantly via the Internet to tens of thousands of analysts and portfolio managers around the world who work in fast-response decision-making organizations.

As a result of these and many other changes, the stock markets—the world's largest and most active "prediction markets"—have become increasingly efficient. So, it is harder and harder to beat the smart, hardworking professionals who set those market prices with all their information, computing power, and experience. So it's much, much harder to beat the market after costs and fees. That is why, among mutual funds, the approximate proportion typically falling behind the market averages has become 60% in any 1 year, over 70% over 10 years, and over 80% over 15 years.

Sadly, most descriptions of "performance" do not even mention the most important aspect of all investing: risk. So, it is important to recall that the many "losers" *under*perform the market by twice as much as the few "winners" outperform. Nor do the data adjust for taxes, particularly the high taxes on short-term gains that come with the now normal high portfolio turnover. Finally, of course, historical performance for funds is usually reported as *time* weighted, not *value* weighted, so the reported data do not show true investor experience. That can only be shown with the value-weighted record of how real investors fare with their real money. It's not a pretty picture.

Nor is it comforting to see the details of how clients—both individuals and institutions—turn negative toward their investment managers after a few years of underperformance and switch to managers with a "hot" recent record, positioning themselves for another round of buy-high, sell-low dissatisfaction and obliterating roughly one-third of their funds' actual long-term returns. (Individuals who actively manage their own investments, notoriously, do even worse.) Unfortunately, this costly behavior is encouraged by investment firms that, to increase sales, concentrate their advertising on funds selected clearly because their recent results—over selected time periods—make good results look even "better." And some fund managers have several hundred different funds, apparently so that they will always have at least some "documented winners" to promote to the public.

In hiring new managers, individual investors notoriously rely on recent past performance even though studies of mutual funds show that for 9 out of 10 deciles of past performance, future performance is virtually random. (Only one decile's past results have predictive power: the worst or 10th decile—apparently because only high fees and chronic incompetence have a reliably repetitive impact on a manager's results.) The sad result is that investors time and again buy after the best results and sell out after the worst is over. Although 83% of plan sponsor investment committees rate themselves "above average" on investment expertise, ironically, the average managers they fired actually achieve slightly higher returns over the next few years than the average managers they hire. And the investment products that institutions move out of tend to outperform the products they move into. This behavior is costly.

Clients may well ask, "How can this be? Didn't our consultants' presentation show that the managers they recommend usually outperform their benchmarks? So shouldn't their managers be earning *something* above the market even after fully adjusting for risk?" Unfortunately for those holding this hopeful view, the data usually shown by many consultants are flawed. By simply removing two biases in the data as conventionally presented—backdating and survivor bias—the apparent record on managers monitored by consultants often shifts down from "better than market" appearances to "below the market" realities. Even large and sophisticated institutions should know who is watching the watchmen.

The grim reality of our first error of commission is that we continue selling what most of us have not delivered and, realistically, will not deliver: "beat the market" investment performance. Most investors have not yet caught on to the fact that they would be better off if they put their investments in low-cost index funds or index-matching Exchange Traded Funds. But that is not the strong "protective moat" against competition that Warren Buffett looks for in a business. One reason investors have not caught on is a major misunderstanding regarding fees.

The Reality of Fees

Most investors still do not realize that investment management fees are not low. Fees are actually very high when seen for what they really are. A fee of 0.5%—when measured as a percentage of the client's own assets—is surely more than 10% of the client's probable average annual *returns*. Because investors can get virtually guaranteed market returns through index funds for less than 10 bps, what they really "buy" when retaining active managers is risk-adjusted *incremental* returns. Calibrated as a percentage of risk-adjusted incremental returns, investment management fees are *not* low; they are high. After 50 years of fee increases, overall investment management fees are now greater than the risk-adjusted incremental returns. This means that investment managers now charge clients more than 100% of the incremental benefits actually produced. This stark reality is surely one strong reason for redefining our professional proposition to our clients with due deliberate speed.

Our Best Opportunity

When they have earned the trust and confidence of their clients, investment counselors can add far more to clients' long-term returns than portfolio managers can hope to produce. This is not a "snap" solution:

Effective investment counseling takes time, knowledge of the complexities of markets, investing, and investors, and hard work. But it can be done and can be done well repeatedly. Successful counselors will help each client understand the risks of investing, set realistic investment objectives, be realistic about saving and spending, select the appropriate asset classes, allocate assets appropriately, and most importantly, not overreact to market highs or lows. Counselors can help their clients stay the course and maintain a long-term perspective by helping them understand what managers are intending to achieve over the long term, understand the predictably disconcerting market turbulence, and be confident that reasonable long-term investment results will reward their patience and fortitude.

Error 2. Incorrectly Ordering Our Priorities

Our second error of commission is that we have allowed the values of our profession to become increasingly dominated by the economics of our business. This may be most evident on a personal level. We should candidly ask ourselves, who would deny the obvious delights of affluence? Our crowd, compared with 50 years ago, live in nicer homes, drive fancier cars, take more interesting vacations, and decorate our larger homes and offices with more remarkable paintings and sculptures. Private planes and "name-it-for-me" philanthropy are not unknown. Realistically, the biggest challenge in our personal finances is not how to get out of debt and pay for our kids' college; it is how to avoid ruining our children's lives by failing to impart the right values for them to achieve success in their own right and by giving them too much too soon.

It is at least possible that the talented and competitive people attracted to investment management have, however unintentionally, gotten so caught up in competing for the tangible prizes that they are not asking potentially disruptive questions about the real value of their best efforts—particularly when they know they are unusually capable and are working terribly hard. Consider the main ways the profitability of investment management has increased over the past 50 years:

- Assets managed, with only occasional short pauses, have risen tenfold.
- Fees as a percentage of assets have multiplied more than five times.
- The combination has proven powerful. As a result of strongly increasing profitability, individual compensation has increased greatly, and . . .
- Enterprise values are way, way up.

A Great Business

As a result of the investment management business having wide profit margins, modest capital requirements, minimal business risk, and virtually assured long-term growth, investment management organizations have become prime acquisition targets for giant noninvestment financial service organizations, such as banks, insurers, and securities dealers. When they choose to remain independent, some firms go public whereas others stay private, but they all recognize the reality that they have become big businesses and thus manage themselves appropriately.

As investment management organizations have been getting larger, it is not surprising that business managers have increasingly displaced investment professionals in senior leadership positions or that business disciplines have increasingly dominated the old professional disciplines. Business disciplines focus the attention of those with strong career ambitions on increasing profits, which is best achieved by increased "asset gathering" even though investment professionals know that expanding assets usually works against investment performance. In the view of senior executives of large financial service conglomerates whose judgments of division-by-division results are understandably profit-focused rather than investment-focused, business success will be determined by the consistency and rate of increase in reported profits. And the bigger the business, the more likely it is that the focus of senior management will be on increasing business profits.

Investing as a Business

Investment professionals searching for long-term value know that intense attention must be paid to current market prices that are always changing and often turbulent. But for the financially focused owners of investment firms, the long-term trends of the investment business offer a very different perspective. Of course, markets fluctuate, sometimes sharply and sometimes substantially, but diversification across asset classes—taking a lesson from portfolio management—reduces the range and frequency of profit fluctuations for a well-managed investment business. More important, the long-term upward trend of all investment markets is strongly favorable, so an astute business manager will realize that profitability is diversified over many time periods. Even within a single decade, the owner of an investment business can absorb market fluctuations and focus on long-term business trends.

The basic trend of nominal market value is clearly upward—at over 5% compounded or more than twice the rate of the overall economy. Add to this the positive impact of incremental sales to current clients and the benefits of entering new markets with established products and developing new products for sale to established clients and the annually compounding upward trend rises above 10%.

A service business that can grow at 10%, requires almost no capital at risk, and can expand extensively while enjoying wide profit margins is, as Mae West so wisely appreciated, "Wunnerful!" In a situation like this, even though investment professionals know from experience that asset size is the enemy, what would any red-blooded business manager do? Would he not recognize the high margins on incremental assets and drive to gather assets, build the business, and sell what is selling?

At investment organizations around the world, the two most important internal changes have not been in investment research or in portfolio management. They have been in new business development (to *get* more business when performance is favorable) and in relationship management (to *keep* more business longer, particularly when performance is not favorable). These changes respond primarily to the realities of the business as a business, not to the needs of the profession as a profession—nor to the needs of our clients as investors.

When business dominates, it is not the friend of the investment profession. If and when, as so very often happens, successful asset gathering eventually overburdens an organization's professional capacities for superior investing, results achieved for investors will fade. In addition, actions aiming to increase an organization's results as a business, such as cost controls, fee increases, and drives for greater "productivity," increase the chances that the organization's professional results will suffer.

Error 3. Dropping Rigorous Counseling

Our third error, also an error of omission, is particularly troubling for all of us who want our work to be recognized as a valuable professional service. In addition to the two errors of commission—accepting the increasingly improbable prospect of beat-the-market performance as the best measure of our profession and focusing more and more attention on business achievements rather than on professional success—we have somehow lost sight of our best professional opportunity to serve our clients well and shifted our focus away from effective investment counseling "because it does not scale." While the largest institutional funds with expert staffs are surely able to take on all their responsibilities without assistance from professionals with training and experience in the complexities of working out the architecture of an optimal long-term investment program, most investors—particularly individuals, but also most investment committees at small and midsize public pension funds, corporate retirement funds, and the endowments of colleges, universities, museums, and hospitals—are understandably not experts on contemporary investing and may not have broad experience. Many need help. All would appreciate having access to the best professional thinking and judgment.

We Can Help

Investment professionals are well positioned to provide important help. Some of the help clients need is in understanding that selecting managers who will actually beat the market over the long term is no longer a realistic assumption. (Yes, some managers will succeed, but discovering which ones in advance has become exceedingly difficult.) Far more important, investors need help to gain a realistic understanding of the long-term and intermediate prospects for different kinds of investments—risk and volatility first, rate of return second—so they will know what to expect and how to determine their strategic portfolios and investment policies.

Still more important, as already noted, most investors need help in developing a balanced, objective understanding of themselves and their situation: their investment knowledge and skills; their tolerance for risk in assets, incomes, and liquidity; their financial and psychological needs; their financial resources; their financial aspirations and obligations in the short and long run; and so forth. Investors need to know that the problem they most want to address and solve is not "beating the market." It is combining these factors into a long-term plan based on each investor's unique reality as an investor.

Although all investors are the same in several ways, they are very different in many more ways. All investors are the same in that they all have many choices and are free to choose, their choices matter, and they all want to do well and want to avoid doing harm. At the same time, all investors differ in many ways: assets, income, spending obligations and expectations, investment time horizon, investment skills, risk and uncertainty tolerance, market experience, and financial responsibilities. With all these differences, investors (both individuals and institutions) need help in designing investment programs that are really well suited to investors' strengths and weaknesses.

Skiing provides a useful analogy. At Vail and Aspen and at other great ski resorts, thousands of skiers are each enjoying happy days, partly because the scenery is beautiful, partly because the snow is plentiful and the slopes are well groomed, but primarily because each skier has chosen the well-marked trails that are best suited to his or her skills, strength, and interests. Some like gentle "bunny slopes," some like moderately challenging intermediate slopes, some are more advanced, and still others want to try out trails that are challenging even for fearless experts in their late teens with spring-steel legs. When each skier is on the trail that is right for her or him and skiing that trail at the pace that is right for her or him, everyone has a great day and all are winners.

We Should Help

Similarly, if investment professionals were to guide investors to investment programs that are right for their investing skills and experience, their financial situations, and their individual tolerance for risk and uncertainty, most of the many different investors could match their investment programs with their own investment skills and resources and regularly achieve their own realistic, long-term objectives. This is the important and not terribly difficult work of basic investment counseling.

The most valuable professional service we could provide to almost all investors is effective investment counseling. With far too few exceptions, most investment managers currently ignore this important work. Such inattention to the one professional service that is most clearly needed by investors, that would be most valuable to investors, and that would, if done thoroughly, enjoy high probabilities of success is more than ironic. It is the largest problem and the best opportunity for our profession going forward.

An Example of Need

The crucial need for investment counseling for individuals has been magnified by the huge shift in retirement security funds from defined benefit to defined contribution plans. Arguably the most valuable financial service ever offered to individuals, defined benefit pension plans provide retirees with regular payouts from long-term, well-supervised investments and require of the beneficiary no investment knowledge or skill, no need for caution at market highs, no need for courage if and when markets collapse, and no concern for outliving the funds.

In contrast, in today's 401(k) plans, millions of participants are on their own to decide portfolio structure. Nearly 20% "invest" entirely in money market funds only because that is how they started out when the balances were small and they have not changed their original allocations. In plans that allow investments in the sponsoring company's own shares, 17% of participants have over 40% of their accounts in that one company. (As Enron, Polaroid, and others have shown, that is potentially painful non-diversification.) For larger numbers of workers, the more serious question is: How many beneficiaries do not realize how much capital it will take to pay out a comfortable monthly amount in retirement, and how many of these will run out of funds in their old age? One norm is to limit withdrawals to 4% of assets a year. For participants in their mid-fifties—with only 10 years to save more—the average balance is now $150,000. At 4%, this produces only $6,000 a year before taxes and inflation, and even at 6% only produces $9,000 a year. Ouch!

Helpful Change

Target date or life-cycle funds convert the "do it yourself" investment *products* into a *service* and are a step in the right direction. So are the low-cost computer models offered by the leading 401(k) managers. Investment organizations that are shifting from product-centric to service-centric strategies report highly favorable professional and business results. They make basic investment counseling scalable and encourage the hope that more will be done. Congress has helped by enabling plan sponsors to advise participants on basic investment decisions. Some of the larger investment managers are taking "toe in the water" steps toward offering advice on which sectors of the market currently appear attractive or unattractive, but they typically leave out the crucial work of understanding each investor's situation and objectives. A few—but only a few—managers are offering an array of investment capabilities and advice on the best mix for specific clients. Much more is yet to be done to close the gap between what is needed and what is made available to investors.

Conclusion: Our Future Promise

Increasing the fit of investment service to the long-term objectives of each investor—moving from *caveat emptor* "product" sales to more durable, shared-understanding *service* relationships—would increase the duration or "loyalty" and thereby the economic value of client-manager relationships. Increasing the duration of client-manager relationships would benefit both clients and investment managers substantially. If the best way to deliver the needed service is to add investment counseling to the existing client-manager relationships to protect and extend them, wouldn't the generous profit margins of the present business absorb the modest expense? Don't we owe it to ourselves and to our profession to redefine our professional mission to include sensible investment counseling so that we and our clients can enjoy a shared understanding and succeed together?

As a profession, let us correct our two errors of commission: defining our mission as "beating the benchmark" and letting the short-run economics of our business dominate the long-term values of our profession. If we correct our error of omission by reaffirming investment counseling in our client relationships we and our clients will both benefit in a classic win–win situation.

Our profession's clients and practitioners would all benefit if we devoted less energy to attempting to "win" the loser's game of beating the market and devoted more skill, knowledge, and time to helping clients recognize market realities, understand themselves as investors, and clarify their realistic objectives, and then stay the course that is best for each of them.

If we take appropriate action, we can enjoy future success as a trusted profession and as individual professionals. While doing right by our clients, we will also be doing right for ourselves when we guide our clients to success in investing's winner's game.

4

The Winner's Game II

The secret to winning the "game" of investing over the long term is to determine each investor's unique objectives and then figure out the policies that will have the best prospects of achieving that particular investor's goals over the long run.

The right investment program for any particular person can look very wrong unless the individual's utility values are understood. Here's a personal example that *looks* wrong.

My grandparents left $10,000 to each of their grandchildren in 1946. While the post-war economy boomed and the stock market rose strongly over the next 15 years, these funds were kept in a bank checking account. Even with 20/20 hindsight, I believe that was the right "investment" policy—for those directly involved. Here's why:

My mother knew what she was doing and why. Her father was a country lawyer in Mississippi who went broke during the Depression like every other lawyer in the Delta region. So, to stay at Northwestern University, my mother borrowed tuition from Kappa Alpha Theta, her fraternity (the term "sorority" was not yet used), and then spent the next 15 years typing students' papers at 8¢ a page and sewing little girls' dresses at $1 per dress to repay those loans.

Mom knew how important it was to have enough for college in the bank. She was determined her children could go to first-rate colleges, so she wanted to be sure we had enough of our own money to cover whatever we couldn't get in scholarships. She believed our small inheritances would be enough to cover what we might need. To risk that assurance and maybe not achieve the "dream" of a college education just to get more than we needed made no sense at all to my mother.

Why, you might ask, not at least put the money into a savings account? Mom had personally experienced the bank holidays of the 1930s and she had read the fine print: Our local savings banks reserved the right to wait 30 days before paying out a withdrawal. And Mom knew that banks could fail in a lot less than 30 days. So our college savings were kept for 15 years in a checking account—so they could be withdrawn immediately if the bank looked shaky.

All things considered, would anyone think my mother's investment policy wrong? Not I. She understood the game and knew how to win—and all four of her children went to fine colleges.

Losers' Game vs. Winners' Game

Generically, a *loser's game* is any game, contest, or activity in which the ultimate victor is determined by the actions of the loser. These contests are not won; they are lost. Amateur tennis is a classic loser's game because most points and most matches are not won. They are lost. You keep hitting balls back to me, but I double-fault or hit shots out or into the net until the set is over, and you are the winner. But you didn't determine the outcome by playing better; I produced the outcome—by playing worse.

In a winner's game, the winner not only wins, but also causes his or her victory as we see when watching the Williams sisters at tennis or Tiger Woods at golf. The encouraging reality is that every investor can be a winner of the winner's game of investing because there is no adversary who must lose in order for you to win. And the requirements for winning are all quite understandable:

- Know the resources available for investment.
- Understand the long-term spending objectives and obligations to be funded.
- Make wise use of *time*, the Archimedes lever of investing.
- Recognize the realistic nature and vagaries of the investment markets—particularly when Benjamin Graham's famous trickster, Mr. Market is out there trying to capture attention.
- Acknowledge the analytical capabilities and the emotional capacities and limitations of the particular investor at those times when rationality will be most serious challenged.

- Concentrate on determining the long-term investment policy most likely to achieve realistic long-term objectives and least likely to fail or cause the investor to fail during the long interim period of investing operations, a time surely fraught with uncertainties, disruptions, and confusions.
- Adapt the long-term policy to significant changes in the investor's financial resources or long-term objectives, if and when they occur.

The Winning Triangle

Most investors will benefit from the self-disciplining exercise of committing to writing their explicit definitions of all three parts of the winning triangle:

1. Current financial resources *for* investments.
2. Future financial objectives *from* investments.
3. The bridging strategy and investment operations designed to take the portfolio most effectively and reliably from item 1 to item 2.

The challenge to the investment profession is becoming increasingly clear. The centerpiece of every long-term investment program is the most underdeveloped level of the game—Level One: Setting the policy normal asset mix.

Part of the benefit of a written investment program is the discipline this gives to our efforts to be rational and rigorous. Part of the benefit comes when we invite serious friends to review and critique our articulation and to offer any challenges they consider significant. And part of the benefit comes from carefully reviewing the written document regularly, typically once each year, to be sure it is as understanding as possible of ourselves and the markets.

Levels of the Game

While most investors take investment services as a blended package, it is important to unbundle the package into separate levels of the game. In making investment decisions, there are five separate levels of decisions for each investor to make individually:

- *Level One*: Asset mix, the optimal proportion of, e.g., equities, bonds, private equity, for the policy normal of the investor's portfolio. This is where investment counseling usually concentrates.

- *Level Two*: Equity mix, the policy normal proportions in various types of stocks: e.g., growth versus value; large-cap versus small-cap; domestic versus international.
- *Level Three*: Active versus index management, deciding on the appropriate method of implementation for the policy normal mix of investments.
- *Level Four*: Specific manager selection, where most investors and most investment committees concentrate most of their time and effort, deciding which firms will manage each component of the overall portfolio, hiring the most promising, and firing the most disappointing.
- *Level Five*: Active portfolio management, changing portfolio strategy, changing managers, security selection, and sometimes even trading.

Investors should recognize that investing is not necessarily a single, bundled package, but can be divided into separate levels and investors can engage in or ignore each level. And investors are free to choose. This freedom of choice is truly splendid because investors can avoid *losing* the loser's game on Levels Four and Five, and can concentrate on *winning* the winner's game on Levels One and Two.

As human beings, particularly if we are successful in other parts of our lives, we are notoriously unable to accept the obvious reality that, on average, we are average, and that our normal experiences will usually be "about average" because we are, as a group, captives of the normal distribution of the bell curve. It amuses us that Lake Wobegon's children are all above average, yet studies show we think we are above-average drivers, above-average parents—and above-average investors. And we do tend to take it personally when our stocks go way up or go way down, even though, as 'Adam Smith' admonished, "The stock doesn't know you own it."

Every investor should recognize the powerful potential impact of luck—not only good luck, but also, bad luck. We can all live through good luck. But bad luck, the apparently random occurrence of adversity, is equally prevalent and its consequences can be far greater.

Levels Are Separable

Knowing that the levels of the game are separable liberates the investor (or the investor's investment manager) to decide whether to be active at each separate level. At least implicitly, the freedom of choice presents a responsibility to choose, because not to decide is to decide. Yet the secret to success, as experience demonstrates again and again, is not playing the loser's game on Levels Four and Five, but instead concentrating on the winner's game on Levels One and Two.

Experienced investors know that the high-to-low order of cost is the mirror opposite of the order of value:

- The most costly and least value-adding level is Level Five with all its active trading—the black hole vortex at the center of the loser's game.
- The least costly and most value-adding level is Level One—determining the optimal asset mix to achieve an investor's realistic long-term goals. Every investor can determine the realistic long-term objective most appropriate to that particular investor's present financial circumstances, capacity for absorbing risk, and future goals and objectives.

Tommy Armour, the great teaching professional in golf, focused on two key propositions:

- Hit the shot that makes the next shot easy. (In flying, the equivalent thought is that "there are old pilots and hold pilots, but there are no old, hold pilots.") Armour urged players to stay within their zone of competence, to play within their own personal game, and not to play against themselves.
- Noting that roughly half of all shots in golf are putts. Armour urged his students to concentrate their practice time on putting—not on the driving range. (Willie Sutton had the same idea about banks: "That's where the money is.")

The sad irony in the investment profession is that most practitioners and most clients devote most of their efforts to Level Five and incur most of their costs competing against a virtually unbeatable array of contending forces: the institutional investors who are too many, too well informed, too talented, too quick to react, too intensely striving to win ever to be beaten over any long period by anything like enough of a margin to cover the costs of playing the game on Level Five.

And the record on Level Four is also quite discouraging. While institutions, with all their expensive advisors and consultants, may experience somewhat less harm by changing investment managers, the poor record for individual investors in mutual funds is unsettling.

Becoming Mr. Market

The long-term passage through the *terra incognita* of future markets is sure to be accompanied by the uncertainties and disruptive challenges of that wily, disconcerting companion we cannot shake: Mr. Market. Emotionally unstable, Mr. Market veers from years of euphoria when he can see only the favorable possibilities of industries, companies, and their stocks to profound pessimism when he's so depressed he can see nothing but trouble ahead.

Mr. Market persistently teases investors with gimmicks such as surprising earnings, startling dividend announcements, sudden surges of inflation, inspiring presidential pronouncements, grim reports of commodity prices, announcements of amazing new technologies, distressing bankruptcies, and even threats of war. These events come from his bag of tricks when they are least expected. Just as magicians use deception to divert our attention, Mr. Market's very short-term distractions can confuse our thinking about investments.

Mr. Market dances before us without a care in the world. And why not? He has no responsibilities at all. As an economic gigolo, he has only one objective: to be attractive. Mr. Market constantly tries to get us to do something—anything, but at least something—and the more activity, the better. Explorers, pilots of single-engine planes, and ocean sailors all know that while adventure and achievement are what laypeople think about, the experienced practitioner's thoughts and actions are centered on the disciplines of defense—not running out of water, not running short of food, not getting lost, not getting frightened—because they know from experience that the essential foundation for a successful offense is a strong defense.

The best defense against Mr. Market's seductive tricks is to study stock market history—just as airline pilots spend hours and hours in flight simulators, practicing flying through dreadful storms, landing at unfamiliar airports, and dealing with mechanical malfunctions so they are well prepared to remain calm and rational when faced with such situations in real life. (They also learn that surprises are not surprising: They are actuarial expectations on a bell curve.)

Three Realities

As more and more individuals become responsible for the investment policy of their retirement assets, particularly via 401(k) plans, it is even more necessary to develop realistic long-term goals and policies that effectively integrate three realities.

The Reality of Current Resources and Probable Additions. We need to know the present value of likely additions to a portfolio (through savings or inheritance) that should be included in our present thinking.

The Reality of the Market's Most Likely Behavior. We need to recognize the market's behavior during and over the period of investment. Two assumptions are reasonable and easy to use:

- The long-term array of past market fluctuations will probably be reproduced over the long-term future.
- If the current level of the market is outside its normal range, the market level will regress toward the mean.

Most investors overemphasize the favorable possibilities, striving to maximize returns with a hold offense. These investors would benefit from giving more attention to their defenses, and to not losing. That's why:

- If mutual fund investors understood the total costs of switching funds, they would know to invest only in funds they truly intend to stay with forever.
- If investors understood the full costs of trading, they would change much less.

All investors will experience uncomfortable fluctuations in the market. That's reality—and fluctuations should not be a major concern. The real concern is with irreversible losses caused by overreaching for speculative possibilities; by taking market risks greater than our capacity to endure major turbulence and maintain consistent rationality; by reaching for managers whose best performance is likely behind them and who are destined to underperform with *your* money; and by going into debt.

The Reality of Future Objectives for Spending from Invested Funds. Most individual investors have some room for maneuvering and can adapt some of their future objectives to the changing realities of financial capacity, so it is often informative to categorize goals and objectives by degree of importance.

For instance, sustaining a given lifestyle is usually more important and less changeable than a large gift to one's alma mater. This is the sort of value weighting that incorporates utility into the assessment of investment objectives because happiness and peace of mind are not simple, quantitative measures. (The difference between success and happiness is worth pondering. Success is getting what you want in life, while happiness is wanting what you get.)

How much regret will you feel if you end up with 20% *over* your goal? How much regret will you feel if you're 20% *under* your goal? Ben Graham's great concept, the Margin of Safety, is essential for long-term investment success because it's not just the end-point that matters; the pathway matters too. Charles Dickens articulated this reality as "Micawber's law": Income of £20 and expenses of £19 and 19 pence equal happiness, while income of £20 and expenses of £20 and tuppence equal misery.

This is why most endowments now use a moving-average spending rule discipline of 5% after covering inflation. (The percentage was originally worked out by James Tobin of Yale to provide intergenerational equity by recognizing investment experience and new gifts and the impact of inflation. His friend David Swensen developed the most rigorous and complete articulation and implementation of solving for the three-way reality in management of the Yale University endowment. He explained this in his great book, *Pioneering Portfolio Management*.)

Know Thyself

Yes, investors are right to be serious students of the markets, particularly the extremes that entice and ensnare, but markets are only part of the recommended curriculum. Know thyself is even more important, and all investors will want to recognize the central lessons of behavioral finance:

- We believe in "hot hands" and "winning streaks" *and* that recent events matter, even in flipping coins. (All three are *not* true.)
- We are impressed by short-term success, as in mutual fund performance.
- We are confirmation-biased, looking for and overweighting the significance of data that support our initial impressions.
- We allow ourselves to use an initial idea or fact as a reference point for future decisions even when we know it is "just a number."
- We distort our perceptions of our decisions, almost always in our favor, so that we believe we are better than we really are at making decisions. And we don't learn; we stay overconfident.
- We confuse familiarity with knowledge and understanding.
- As investors, we overreact to good news and to bad news.
- With all this going against us, it's no wonder that we get seduced away from concentration on the winner's game of investing and into the loser's game, particularly since Mr. Market is clearly one of the most

entrancing seducers of all time. Investors, like dieters and teenage drivers, will be wise not to expect too much of themselves, particularly when superior personal behavior would be necessary to achieve superior results.

If Mr. Market can't get you to be overly optimistic by showering you with good news and promises, then can he worry and even scare you with bad news and threats? We all have weaknesses, and Mr. Market knows where and when to push our buttons.

Risk tolerance differs for each investor. And the worst time to learn your risk tolerance—the limit to which you can absorb risk and uncertainty without experiencing the anxieties that produce irrational behavior—is when you are there for the first time or are without preparation. This is why fire drills make sense, and why investors will benefit from studying past market behavior, so they can estimate their own "what if" behavior and protect themselves from getting caught outside their personal comfort zone.

Utility likewise differs for each investor. Having $100,000 extra is not the reciprocal of being short by $100,000 any more than having an extra gallon of gas in the tank when you arrive at your destination is the reciprocal of running out of gas 16 miles from home. Each investor will benefit from an explicit understanding of his or her utility function.

Time, the Archimedes lever in investing, wants to be your helpful friend *if* you can be patient. If you invested $1.00 in the S&P 500 through the 1990s, you would have made $5.59. But if you missed just 90 big days in that decade, you would have *lost* money. And if you missed just 60 months out of the 75 years ending in 2000, your total return for that long, long period would be zero. The obvious lesson: To get the long-term return you have to be there when the market moves—and these best days or months occur when least expected.

Everyone Can Win

If all investors followed the investment policies that would be best for them, they would have no conflicts with any other investor's best-fit policies. The only assumption behind this categorical statement is that investors differ in risk tolerances and in time horizon, and emotional capacities, and the consequences of just these two types of difference produce an almost infinite variety of combinations of risk restraints, investment objectives, and investment capabilities. For each set of variables, there is an optimal best-fit investment policy.

With the beginning and the ending reasonably well defined, the investor can then try to estimate the most reasonable expectation for investments over the intervening time span to see how realistic it is to expect the starting funds to achieve the investor's objectives after that most probable investing experience. If this three-part cut-and-try process works, fine. If the fund comes up short, the investor will want to consider seriously saving more or reducing the aggregate goals.

The really hard part is not figuring out the best feasible investment policy combination. While it takes some time and analytical discipline, this part of the problem-solving is straightforward engineering. The really hard part is managing ourselves: our expectations and our interim behavior. As Walt Kelly's Pogo puts it: "We have met the enemy and it is us." Most investors are too optimistic about the long run and much too optimistic about how well they will do compared to the averages, so they set themselves up for disappointment.

Even worse, most investors do harm to their longer-term investment results by trying and trying again to do "better": changing managers and changing asset mix at the wrong time and in the wrong way. Disappointed by a few years of poor performance from managers we were attracted to by their good performance of prior years, we miss the recovery when the manager's type of stocks does well, and we catch the down-leg of the newly chosen manager whose results are simply regressing to the mean. The record on market timing is even worse. Investors' self-destructive attempt to do better is shown starkly in the results of the mutual fund investor switching noted above.

Where can and should the individual or the institutional investor turn for counsel on the long-term investment policy that is right for that particular individual or that specific institution? Where would you send your mother's best friend? Where would you send the trustees of your alma mater? Where would you want your grandchildren to go for investment counseling? Is it really just *caveat emptor*?

If you find these questions difficult to answer, you may share with me the view that the investment profession has an important opportunity to develop our capabilities in investment counseling and make them much more widely available. Three parts of investment policy are important:

1. Deciding the right asset mix for the particular investment fund.
2. Accepting and working with the reality that each investor's long-term gross returns for each asset class will very likely be "average" for

that asset class—minus manager fees, taxes, and costs of operations—and accepting the reality that underperforming is much more likely than outperforming.

3. Sustaining policy commitments at market highs and at market lows, exactly when that rascal Mr. Market is doing his very best to do his worst.

Loser's Game Getting Worse

The importance of each investor concentrating on winning the winner's game with sensible long-term investment policies is matched by the daunting realities of changes in the investor's environment that make the loser's game all the harsher and more forbidding. Changes in the way institutional portfolios are managed are substantial. And because they are simultaneous, they are compounding.

Because the business consequences of the Loser's Game are becoming recognized by investment managers, they are moving toward the norm of hugging the index and charging full fees for managing high-turnover portfolios based on largely the same information—with little chance of outperforming competitors who are equally skillful, have equal access to information, and are equally quick to respond to changing information or interpretation by buying or selling.

Making your own plan is the best, and probably the only, way to win the winner's game. And it's easy if you can ignore that rascal Mr. Market and the crowd that follows him as they play the Loser's Game. By correctly defining each investor's unique investment objectives and determining the realistic investment policies for achieving those objectives, each investor can avoid the Loser's Game and win his or her own Winner's Game.

Source: *The Journal of Portfolio Management*, Spring, 2003.

5

The Rise and Fall
of Performance Investing

Performance or active investing enjoyed a remarkably long lifecycle but today the costs and fees of active investing are so high and the incremental returns so low that the Money Game is no longer a game worth playing. Investors— both institutions and individuals—are increasingly shifting toward indexing. As acceptance of indexing grows, clients and managers have an opportunity to stop focusing on price *discovery (which has made our markets so efficient) and refocus on* values *discovery, whereby investment professionals can help investors achieve good performance by structuring an appropriate, long-term investment program to each investor's true goals and staying with it.*

Charles Darwin correctly lamented that his transformative theory of evolution would not be accepted during his lifetime by most of the scientific community. General acceptance, he saw, would have to wait until his friends and colleagues—captives of their prior work, stature, and success as traditional biologists—had been replaced by others not dependent on sustaining the status quo. Similarly, most active "performance" investment managers today are so attached to their work, stature, and success that many do not yet recognize a seismic change in their world. The dynamics that produced the rise of active investing to prominence also carried the seeds of its inevitable peaking, to be followed by an increasingly recognizable decline, first in the benefits accruing to clients and then in benefits to practitioners.

As we all know—but without always understanding the ominous long-term consequences—over the past 50 years, increasing numbers of highly talented young investment professionals have entered the competition for a faster and more accurate discovery of pricing errors, the key to achieving the holy grail of superior performance. They have more-advanced training than their predecessors, better analytical tools, and faster access to more information.

Thus, the skill and effectiveness of active managers as a group have risen continuously for more than half a century, producing an increasingly expert and successful (or "efficient") price discovery market mechanism. Because all have ready access to almost all the same information, the probabilities continue to rise that any mispricing, particularly for the 500 large-capitalization stocks that necessarily dominate major managers' portfolios, will be quickly discovered and swiftly arbitraged away into insignificance. The unsurprising result of the global commoditization of insight and information and of all the competition is the increasing efficiency of modern stock markets that makes it harder to match the market indexes and much harder to beat them, particularly after covering costs and fees.

Fifty years ago, beating the market (i.e., beating the competition: part-time amateurs and over-structured, conservative institutions) was not just possible, it was probable for hard-working, well-informed, boldly active professionals. Institutions did less than 10% of total NYSE trading, and individuals did more than 90%. Those individual investors not only were amateurs without access to institutional research but also made their decisions—fewer than one a year—primarily for such outside-the-market reasons as an inheritance or bonus received *or* a down payment on a home or college tuition to pay. Today, the statistics are upended.

More than 95% of trades in listed stocks, and nearly 100% of other security transactions, are executed by full-time professionals who are constantly comparison-shopping inside the market for any competitive advantage. Armed with research and a continuous flood of global market information, economic analyses, industry studies, risk metrics, company reports, and superb analytical models, all investment professionals now have access to more market information than they can possibly use. And with Regulation Fair Disclosure (Reg FD), the US SEC insists that all information be disclosed to all investors at the same time. Each of the many individual changes has been important. The compounding change of all the many changing factors over the past 50 years has been astounding.

Although clients put up all the capital and accept all the market risks, the sought-after "performance" for clients—incremental returns above the market index—has been faltering. Meanwhile, active investing has become for investment managers one of the most financially rewarding service businesses in history.

To be sure, the degradation of performance investing was not like a light switch but, rather, a rheostat. Even now, a few specialist managers appear to have found creative ways to exploit the very market forces that confound most large active managers. However, such managers are small in capacity, hard to identify in advance, and limited in how much they will accept from any one client (or are closed to new accounts) and so they cannot accommodate more than a modest fraction of potential institutional demand. Meanwhile, most large investment managers are obliged by their size to invest primarily in the 500 stocks most widely owned and closely covered by experienced portfolio managers and expert analysts.

A Brief History of Performance Investing

The key to understanding the profound forces for change in active investing, particularly in the results produced for investors, is to study major trends over the long term. Fifty years ago, as performance investing was just getting started, insurance companies and bank trust departments dominated institutional investing. They were deliberately conservative and hierarchical, controlled by investment committees of senior "prudent men"—still haunted by the Great Depression, World War II, the Korean War, and the Cold War—who were understandably risk-averse. Meeting for a few hours once or twice a month, these worthies promulgated an "approved list" from which junior trust officers cautiously assembled buy-and-hold equity portfolios dominated by utilities and blue-chip industrials such as U.S. Steel, General Motors, DuPont, and Procter & Gamble plus a few seasoned growth stocks, such as Coca-Cola and IBM. Dividends were sought, taxes were avoided, and high-grade bonds were purchased in laddered maturities. Trading was considered "speculative."

But, change was coming. As Fidelity and other mutual fund managers achieved superior rates of return, "performance" mutual fund sales boomed. Pension funds noticed and wanted in on the winning.

Corporate pension assets, initially accepted by major banks as a "customer accommodation," had been accumulating rapidly. Money center banks soon became enormous investment managers and, with fixed-rate commissions surging, major consumers of brokers' research and Wall Street's emerging capabilities in block trading. New investment firms were organized to compete for the burgeoning pension business—some as subsidiaries of mutual fund organizations, but most as independent firms. Their main proposition: active management by the most talented young analysts and portfolio managers, who would be first to find and act on investment opportunities and would meet or beat the results of the so-called performance mutual funds. Better yet, the portfolio managers would work directly with each client.

Early practitioners of performance investing experienced significant impediments and costs that would be strange to today's participants. Block trading was just beginning and daily NYSE trading volume was only one-third of 1% of today's volume; thus, trades of 10,000 shares could take hours to execute. Brokerage commissions were fixed at an average of more than 40 cents a share. In-depth research from new firms on Wall Street had barely begun. Computers were confined to the "cage" or back office.

Although overcoming these difficulties was not easy, for those who knew how, the results were grand. Aspirations of investors shifted from preservation of capital to performance and "beating the market." A.G. Becker and Merrill Lynch created a new service that measured, for the first time, each pension fund's investment performance against that of competitors and showed that the banks' investment performance was often disappointing compared with that of the new firms.

A new kind of corporate middle management role emerged: the internal manager of external investment managers of pension funds. Supervising a large pension fund's 10, 20, or even 30 investment managers, and meeting each year with another 25–50 firms (each hoping to be chosen), and then selecting the "best of breed"—all required the expertise of full-time specialists, often aided by external investment consultants.

The rapidly accumulating pension funds began pouring their money out of the banks and into the new investment firms that promised superior performance. With dozens of selection consultants scouring the nation to find promising new investment managers for their large clients, getting business came easier and faster for promising new investment firms. Increasing numbers of energetic investment managers formed new firms—or new pension divisions in established mutual fund organizations—to pursue the pension funds' demand for superior performance. Adding insult to injury, the new investment firms were often populated with the banks' "best and brightest" fleeing from trust department procedures they found stultifying and financially unrewarding.

The opportunities for superior price discovery were so good in the 1970s and 1980s that the leading active managers were able to attract substantial assets and—not always, but often—deliver superior performance. But as the collective search for mispricing opportunities attracted more and more skillful competitors—aided by a surging increase in computers, Bloomberg terminals, e-mail, algorithms, and other extraordinary new data-gathering and data-processing tools—price discovery got increasingly swift and effective.

With all these changes, the core question was not whether the markets are *perfectly* efficient but, rather, whether they are *sufficiently* efficient that active managers, after fees and costs, were unlikely to be able to keep up with, and very unlikely to get ahead of, the price discovery consensus of the experts. In other words, after 50 years of compounding changes in investment management and in the securities markets *and* given the difficulty of successful manager selection *and* the poor prospects for truly superior long-term returns, do clients have sufficient reason to accept all the risks *and* uncertainties and costs and fees of active management?

The pricing of investment management services has had an interesting history and until recently a single direction—up. Before the 1930s, conventional fees were charged as a percentage of the investment income received in dividends and interest. During the 1930s, Scudder, Stevens & Clark shifted the base for fee calculation to a 50–50 split—half based on income and half based on assets. Still, the level of fees was low. In those days, investment counseling might have been a fine *profession*, but it was certainly not a great *business*. Those going into investment management typically hoped to cover their costs of operation with client fees and then make "some decent money" by investing their own family fortunes. Bank trust departments, often restricted to very low fees by state legislatures seeking to protect widows and orphans, traditionally charged little or nothing. Fees of only 0.1% of assets were common.

With the formation of new investment firms in the 1960s, the terms of competition changed in ways that surprised the banks and insurers. With their long experience in such institutional financial services as bank loans, cash management, and commercial insurance, they knew to expect tough price competition and aggressive bargaining by major corporate customers and they knew how to compete on the basis of costs.

But in the new era of performance investing, pension management had been converted from a *cost*-driven market into a *value*-driven market, with value determined primarily by expectations of superior future investment performance. Superior investment returns could reduce annual contributions—and thus lift reported earnings—by reducing the annual cost of funding pensions. The new managers found that they could easily charge much more than banks and insurance companies charged because higher fees were seen as a confirmation of the expected superior performance. Compared with the magnitude of the predicted superior performance, the fees for active investment simply did not seem to matter; any quibbling about fees was dismissed with such comments as, "You wouldn't choose your child's brain surgeon on the basis of price, would you?"

Decade after decade, assets of mutual funds and pension funds multiplied and at the same time—instead of going down, as might be expected—fee schedules for active investment management tripled or quadrupled. With this combination, the investment business grew increasingly profitable. High pay and interesting work attracted increasing numbers of highly capable MBAs and PhDs, who became analysts and portfolio managers and, collectively, more competition for each other. Meanwhile, particularly during the high returns of the great bull market of the last quarter of the twentieth century, investors continued to ignore fees because almost everyone assumed that fees were unimportant.

Fees for investment management are remarkable in a significant way: Nobody actually pays the fees by writing a check for an explicit amount. Instead, fees are quietly and automatically deducted by the investment managers and, by custom, are stated not in dollars but as a percentage of assets. Seen correctly—incremental fees compared with incremental results—fees have become surprisingly important. This view can best be seen by contrasting conventional perceptions with reality.

Fees for equity management are typically described with one four-letter word and a single number. The four-letter word is "only," as in "only 1%" for mutual funds or "only half of 1%" for institutions. If you accept the 1%, you will easily accept the "only." But is that not a serious deception? "Only 1%" is the ratio of fees to assets, but the investor already has the assets, and so active investment managers must be offering to deliver something else: returns. If annual future equity returns are, as the consensus expectation now holds, 7–8%, then for what is being delivered to investors, 1% of assets quickly balloons to nearly 12–15% of returns. But that is not the end of it.

A rigorous definition of costs for active management would begin by recognizing the wide availability of a market-matching "commodity" alternative: low-fee indexing. Because indexing consistently delivers the market return at no more than the market level of risk, the informed realist's definition of the fee for active management is the *incremental* fee as a percentage of *incremental* returns after adjusting for risk. *That* fee is high—very high. If a mutual fund charging 1.25% of assets also charged a 12b-1 fee of 0.25% and produced a net return of 0.5% above the benchmark index each year—an eye-popping performance—the true fee would be very nearly 75% of the incremental return before fees! Because a majority of active managers now underperform the market, their incremental fees are actually over 100% of long-term incremental, risk adjusted returns. This grim reality has largely gone unnoticed by clients—so far. But "not yet caught" is certainly not the strong, protective moat that Warren Buffett wants around every business.

The challenge that clients accept when selecting an active manager is not to find talented, hard-working, highly disciplined investment managers. That would be easy. The challenge is to select a manager sufficiently more hard-working, more highly disciplined, and more creative than the other managers—managers that equally aspirational investors have already chosen—and more by at least enough to cover the manager's fees and compensate for risks taken.

As the skills of competitors converge, luck becomes increasingly important in determining the increasingly meaningless performance rankings of investment managers. Although firms continue to advertise performance rankings and investors continue to rely on them when selecting managers, evidence shows that such rankings have virtually zero predictive power. As price discovery has become increasingly effective, and thus securities markets have become increasingly efficient, any deviations from equilibrium prices—based on experts' consensus expectations of returns, which are based on analyzing all accessible information—have become merely unpredictable, random noise.

Investment professionals know that any long-term performance record must be interpreted with great care. Behind every long-term record are many, many changes in important factors: Markets change, portfolio managers change, assets managed by a firm change, managers age, their incomes and interests change, whole organizations change. The fundamentals of the companies whose securities we invest in also change. Forecasting the future of any variable is difficult, forecasting the interacting futures of many changing variables is much more difficult, and estimating how other expert investors will interpret such complex changes is extraordinarily difficult.

A Clear Alternative

For many years, the persistent drumbeat of under-performance by active managers was endured because there were no clear alternatives to trying harder and hoping for the best. Often blinded by optimism, clients continued to see the fault as somehow theirs and, so, gamely continued to try to find Mr. Right Manager, presumably believing there were no valid alternatives. Now, with the proliferation of low-cost index funds and exchange-traded funds (ETFs) as plain "commodity" products, there are proven alternatives to active investing. And active managers continue to fail to outperform. The grim reality is how few funds have outperformed their indices after adjusting for survivorship.

After a slow beginning, some clients are increasingly recognizing that reality and taking action. Yet, many clients continue to believe that their managers can and will outperform. (The triumph of hope over experience is clearly not confined to repetitive matrimony.) Even though no major manager has done so, the average US institutional client somehow expects its chosen group of active investment managers to outperform annually, after fees, by a cool 100 bps. As Figure 5.1 shows, corporate and public pension funds are only slightly less optimistic, whereas

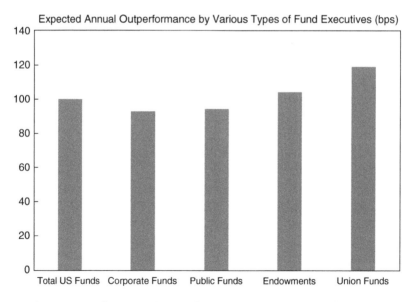

Figure 5.1 After-Fee Outperformance Expectations for Active Investment Managers

endowments and unions are somewhat more optimistic. Among pension fund executives, the elusive magic of outperformance is now the most favored way to close funding gaps.

In 2012, Eugene Fama summarized his study of the performance of all domestic mutual funds with at least 10 years of results:

Active management in aggregate is a zero-sum game—before cost ... After costs, only the top 3% of managers produce a return that indicates they have sufficient skill to just cover their costs, which means that going forward, and despite extraordinary past returns, even the top performers are expected to be only about as good as a low-cost passive index fund. The other 97% can be expected to do worse.

Quantitative observers might point out that only 3% of active managers' beating their chosen markets is not far from what would be expected in a purely random distribution. But qualitative observers would caution that odds of 97 to 3 are, frankly, terrible—particularly when risking the real money that will be needed by millions of people in retirement or to help finance our society's most treasured educational, cultural, and philanthropic institutions. The long-term data repeatedly document that investors would benefit by switching from active performance investing to low-cost indexing. This rational change, however, has been exceedingly slow to develop, raising the obvious question: Why?

Understanding the Social Acceptance of Innovation

The problem of acceptance that Darwin faced is not confined to biology or science in general; as Thomas Kuhn explained in his classic book, *The Structure of Scientific Revolutions*, it is universal. Those who have succeeded greatly in their fields naturally resist—often quite imaginatively and often quite stubbornly—any disruptive new concept. They resist for two main reasons. First, most new hypotheses, when rigorously tested, do not prove out, and so leading members of the establishment are often dismissive of *all* new ideas. Second, members of the establishment in any field have much to lose in institutional stature, particularly their reputations as experts, and their earning power. They depend on the status quo—their status quo. Thus, they defend against the new. Usually, they are proved right, and so they win. But not always.

Percent

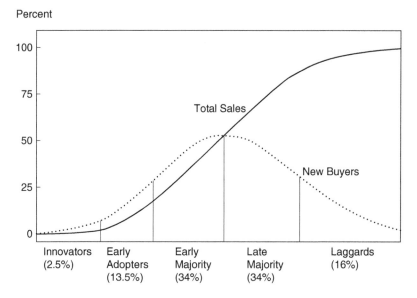

Figure 5.2 **Who Buys In When**

In his scholarly book *Diffusion of Innovations*, Everett M. Rogers established the classic paradigm by which innovations reach a "tipping point" and then spread exponentially through a social system, as shown in Figure 5.2.

Most members of a social system rely on observing the decisions of others when making their own decisions and repeatedly follow a five-step process:

1. Becoming aware of the innovation.
2. Forming a favorable opinion of the innovation.
3. Deciding whether to adopt the innovation.
4. Adopting the innovation.
5. Evaluating the results of the innovation.

Deciding to act or not to act (the third step) depends on confidence in the benefits, compatibility with past habits and norms, and anticipation of how others will perceive the decision—particularly, whether they will approve.

Successful innovations steadily overcome resistance and gain acceptance through a process that is remarkably consistent, but the pace of change differs markedly from one innovation to another. For example, conversion to hybrid seed took a majority of corn farmers 10 *years*, whereas a majority of doctors adopted penicillin in less than 10 *months*. The speed with which new and better ways of doing things are adopted is a function of several contributing demand factors: how large and how undeniable the benefits are, the speed with which benefits become visible, the ease and low cost of reversing a mistake, and the quality of the networks by which information and social influences are communicated and expressed. Resistance to change is a function of the uncertainty about the benefits of the innovation, the risk of economic loss or social disapproval the new adopter might experience, the risk tolerance of the prospective adopter, and the speed with which rewards and benefits will be known.

Combining Kuhn's and Rogers's theories on innovation provides a way to understand the increasing acceptance of performance investing in the 1960s and 1970s, its maturity in the 1980s and 1990s, and the gradual decline in demand for it and the slow but accelerating shift to indexing.

Demand for indexing has been retarded by several factors that still encourage investors to stay with active management: the human desire to do better by trying harder; the "yes, you can" encouragement of fund managers, investment consultants, and other participants who make their living as advocates of "doing better"; and investment committees' focus on selecting the one or two "best" managers from a group of preselected "winners" chosen by consultants. Advertising notoriously concentrates on the superior performance of a small and ever-changing minority of managers. Media coverage centers on reporting the latest winners. (If you watch stock market reports on TV, note how much the news casters sound like sportscasters.)

However, little is said by the insiders about the numbing consistency with which a majority of active managers fall short of the index or how seldom the past years' winners are winners again in subsequent years. Glossed over, too, is how hard it is to identify future winners when many investment committees and fund executives apparently believe they can somehow beat the odds by switching from manager to manager. Extensive data show that in the years after the decision to change, the recently fired managers typically outperform the newly hired managers. Other than choosing managers with low fees, no method has been found to identify in advance which actively managed funds will beat the market.

Of course, recognition of the ever-increasing difficulty of outperforming the expert consensus after substantial fees and costs of opportunities has not come quickly or easily, particularly from the active managers themselves. We cannot reasonably expect them to say, "We, the emperors, have no clothes," and to give up on performance investing when they are so committed to active management as a career, work so hard to achieve superior performance for clients, and are so admired for continuously striving. Nobel Laureate Daniel Kahneman, author of *Thinking, Fast and Slow*, described the socializing power of a culture like the one that pervades active investment management:

> We know that people can maintain an unshakable faith in any proposition, however absurd, when they are sustained by a community of like-minded believers. Given the competitive culture of the financial community, it is not surprising that large numbers of individuals in that world believe themselves to be among the chosen few who can do what they believe others cannot.

Many puzzling examples of less-than-rational human behavior can be explained by turning to behavioral economics, where studies have shown, with remarkable consistency, that the Pareto principle, or 80/20 rule, applies to most groups of people when asked to rate themselves "above average" or "below average." As we see ourselves, most of us hail from America's favorite hometown: Lake Wobegon. Over and over again, about 80% of us rate ourselves "above average" on most virtues—including being good investors or good evaluators of investment managers. This finding may be the key to explaining why indexing has not been pursued even more boldly.

Summing Up

The ironic triumph of active performance investors, who are so capable of price discovery, is that they have reduced the opportunity to achieve superior price discovery so much that the money game of outperformance after costs and fees is, for clients, no longer a game worth playing. The obvious central question for our profession—for each individual and each firm in active investment management—is, when will we recognize and accept that our collective skills at price discovery have increased so much that most of us can no longer expect to outperform the expert consensus by enough to cover costs and management fees and offer good risk-adjusted value to our clients?

Another central question is, when will our clients decide that continuing to take all the risks and pay all the costs of striving to beat the market with so little success is no longer a good deal for them? These questions are crucial because to continue selling our services after passing that tipping point would clearly raise the kind of ethical questions that separate a proud profession from a crass commercial business.

Ideally investment management has always been a "two hands clapping" profession: one hand based on skills of price discovery and the other hand based on values discovery. Price discovery is the skillful process of identifying pricing errors not yet recognized by other investors. Values discovery is the process of determining each client's realistic objectives with respect to various factors—including wealth, income, time horizon, age, obligations and responsibilities, investment knowledge, and personal financial history—and designing the appropriate strategy.

As a business, active investment management has been a booming success for insiders, but truly professional practitioners want both a great business and an admired profession. Sadly, our collective decisions and behavior, far more than most insiders seem to realize, show that in what we do versus what we say, many of us put "great business" far ahead of "admired profession." Part of the reason we have been able to put business first is that most clients do not seem to realize what is really going on and also we insiders do not see, or pretend not to see, our emerging reality all that clearly either.

One way to test our thinking would be to ask the question in reverse: If your index manager reliably delivered the full market return with no more than market risk for a fee of just 5 bps, would you be willing to switch to active performance managers who charge exponentially more and produce unpredictably varying results, falling short of their chosen benchmarks nearly twice as often as they outperform—and when they fall short, lose 50% more than they gain when they outperform? The question answers itself. And that is the question each client should be asking—and more and more apparently are asking—before shifting, however warily, to ETFs and index funds. Demand for indexing (Figure 5.3) and ETFs (Figure 5.4) is accelerating.

Assets ($ billions)

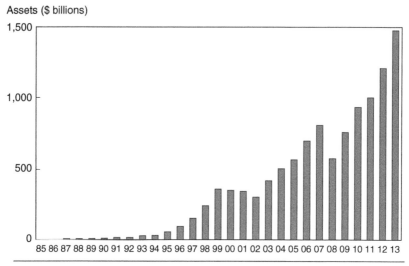

Note: Data for 2013 go through September.

**Figure 5.3 Total US Index Mutual Funds Assets, January
1985–September 2013**

Assets ($ billions)

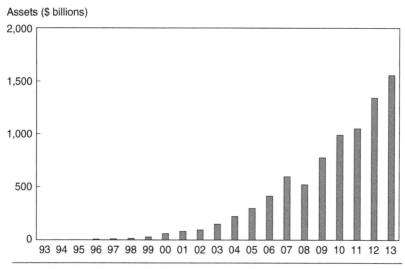

Note: Data for 2013 go through September.

Figure 5.4 Total US Industry ETF Assets, January 1993–September 2013

Conclusion: Looking Forward

The double whammy of fee compression for active investing and an increasing shift into low-cost indexing will surely depress both the economics of the investment business and the income of individual practitioners. Fortunately, we still have an opportunity to rebalance what we offer clients by re-emphasizing the once-central part of our "two-handed" profession: values discovery, by which every client can be guided through the important questions to an appropriate investment strategy and helped to stay on course through the inevitable market highs and lows.

The "winner's game" of rigorous, individualized value discovery and counseling may not be as financially rewarding to investment managers as the performance "product" business based on price discovery, but as a profession, it would be far more fulfilling. It is an admirable way forward that would inspire client loyalty—with all the attendant long-term economic benefits—and would provide practitioners with deep professional satisfaction. Although not as exciting as competing on price discovery, investment counseling based on values discovery is greatly needed by most investors and surely offers more opportunities for real long-term success to both our profession and our clients.

Source: Charles D. Ellis (2014) The Rise and Fall of Performance Investing, *Financial Analysts Journal*, 70:4, 14–23, copyright © CFA Institute reprinted by permission of Taylor & Francis Ltd, http://www.tandfonline.com on behalf of CFA Institute.

6

Seven Rules for More Innovative Portfolio Management in an Age of Discontinuity

Peter Drucker was a friend and a regular consultant to Greenwich Associates. He was a superb writer and always a provocative, original thinker. As active investing centered on the portfolio manager was in ascendancy in the late 1960s, this good-humored piece borrowed and applied some of Drucker's ideas and insights. Readers will smile at the admonition—over 50 years ago—that charging high fees was a good way to attract the best clients.

Peter Drucker's new book, *The Age of Discontinuity,* is an appropriate source of "scripture" for a consideration of how to get organized for managing large, aggressive equity portfolios, because recognizing, evaluating, and capitalizing profitably upon the discontinuities of our age are truly the mission of portfolio management organizations.

"We have learned, by and large, how to use organization to do efficiently what we already knew how to do," Drucker writes. "This is a tremendous step forward, and one on which our present society rests.

We now need to make possible organization that can *innovate* . . ." An innovative organization requires a different structure in the relationships between people. It requires an open-team organization rather than a closed-command organization, and it requires flexibility in relationships. Team structure is largely unknown to classical organization theory—though a jazz combo or, for that matter, a surgical team in the operating theater both exemplify it.

The innovative organization needs a new attitude on the part of the people at the top. In the traditional pyramidal command managerial organization, the top people sit in judgment; in the innovative organization, it is their job to encourage the development of new ideas. It is the job of the top people in the innovative organization to try to convert the largest possible number of ideas into serious proposals for effective, purposeful work. It is not their job, as it is in the traditional managerial organization, to say: "This is not a serious proposal." It is their job to say: "What would this idea have to become for it to be taken seriously?" Drucker concludes that "no idea for the really new ever starts out as a realistic, serious, thought-through, worked-out proposal. It always starts out as a groping, a divining, a search."

The need to organize "knowledge workers" to produce and implement innovative thinking is particularly acute for investment management organizations seeking to achieve superior performance. Performance depends upon three extremely difficult feats:

- Identifying truly major changes in the market, in industries, and in companies.
- Acting before recognition by others has already changed market prices.
- Committing enough capital to perceived changes to make a major impact on the portfolio.

Most of us know this triple crown is not easy to win, although some organizations do not yet seem to understand why it might be difficult. In any event, let us draw some guidelines that are useful to the investment management organization which does not have a heroic genius who can do it all alone. We are concerned with the investment firm that has bright, well-educated, ambitious, responsible people who are good, but not perfect.

To help such a capital management group achieve superior performance on a regular basis, I propose seven laws. While it may sound all too obvious to say we ought to define where we want to go before starting off, very few investment managers can answer with clarity or conviction such basic questions as: What are you organizing for? What are you trying to do? Without defining your goals, you cannot possibly know how well you are progressing. Hence, the first law is:

- *Poorly defined standards of performance make poor performance standard.*
  Very few investment managing organizations can effectively perform superior services for all types of clients. Diverse client goals and needs are a great centripetal force, and the people and methods required to meet each of these contrasting needs are not harmonious. Any attempt by one organization to serve several kinds of investors will almost automatically result in mediocre accomplishment. And when this happens, the most desirable client—the one who is willing to pay handsomely for performance—will go elsewhere. Hence, the second law:
- *Bad clients drive out good.*
  The third law requires no explanation:
- *The customer is always wrong.*
  Since you can only perform well as a "creative" for a rather small number of clients, you might just as well do this for those who like to pay well for the services you render. Really, there is no *excuse* for low fees; if we cannot earn high fees, we are just playing around with our clients very precious money—rearranging the deck chairs—and should quit the business. Clients who do not understand higher fees are almost inevitably the same clients who are a nuisance to work with, expect too much, and criticize your best efforts at the worst times and places.

  On the other hand, high fees have the happy effect of attracting that ideal client who expects to pay for what he gets. There is also a peculiar snob appeal to paying a higher fee. (The success of private hedge funds bears eloquent witness to these thoughts.) Hence, law number four:
- *High fees repel bad clients and attract good ones.*
  A superb investment manager does very little. At most he will make only two or three really worthwhile decisions in a year, and two or three important decisions is more than enough to assure outstanding performance. No more are needed. Yet, most investment managers intentionally try to make hundreds of decisions annually. They like to think that long hours, high piles in the "in" and "out" boxes, stacks of telephone messages, and a lot of personal hustle are good. It shows we work hard. But the decisions made by these harried managers are

almost necessarily *inferior* decisions in that they can only be used once or twice in specific transactions.

What we need are more *superior* decisions—decisions that are used over and over again in different areas and at different times because the creative energy unleashed by these rare superior decisions is so powerful. The fifth law thus follows:

- *Small decisions obfuscate major decisions.*

The environment in which we work is the most dynamic known to man. Social, political, technical, religious, international, climactic, cultural, and competitive changes must all be considered continuously. Consequently, we must be flexible in response and swift to take the initiative. In general, an organization designed for *efficiency* in our business is not particularly *effective*. Analysts who are long-established experts in particular industries all too often become financial bigots who have spent years confirming and refining their prejudices. Ours is the business of change, and rigidity is not helpful. Hence, the sixth law:

- *Experience can be a bad teacher.*
- We must prepare ourselves for creative excellence. While the data is a bit sketchy, it consistently supports the conclusion that the less intensively we work, the more we contribute. I know of only three money managers who have been away from their offices for at least three months (one for a leisurely convalescence, one for a series of long trips abroad, and one for a political campaign). In every case, their associates found the value of their contribution in the remaining nine months to be far greater than usual. In every case, these investors made very few decisions. But they were all superior decisions because they had made time for deep reflection and new ways of thinking that had major impact. Thus, as rational people, we must conclude that long and frequent vacations are essential to outstanding performance. The seventh and final law brings this brief article to its conclusion:
- *Work and achievement do not mix.*

Source: *Institutional Investor*, April, 1969.

7

Will Success Spoil Performance Investing?

Written over 50 years ago, this piece celebrated the remarkable long-term "bell curve" business cycle that would take active "performance" investing from a surging young growth business up and over its apex in the 1980s and on to the steady decline—for consumers, if not for producers—by the turn of the century. Ironically, the factors that would lead to its inevitable self-destruction were buried within what most of us—over 50 years ago—saw back then as clear indicators of progress.

Big Money is on the move. It has been a long time since the Great Depression, which was the Ice Age of the U.S. economy, during which the investment principles and practices of Big Money got solidly frozen. But now, with competitive pressures for good performance heating up, the glacial Establishment is rapidly melting around the edges. And it is beginning to slide.

Traditionally conservative institutions—banks, trust companies, university endowments, pension funds, insurance companies and the more staid mutual funds—are moving at an accelerating pace towards the performance method and philosophy. Technicians, traders, young portfolio managers, incentive pay and talk of highflyers are surprisingly common within the marble halls of these once staid bastions of fiscal tradition. Performance investing has come from suspected intruder to accepted darling among the nation's major institutions and their customers.

The ascendancy of performance investing is due to achieved results. And results in recent years have been very good. Perhaps too good. Possibly, even probably, its great success will soon spoil performance investing.

Before discussing the developing problems for performance "investing," it is worth defining what it is. Performance investing is an aggressive, eclectic, intensively managed effort to continuously maximize portfolio profits. Performance investing goes far beyond such quotable quotes and slogans as: "Don't marry stocks; love 'em and leave 'em." "It's a fashion business, so don't buck the trend, ride it." "Go where the action is." It's a tough, highly competitive, brain-draining, fast-moving and wide-ranging struggle to beat the pack. And to beat most of the other young lions.

The Successful Performance Investor

The performance fund manager operates somewhere between the extremes of tape reading traders and very long-term holders. Traders try to combine high turnover with very small profit increments per decision: long-term holders with low turnover depend on much larger price changes per decision. The successful performance investor combines the best of both, capturing the larger mark-ups than traders and turning over his inventory faster than long pull investors.

The performance investor specializes in identifying and acting quickly upon the factors that he feels will probably change stock prices, seeking to buy or sell before the general market reacts to these developments. To operate effectively, the performance fund manager must have access to current information on a very great many companies and stocks in order to find openings in the market to ply his trades. Charts and other technical studies of prices and volume can be analyzed to catch changes in supply and demand. Quarterly earnings become critical. Bits and pieces of information of all kinds must be acquired and processed, and this requires a very wide network of helpers who call in with data, rumors, ideas, etc. He must be mentally and emotionally capable of making a great many more decisions with less complete knowledge than his longer-term competitors. Performance investing is not nearly as easy as it looks to some of the noncombatants.

Not only is performance investing hard to do, the most effective practitioners face serious problems. These are the problems that raise the question: will success spoil performance? The performance investor is trying to capture the profits available for early recognition of changing value that will cause rapid change in stock prices. But the total potential profit available is limited because the performance funds do not, in the long run, make the market; they can only operate in and upon the market made by other longer-term investors. Since the performance pie is not indefinitely large, when too much money chases pieces of that pie, the rate of return per dollar invested must fall. Performance techniques would simply get less and less "performance."

Second, as the number of funds operating in the performance manner increases, portfolio managers, who want to "get in early," are obliged to act sooner and sooner. This means that they act with less and less certainty that the expected positive or negative development will actually happen. And this lowers the probabilities of being right, which reduces the profits.

Third, the most successful funds may get swamped with money. As they rack up profits, more and more investors jump on the razz-matazz bandwagon and new money flows in, these funds can get too big for their own kind of game. For example, if market liquidity limits holdings to $1 million in a small "hot" stock, a $50 million fund can go after it. But a $500 million fund would need positions of $10 million in such a stock—a dangerous amount to liquidate. So the large fund manager is limited to stocks with bigger and bigger capitalizations.

Giant Fund Manager Disadvantaged

But even in the most liquid stocks, a $1 billion fund has trouble cutting in and out of positions that may average $15 million (300,000 shares of $50 stock). That much stock is hard to buy and hard to sell. So the giant fund manager just can't act on the frequent, but small profit opportunities that come along because the costs of moving big blocks may be more than the profit opportunity identified.

These are some of the major problems facing the best performance funds. If performance investing is doomed to follow the typical phases of development, maturation, and decline, the first two phases are easily described.

During the first phase, the creative impact of the pioneers results in the development of a new, iconoclastic approach to equity management that is disparaged and/or rejected by the Establishment. But the approach works well and earns high portfolio profits. It can't be ignored. Public acceptance leads to grudging, then intrigued acceptance by other institutions. Good investment results cause accelerating endorsement by the

Establishment which, paradoxically, may doom the darling to dreary disappointment.

The third phase is decline. The problem with success is simple: You get too big, almost "money bound."

Individual funds have grown enormously in the past decade, and the number of new and old portfolios committed to performance is expanding rapidly too. The result is a geometric increase in the amount of money trying to exploit the performance opportunity. The problems of success are most acute for the individual fund whose success has caused a financial form of elephantiasis. Limit to "big capitalization" stocks and paying high tolls to get in or out of each position, their performance gets hurt. In the good old days, there was plenty of room for everybody who wanted to try fleecing the public and the slower institutions, but now former comrades in arms are by necessity trying to fleece each other. There is not enough profit to go around. Success is beginning to spoil performance.

Two solutions or offsets are worth considering because there are two different problems. What can help the individual performance fund? And what can help the performance funds as a group?

Three answers have been offered to the problem of an individual fund's size: limit the size of the fund by closing down new sales when a size such as $100 million is reached; start new funds as the old get too big; and try to convince shareholders to accept lower rates of return. Each of these methods is being tried and they seem to work for a few individual funds.

In addition, there is a good chance that the problems facing performance funds as a group can be at least deferred This prospect is inherent in the increasing acceptance of the performance goal by the very large institutions such as banks, pension funds, endowments, and insurers. Their movement into the field brings relief in several ways:

First, the market is made more liquid by having more active participants. This allows larger and larger holdings to be bought and sold quickly and without undue disruption of price.

Second, with more money looking for high profits, stock prices react faster to changing expectations. The payoffs for good selections come faster, which can dramatically increase the annual rate of return of each investment.

Third, the traditional institutions are buying into the kinds of stocks the performance funds already own. This raises the general P/Es of "performance" stocks while selling down the prices of traditional

"Dow Jones" Issues. This shifting process is lifting prices in that area of the market where performance investors operate, giving them an extra advantage in their efforts to surpass the market averages.

Liquidity Loses Usefulness

While each of these elements of change is helpful to the performance investors, they can't and won't help for very long. Greater liquidity loses its usefulness when too many funds try to do the same thing at the same time. Getting the bigger profit from faster price moves depends on buying early, and the younger generation at the traditionally slow institutions are anxious to be early too. Competition for leadership could get tough. Finally, switching from "slow" to "go" stocks is not going to take forever and its relative impact on multiples may be diminishing already.

Unless the traditional institutions both insist on trying performance investing and consistently fail to be very good at it, winning them over may eventually compound the problems of success which "performance investing" already faces. The decline phase of performance may be delayed a bit and then be made all the more inevitable. The general concept of performance investing may also come in for strong abuse if the big institutions, in trying to learn the game, are hurt badly. Many of these traditional capital pools are already too large, have administrative problems that prevent quick reactions, and are not staffed by aggressive "swingers" who will thrive on the competitions, challenge, and excitement of the high-performance game. It now appears that many conservative funds are being seduced by the siren song and are starting to play a game that they are ill prepared for.

Whatever the facts of individual funds or the general view of performance investing, it does seem clear that the business of managing institutional money has been permanently changed away from capital preservation. Performance investing is surely not the only way to get good portfolio profits, but it must be given credit for forcing money managers to try harder. The risk is that money managers may try too hard, relative to their own abilities and market opportunities and begin to stumble.

8

To Get Performance, You Have to Be Organized for It

In an era of rapid change over 50 years ago, investment managers with aggressive "open" ways of operating were able to exploit the changes. But that environment would not last long. The beliefs underlying this article would, over time, become obsolete. (Note: Four years out of business school, I was working for a securities firm at the time and was declared too inexperienced by one year to take the third exam to become a Chartered Financial Analyst. This article was made the basis for a three-hour essay question on that exam: "Please comment.")

Performance-oriented managements have captured virtually all the attention of both individual and institutional investors in recent years and their investment records have been enviable. Are these records luck? Or speculative good fortune? Or only temporary?

Better research and more astute portfolio management are part of the answer, but only part. Like successful companies in other fields, the most rapidly growing and highly regarded investment companies are developing innovative strategies to make the best use of changes in the business environment. Investment managers who seek comparable results should understand the key changes in methods, purposes, and organization which produce sustained superior portfolio performance.

The successful new capital managers have achieved superior operating results because they are better organized for performance than more traditional investors. Their approach is strategic. Effective corporate strategy anywhere usually involves several phases:

- Specify the goal.
- Identify problems and opportunities presented by the environment.
- Determine the internal strengths and weaknesses of the enterprise.
- Develop policies that minimize problems and exploit opportunities.

The single objective of the new investment management is to maximize the profitability of capital under management. Capital productivity (not capital preservation) dominates the structure and activities of the entire organization, and the efforts of every individual are aimed at contributing to portfolio profit.

Traditional investment managers often have a strikingly different set of goals: Capital preservation (not profitability) is their economic objective. An image of quality and conservatism is sought and protected. They avoid risk. Naturally, these other goals can and often do conflict with a determined effort to maximize money-making.

How the "New" Managers Operate

The new managers are convinced that the traditional organizational structure has important weaknesses that can be reduced or eliminated by changes in management organization and method.

Traditional investment management is oriented towards long-term investments; relies on a committee of senior officers to make all investment decisions at weekly or semi-monthly meetings; depends primarily on a staff of in-house analysts for information and evaluation; and conducts its affairs in private. Since the principal investment objective is capital preservation (rather than capital productivity), caution and conservatism tend to characterize the decision process and the portfolio.

An investment committee has two important and useful capabilities. First, serious errors in judgment seldom survive its open review, because a committee composed of those with diverse experience can usually raise most potentially significant questions. Second, an effective committee can establish sound basic policy. But this does not mean that the committee should also make such operating decisions as security selection, and the degree of emphasis given individual securities.

In portfolio management, time is money, and the necessarily slow decision process of a committee can be very expensive to the portfolio. Memoranda prepared for committees take analysts' time away from productive research efforts. Formal procedures delay actions, often until it is too late to act at all because of price changes. Committee decisions are not easily reversed (although market liquidity allows it) with the result that tentative, experimental purchases are virtually impossible. Profit opportunities provided by market swings must be ignored, and only long-term opportunities can be considered.

Committees Can't Control

Since a committee can only make a few decisions each meeting, they tend to manage portfolios by exception, selling "bad" stocks and buying "good" ones. The new management wants portfolio management by control and recognizes that investment decisions are seldom clearly identified in blacks and whites, but rather appear in varying shades of gray, which warrant almost continuous change in the emphasis placed on various securities. The committee system makes it difficult to assign personal responsibility and measure results. It's not clear who can take credit for good decisions, and who can be held accountable for poor decisions?

An individual investment manager working full-time on the problems and opportunities facing his portfolio can exercise management by control. The logic is in the mathematics of time. A committee that meets for two or three hours 50 times a year cannot make nearly as many astute decisions as an executive working 50 or more hours, 50 weeks a year.

Moreover, if the committee attempts to run the portfolio, it will seldom give adequate time and attention to its major policy responsibilities and will also make inferior operating decisions. So the new management clearly separates policy decisions from operating decisions by assigning operating authority to a single executive or portfolio manager. The capacity to make more decisions allows more aggressive management and allows the portfolio to capture that many more increments of profit. The portfolio manager need not wait for a committee meeting; decisions can be quite informal; he avoids the delays inherent in the preparation of a formal presentation to an investment committee; and he can act decisively.

Why Individuals Outperform Committees

The competent individual has important advantages over a committee in making investment decisions. Since he devotes all his time and energies to the success of the portfolio, it stands to reason that he'll know more about each constituent security, why it was bought, why it is held, and why it might be sold.

Since portfolio management is more art than science, and since committees are notoriously not artful, the single portfolio executive who is personally skilled in this art will enjoy a significant competitive strength. He can exploit his intuition, inventiveness, and sense of the market because he is judged, not on how well he can explain his programs, but on results in the marketplace.

Moreover, since the portfolio manager is judged on the profitability of the portfolio as a whole, he is more clearly motivated to take sensible risks where the rewards are commensurate. He can act boldly, innovate, and see initiatives to increase portfolio profits. By giving the portfolio manager the authority and direct responsibility for operating decisions, the new managements obtain the advantages of an individual in making and executing decisions while preserving the policy-and-review capabilities of a committee.

How "New" Management Gets Information

The new investment management organizations strive not only to be highly effective at making profitable decisions, but also skillful at acquiring and evaluating the information upon which decisions must be based. The traditional approach to data collection and appraisal relies upon a permanent private staff of analysts who study statistics, visit managements, and write reports recommending purchases and sales to the investment committee. The research process is treated as proprietary and confidential and is considered the sole responsibility of the in-house staff.

While this internal resource can be highly valuable, it can all too often lead to a constriction on the flow of information to the decision-maker. A major opportunity for improved portfolio profit is presented in the best research and security evaluation supplied by brokers. The view that broker research has great value is coupled with a clear awareness of the service buying power of commission generated by the portfolio. The commission buying power is managed carefully and expended to acquire that brokerage research and judgment that will add the most profit to the portfolio.

Another major innovation in capital management is the way in which broker research is integrated into the capital management process. A communications gap exists between the growing store of brokers' research knowledge and the operating needs of the portfolio manager. The portfolio manager who best bridges this communications gap will have an advantage over his competitors.

Bypassing the Staff Analysts

Whereas the traditional management group insists that all broker research go to the staff analysts, the new approach channels an important part of this information and opinion flow directly to the portfolio manager. This practice derives from an appreciation of subtle human differences between analyst and portfolio manager, their positions within the organization, and how they respond to external opinion.

For many good reasons, staff analysts are usually not well suited to appreciating the merits of broker recommendations. A good analyst is necessarily skeptical and tends to discount what others say. Professionally, he distrusts and disparages relying on the work of others. He knows too much about the particular stocks he follows closely to be impressed by a summary description of other securities, and his professional satisfaction often depends more on the breadth and depth of his company and industry knowledge than on the profitability of recommended purchases and sales. His career development typically depends more upon the consistent accuracy of his earnings projections in research reports than upon the frequency and magnitude of his contributions to the portfolio's profitability. Each year he makes far fewer recommendations than a portfolio manager makes decisions and therefore has a smaller set of commitments over which to obtain a satisfactory average of profitability. And he has less opportunity to reverse his decisions, so he must realistically be more confident of each individual security endorsement. For all these reasons, a staff analyst is ill-suited by position, responsibility, and interest to effectively exploit broker research.

The Open-Minded Manager

In contrast, the portfolio manager must always rely heavily on the knowledge and appraisals of others, whether they be internal staff analysts or external broker analysts. He is just as receptive to one analyst as he is to another if they can equally increase the profits of the portfolio.

His principal skill is in seeing the positive potential in a given situation rather than in identifying possible negatives. Consequently, the contemporary management philosophy offers the portfolio manager wide access to ideas and information, which he may pass on to a staff analyst for review and evaluation if he is interested but not yet convinced or may act upon immediately if he sees opportunity.

Another approach for in-house analysts is to redefine responsibility so that each analyst sees himself as an assistant portfolio manager and concentrates his efforts on flowing profit-making ideas into the portfolio. In this new role, in-house analysts can see broker research as an opportunity to save time, broaden knowledge, and use the best opinions of others. The assistant portfolio manager-analyst will build upon the work of these external analysts rather than recreating their original research, with the strong probability that his annual profit contribution to the portfolio will be greater than if time, efforts, and talents were devoted to independent research.

Beyond recasting the communications net to capture more value from external research, the new management considers outside investment capabilities as an opportunity to improve internal portfolio performance by integrating their knowledge and judgments into the portfolio's management. The most helpful brokers are taken in as effective partners in the management of the portfolio. Their opinions are sought on possible changes in investment policy as well as possible changes in holdings. The result of this "open door" policy is to expand greatly the number of competent persons contributing to the profitable management of the portfolio. With a good understanding of how the portfolio is managed, these outside partners can focus their efforts on providing the particular information and suggestions that are most valuable to the particular portfolio at a particular time.

Market Action Is an Indicator, Too

Trading is an important profit opportunity, and one member of the management team ought to have complete responsibility for it. The experienced trader, involved continuously with the market, not only knows quoted prices but has useful insights into the structure of supply and demand. With this superior market knowledge, the trader is often able to contribute significantly to the profit goal by advising the portfolio manager on timing of actions and on unusual opportunities to buy or sell created by temporary imbalances of supply and demand in the market.

New methods have been used to improve the profitability of open market operations, such as large block transactions that allow rapid redeployment of funds in large amounts at specific prices, and sales of blocks to brokers who make position bids by putting their own capital at risk when the market will not immediately absorb a large supply of shares.

Performance Pays the Performers

The management goal of portfolio profitability is supported with pay and other incentives closely related to an individual's ability to contribute to portfolio profitability. The most important job in terms of income, professional responsibility, prestige, and influence is that of portfolio manager. The personal, non-financial incentives are also important in these free-form, multi-profit-center managements in which each person functions as an entrepreneur, and ability to contribute to portfolio profitability is quickly recognized and quickly rewarded. As a result, the new managements have attracted unusually able, hard-working, and creative young people, and then stimulated them to achievements at or near their potential. As in most fields of organized endeavor, the essential ingredient for sustained superior results is the ability and effectiveness of the people in management, and the new concept of capital management has emphasized the importance of profit-making people.

In summary, having observed and worked with dozens of different investment organizations, I am convinced that the superior record of achievement of a still small but rapidly growing number of capital managements results from their clearer, deeper, and broader understanding of the environment in which they operate and a careful organization of internal strengths to achieve maximum portfolio profits. The flow of new monies to these new managers is impressive evidence that the sophisticated public recognizes their success. Investment managers that are organized along more traditional lines should seriously consider the nature and importance of the new approach to capital management.

Source: *Institutional Investor,* January, 1968.

9

Investing Success in Two Easy Lessons

If we are always looking for insights into investing's secrets, we will find them, even in unusual places. Here are two good lessons: one found while watching the Munich Marathon and one found in a Wall Street admonition by a dignified, successful senior.

Successful investing should be easy. Obviously, it's not. But in over 40 years, mostly in the privileged position as trusted advisor to the leaders of major investment and securities firms, two investment lessons stand out for me as particularly valuable and easy to use. Anyone who "gets it" on these two easy lessons will do well. Like career "bookends," one came early and one late in over four decades of continuous learning about investing.

In Munich, while visiting my son Chad and his wife Trish a few months ago, we agreed to cheer for their friend who was running in the Munich marathon. That friend had run several marathons, so she had a realistic plan and knew that at about eleven, she would pass a particular church, so we were stationed there and, right on schedule, she came by. We cheered lustily, she waved and was quickly gone.

We went off to lunch at a Wursthaus and then took the tram out to Olympic Park. As we walked from the tram station to the stadium and the marathon's finish line, we passed a trio of cheerful Kenyans who had

already completed the race—probably coming in 1st, 2nd, and 3rd—
and were going home. It would be nearly an hour before our friend
would finish.

The organizers of the Munich Marathon had arranged an attractive
way to finish:

> Runners would come into the stadium through a tunnel that was filled
> with vapor and then burst out into the sunlight as they entered the
> Olympic stadium with only one short lap around the stadium left to
> go. The runners, nicely encouraged, loved it.

Sitting in the stadium with a few hundred other fans, we enjoyed
watching runners individually and in small groups come through the
portal entrance and into the stadium for the final lap to the finish line.
The runners were all different in age, dress, and running style but in one
particular way, they were all the same.

Runner after runner—on entering the stadium, seeing the crowd,
and hearing the scattered but friendly applause—reached high overhead
with both arms in the traditional triumphal Y and held it for at least half
a minute, running out the final lap, grinning in victory.

At first, it seemed strange. Didn't they know the Kenyans had won
long ago? As time went by—and we were in the stadium for nearly two
hours because our friend had caught a cramp and had to slow down—it
might have seemed stranger and stranger to see later and later runners
act like champions, heroes, and winners. Then it hit me: They *were* winners. They were *all* winners because each runner had achieved her or his
own realistic objective.

Some finished in less than three hours; some in only three hours; or
"only" three and a half hours. Others beat their prior best time. Some
won simply by completing the whole marathon, some for their first time
and others for their last time.

The powerful message: Each successful runner had achieved his or
her own realistic objective, so each one was a true winner and fully entitled to make the big Y and run the victory lap.

If, as investors, we would think and act the same way: understanding
our capacities and our limits, we could plan the race that is right for us
and, with the self-discipline of a long-distance runner, run our own race
to achieve our own realistic objectives. In investing, the good news is
clear: Everyone can win. Everyone can be a winner.

The secret to winning the Winner's Game in investing is simple:
Plan your play and play your plan to win *your* game. And if we don't

think and work that winning way in investing, we will, by default, be playing the Loser's Game of trying to "beat the market," a game which almost every investor will eventually lose.

My other favorite investing insight came first over 40 years ago. A freshly minted MBA, I was in a training program in Wall Street.[1] As part of our training, we were to meet each Thursday for the hour before lunchtime with the heads of various departments—syndicate, block trading, research, municipal bonds, etc.—for an introductory explanation of each unit's work.

One day, we were happily surprised to learn that the senior partner had agreed to take a Thursday slot to discuss the larger picture. Mr. Joseph K. Klingenstein—known to his friends as "Joe" and to us as "JK" *except* when he was or might be present, in which case he was always "Mr. Klingenstein," wore pince-nez glasses and was patrician, dignified, and erect.

As Mr. Klingenstein spoke about the history of his firm and of Wall Street and its traditions, we listened quietly but not, I fear, very conscientiously. Then five minutes before noon, Mr. Klingenstein had finished his talk and asked, "Do you young gentlemen have any questions?"

Silence.

The silence was broken by the brightest and certainly the most outspoken of our little group. "Yeah, Mistah Klingenstein, I've got a question for you.

"You're rich, Mr. Klingenstein. We all want to be rich too, Mr. Klingenstein. So, what can you tell us from all your experience, Mr. Klingenstein, about how to get rich like you, Mr. Klingenstein?"

Of course, you could have heard the proverbial pin drop—or a butterfly land on a marshmallow. We were mortified. Such a way to speak to such a very great man!

Joseph K. Klingenstein at first appeared angry, perhaps *very* angry. But then, to our great and collective relief, it became clear that he was silent because he was thinking—thinking very carefully about his many investment experiences. Then, looking directly at his questioner, he said very simply and clearly, "Don't lose."

After JK rose and left the room, we all went off to lunch, where we agreed, "If you ask a simple question, you'll get a simple answer." By "simple," we meant stupid.

---

[1] At Wertheim & Co.

As the years have passed, Mr. Klingenstein's advice has come back to me again and again. Now, I know that in two simple words JK gave us the secret of investing successfully for the long term. While all the chatter and excitement is about big stocks, big gains, and "three-baggers," long-term investment success really depends on *not losing*—not taking major permanent losses.

We all know that a 50% loss requires a *double* just to get even, but still we strive for the Big Score, knowing full well that accidents happen most often to too-fast drivers; that Icarus got too close to the sun; that Enron, WorldCom, and many dotcoms had very high "new era" multiples before their obliteration.

Large losses are forever in investing, in teenage driving, and in fidelity. If you avoid large losses with a strong defense, the winnings will have every opportunity to take care of themselves. And large losses are almost always caused by taking too much risk.

If, as investors, we could learn to concentrate on wisely defining our own long-term objectives and learn to focus on not losing as the most important part of each specific decision, we could all be winners over the long term. And if it's too late for any of us because our best years are behind us, it's not too late to tell our children or grandchildren Mr. Klingenstein's great lesson.

Source: Charles D. Ellis (2005) Investing Success in Two Easy Lessons, *Financial Analysts Journal,* 61:1, 27–28, copyright © CFA Institute reprinted by permission of Taylor & Francis Ltd, http://www.tandfonline.com on behalf of CFA Institute.

10

The End of Active Investing?

While China's stock market continues to be dominated by retail investors, most other markets are now overwhelmingly dominated by professionals—all with superb information, powerful computers, Bloomberg terminals, and Internet access to an enormous flow of information. And each active manager has the same big problem: all the other experts have the same wonderful resources, too. As a result, after costs of operations and fees, most professionals fall short of the market over the long term—and most of the few who did not fall short in the past 15 years will fall short in the next 15. Active investing rose to fame 60 years ago, had a wonderful run, but just may have seen its era ending in recent years.

Since index funds deliver the market rate of return through a widely diversified portfolio with no more than the market level of risk, the only justification for actively managed funds must be either more returns or less risk—or both. That justification is increasingly recognized as the investment world's version of the triumph of hope over experience.

During the 1960s and 1970s, most actively managed "performance" funds were able—more years than not and almost always over longer periods—to produce superior returns. Clients loved it. And, as money poured in and fees were raised, investment managers prospered. If nothing had changed over the past half-century, active investing would still be triumphantly successful.

But things have changed. New investment companies were created, prospered, and expanded rapidly. Established ones reorganized and then prospered too. Darwinian evolution drove inferior institutional managers out of the market and strong firms made themselves even stronger. As the competitive norm rose higher during the 1980s and 1990s, the capabilities required for even moderate success continued to rise. Today, actively managed funds are not beating the market. The market is beating them. And the long-term trend for active management is grim.

The seriously distorted conventional data on the performance of active managers are now being corrected by adding back into the record the results of funds that, because they performed so poorly, had been closed or merged into other funds and then deleted from the conventional records. This corrected data has important messages for investors.

Actively Deficient

Three points are crucial. Over 10 years, 83% of active mutual funds in the US fail to match their chosen benchmarks; 40% stumble so badly that they were terminated before the 10-year period was completed and 64% of funds drift away from their originally declared style of investing. These seriously disappointing records would not be at all acceptable if produced by any other industry. And while these are US statistics, since international institutions dominate all stock markets, they are all moving in a similar direction (Table 10.1).

The forces of change causing these shabby results for active managers are numerous and undeniably powerful. Over 50 years, trading volume on the New York Stock Exchange has increased 5000 times—from 3 million shares a day to over 5 billion (while trading in derivatives has gone from zero to now exceed the stock market in value). Investment

Table 10.1 Percentage of International Funds That Lag Behind Benchmarks

Fund category	Benchmark index	10-year percentage failure rate
Global	S&P Global 1200	79.2
International	S&P International 700	84.1
International small cap	S&P Developed Markets, ex-US Small Cap	58.1
Emerging markets	S&P/IFCI Composite	89.7

Source: S&P Dow Jones Indices. Data periods ending December 31, 2015.

research has increased substantially. Today's leading securities firms have as many as 600 company analysts, industry analysts, market analysts, commodities and foreign exchange experts, economists, demographers, and political analysts located in offices in major cities all over the world. The number of Chartered Financial Analysts is up from zero to 135,000, with another 200,000 studying for the CFA exams.

Instant communication of all sorts of information via 325,000 Bloomberg terminals, the Internet, and blast faxes ensure that all investors worldwide have immediate, equal access to a global cornucopia of information, analysis, and insight. With SEC Regulation FD (for "fair disclosure"), any investment information made available to any investor must be simultaneously made available to all investors. This eliminates what was once the "secret sauce" of active investors: getting the "first call" with new information, insights, or judgments.

The number of professionals engaged in price discovery has, over half a century, exploded from an estimated 5,000 to over 1,000,000. Hedge funds, the most intensive and price-sensitive market participants, have proliferated and now execute nearly half of all buying and selling. Algorithmic trading, computer models, and early versions of artificial intelligence are all increasingly powerful factors. As a result, institutional investors have collectively created a global expert information network that produces the world's largest and most effective continuous prediction market.

The only way for active investors to outperform is to discover and exploit pricing errors by other expert professionals, all having the same information at the same time with the same computers and teams of experts having much the same talent and drive. The difficulty of sustaining a significant competitive advantage at price discovery continues to increase.

Standing Out?

Curiously, the most powerful force for change has gone largely unnoticed. In the US, institutional trading has gone steadily upwards over the same half century from a market share of 9% to 20% to 50% to 80% and now over 90%.

While institutional trading volumes may have advanced in an almost straight line, the difficulty of achieving superior performance when selling only to, or buying only from, near-equal competitors—all active participants in the same giant, swift, global information network—has been accelerating. The difficulty of outperforming the expert pricing consensus which is the market has been accelerating up an exponential "power law" curve.

Like the Doppler effect on an approaching train's whistle, the impact of professionals increasingly trading only with other professionals—all nearly equally well armed and equally well-informed—has made and will make it increasingly hard for them to outperform the market they and their peers collectively dominate as the corrected data on funds now shows.

Surely, some active managers with unusual skills or practices will outperform, but they will not be competing directly with the many conventional active managers. These active managers will have developed and focused on a market segment with fewer competitors and will excel in it. Nor will future "winners" be easy to identify in advance.

When price volatility or a bull market in small company stocks or a bear market in large capitalization stocks develops, we can be sure stories will appear claiming that "active is back," filled with admiring interviews of the new heroes of the sector. Their case will require focusing on the lucky winners while ignoring the equally unlucky losers in the wide dispersion of results so predictably caused by the statistical "law of small numbers."

Even as evidence piles up that forceful changes are closing in and threaten to confound more and more active managers, most investors still will not recognize the reality—or will say they don't. But as Winston Churchill once said: "We must look at the facts because the facts are looking at us." Like climate change and other complex systemic changes, the evidence needs careful analysis to separate long-term secular trends from medium-term cyclical fluctuations around those secular trends—and both of these from meaningless short-term, random statistical "noise."

Sorting out the profound from the probable—and both of these from the ephemeral—will be sufficiently difficult for most clients that clever sellers will be able to find and merchandise highly selective, semi-plausible supportive "evidence." We've seen this movie before in the way Big Tobacco cast doubt over the evidence that smoking causes cancer or the oil industry raised doubts about climate change.

The Good Old Days

Active managers had their halcyon days in the 1960s, when they did less than 10% of the trading in the US and were almost always competing at price discovery with amateur individual investors with little or no research or investment expertise who averaged just one trade a year, and who bought or sold for reasons *outside* the market: to invest a bonus or inheritance received or to raise money to buy a home or pay college fees for their children.

Back then, most institutional investors were the trust divisions of regional banks buying blue-chip "dividend" stocks held over the long term to avoid taxes and bond portfolios with laddered maturities. They were not challenging competition.

In those days, it was not unusual for active managers to beat the market by 200–300 basis points each year. Would investors mind paying 1% of assets to get double or triple that much in higher returns? Of course not.

Then, in the 1980s and 1990s, interest rates declined from 12% to 4% as the Fed, having broken inflationary expectations by pushing interest rates to record levels, let them normalize. Stock and bond prices began a long upward surge, with annual returns to investors of 10%, 12%, and 14%. Would investors mind paying 100 basis points while getting such splendid returns? No!

But today, if stock market returns over the next several years average only 6–7% and bond returns only 2–3% (as the consensus expects), will investor clients still be happy to pay over 100 basis point in fees (and nearly as much in operating costs) when most active managers continue to underperform their own benchmarks? Index funds repeatedly and predictably produce market-matching returns with no more than market-matching risk and charge less than 10 basis points. Will investors be willing to pay 90–120 basis points *more* to get active management when it typically produces *less* than market rates of return with both more risk and more uncertainty?

Before answering that pair of central questions, readers may want to consider four phases in the history over the past half century of active investment management.

- **Phase One (1960–1980)**: active managers compete principally against individuals and conservative mutual funds and trust institutions. Results: 200–300 basis points of superior performance are common. Index funds get no attention.
- **Phase Two (1980–2000)**: active managers ride a strong bull market, which pleases clients greatly, but can only achieve enough incremental performance to offset their costs and fees. Index funds get some attention.

- **Phase Three (2000–2010)**: active managers no longer earn back all their operating costs and fees. Index funds experience increasing interest and demand. Switching from active management to indexing increases from a low base level.
- **Phase Four (2010–)**: increasing numbers of active managers—particularly larger firms that must invest mostly in large capitalization, widely owned stocks covered by many analysts and mostly correctly priced—underperform an almost completely professionalized market, with prospective returns averaging only 7%. Objective observers conclude that fees and other costs can no longer be dismissed as "inconsequential." Demand for low-cost indexing steadily accelerates.

Active investment managers and their clients had little or no difficulty with each other during Phases One and Phase Two. Even in Phase Three, memories of better times in the past blended with understandable hopes for a return to past years' favorable experiences—without insisting on any explanation of how that might actually be achieved. Investors waited patiently, hoping for better returns.

Phase Four is different. Clients are inevitably learning that the key question is not, "Can we find an investment firm of super-bright, hard-working, skillful managers who will work hard for us?" The obvious, but useless, answer to that question is Yes! But that is not the right question. The crucial question is, "Can we find significantly *more* skillful, *more* hard-working, *more* creative active managers?" Alas, the answer to that question for most investors is clear: No.

Poor Value

The fees conventionally described as "only 1%" of *assets* are better seen for what they really are in a 7% return market—15% of *returns*. Worse, try taking incremental fees as a percentage of incremental returns—both versus indexing. When you do, incremental fees for active investment management are now actually over 100%—a price-to-value ratio seldom seen and rarely substantial.

Dismal reality will not confront all active managers equally nor simultaneously. Managers least at risk will be those delivering the best results or having the best client relationships or the least demanding clients—or both. Also, managers with clearly differentiated capabilities in advanced mathematics or clearly longer fundamental research time horizons will be under less pressure.

The greatest pressure will be on large, conventionally active managers of portfolios necessarily dominated by the same large stocks that are most widely owned and most carefully priced by the professional consensus. Meanwhile, the "vice of destiny" will continue to squeeze in on layer after layer of full-fee active managers.

Historically, most products and services that have commanded prices that produce unusually high profit margins in free, open, and competitive markets have been unable to sustain their exceptional profitability. So far, the business of active investing has been remarkably successful—for the active managers. But the remarkable success of the business; as distinct from the profession, continues to attract more and better competitors, information, and technologies. This makes superior returns ever harder to achieve. And, in a lower rate of return market, this problem is increasingly visible to growing numbers of clients.

As the negative evidence continues to accumulate and the forces driving active investing's underperformance continue to be better understood, increasing numbers of clients will realize that in toe-to-toe competition versus near-equal competitors, most active managers will not and cannot recover the costs and fees they charge.

As indexing repeatedly earns higher returns at lower cost and with less risk and less uncertainty, the world of active management will be taken down, firm by firm, from its once dominant and exalted position. The painful process will be seen in retrospect as the inevitable result of the increasingly visible impact of external and internal forces of change. As T.S. Eliot wrote in 1925: "This is the way the world ends. Not with a bang but a whimper."

Source: *Financial Times,* January, 2017.

11

In Defense of Active Investing

This whimsical piece made gentle fun of the active investors' curious scramble to find various less-than-credible reasons to believe they must be doing the right thing. Of course, for indexers—who "free ride" on all the skillful work active managers do—they <u>are</u> doing the "right thing" by making indexing not only feasible, but also lower in costs and fees and higher in returns—and for individual investors, lower in taxes too.

Investment management is at once both a profession and a business, so it cannot be surprising that these two disciplines can come into conflict, particularly when gradual trends of change have conspired to bring such conflict forward slowly and quietly. Ironically, the driving force has been the increasing excellence of the skilled professional practitioners who have done so much so well in the exceedingly hard work of price discovery. Their collective success has made it increasingly difficult for any one manager or firm to be so consistently superior to the consensus of the other experts that it can repeatedly outperform that market pricing system, particularly in large, diversified portfolios and after costs.

Some will say that the crossing of the Rubicon, beyond which most active managers fall short of the market (after costs and fees), happened years ago. Others will say the crossing was more recent. And a few will believe it has not yet happened or, at least, has not yet happened to them.

During a long transoceanic flight, I found myself dozing while quietly reflecting on this question and the more than 50 years I've enjoyed the privileges of having a wide circle of friends in the profession and my full share of the economic benefits of being in the right place at the right time. As best I can recall, these were the thoughts that came to mind during my high-altitude reverie.

★★★★

Something should be said. Active investing has been subjected to increasing abuse, particularly by those whose opinions are driven by the persistent accumulation of hard data and logical arguments. As we all know, active investing is on the defensive—even, some skeptics claim, "on the ropes"—having suffered a series of setbacks and increasingly virulent attacks. Especially scornful personal abuse has been aimed at active investing's few remaining advocates.

The time has come to mount a defense, not by the usual citing of occasional exceptions or by dismissing the challengers with colorful pejoratives but, rather, by looking at the broader picture and pointing out the many indirect benefits that skeptics—with their narrow focus on just "beating the market" for clients—apparently continue to miss.

The recent past has been a particularly mean-spirited time for active managers owing to a rare market phenomenon: Small-cap stocks have performed poorly. For the 12 months ended 30 September 2014, the Russell 1000 Index (large-cap stocks) rose more than 19% while the Russell 2000 Index (small-cap stocks) rose less than 4%. This unusual diversification in performance has recently penalized active managers, who often invest 10–30% of their portfolios in small-cap stocks, and this factoid is being overexploited by the usual active-investing deniers. The "active attackers" are in full throat now as they gloat over such seemingly decisive data. Although sensitive defenders of active investing can retort that "it's always darkest before the dawn" and cite the long history of how consensus conviction has almost always been wrong, the best defense is more robust. Before I present the case for the defense of active investing, however, let's briefly review the so-called case for the prosecution.

First came the academics, armed with their arcane null hypotheses, statistical inferences, and long equations littered with Greek letters. Most practitioners could safely ignore them, confident that nobody with a seat at the high table was all that interested in "ivory tower" mumbo jumbo. Active managers were certain that no practical men of affairs knew about, much less read the obscure academic journals in which those in the cloister publish and reference each other's articles. Meanwhile, active managers could, if pressed, dismiss these attacks as a modern version of Bishop Berkeley's quaint question, "If a tree fell in the forest with nobody there to listen, would it make any noise?"

Next came performance reporting and all sorts of odious comparisons. Fortunately, as Nate Silver continues to explain, the numbers we see combine both the signal and the noise in a never-ending cloud of mystery that invites manipulation: Change the base year, change the benchmark or standard of comparison, or report gross of fees rather than net. Or, in especially awkward situations, explain that certain surprisingly disappointing people have been replaced, so all will now be better. If necessary, show again that most managers with superior long-term results have had three long years of underperformance, or explain that Morningstar's ubiquitous star ratings, like all records of past performance, really have no proven predictive power and that staying the course is often wiser than switching horses in midstream.

More recently, the world of active investing has been under attack in reports that a majority of funds fall short of their benchmarks *and* that the trend is toward larger proportions of actively managed funds falling short *and* that the magnitude of underperformance substantially exceeds the magnitude of outperformance. Even worse, investment consultants are being accused of enhancing their favorable records by such standard manipulations as backdating to delete failed managers no longer covered or including the histories of strong managers they have recently added to their recommended manager lists. Outside observers repeatedly refer to these two concerns, both are blithely banished from the banter of those paid to advise on the selection of active managers.

A particularly painful attack on active managers purports to show that most are only masquerading as true actives when most of their portfolios—60%, even 80%—replicate index funds and only 20–40% of the whole portfolio is "active share." Thus, the active minority of their portfolios must earn back the fees charged on the whole. If active share was 25%, then that share's burden, based on a total 1% fee, would be nearly 4% a year. If market returns were, say, 8%, the active share would have to achieve 50% more than market returns just to cover costs and break even. Yes, it could be done by some managers sometimes, but not regularly by any managers over the long term.

To active investors, it must be painful to see "index huggers" bite the hand that feeds them by assuring their ability to index. After all, the indirect benefits of active investing all swing on the hinge of one great reality: active investors are so numerous, skillful, independent, and superbly well informed, so well provided with information, analyses, opinions, and judgments by an extraordinary array of experienced experts; so well-armed with advanced information-processing devices and so eminently capable and highly motivated economically that they have succeeded at "price discovery" beyond our poor powers to add or detract.

All is fair in love and war *and* marketing. So, active investors can take great pride in their PR masterstroke of hanging on index funds the dreaded verbal albatross "passive." Would any among us ever want to be called passive? (Try it. "This is my husband. He's *passive*." Or: "Our team captain is *passive*.") Of course not! Throughout our society, *passive* has a major negative connotation while *active* has a major positive connotation.

In addition, some overzealous fund companies dedicated to active investing have made matters worse by their extensive advertising of those few funds that have recently enjoyed good results. Although all professionals know it takes many years of superior performance to prove that skill, not luck, is causal, the vast investing public is unwilling to wait. And most are so unsophisticated when it comes to statistics that they don't realize how dangerous selective sampling can be. So, performance envy runs rampant and investors mutter, "I'll have what *he's* having!"

Thus, defenders of active investing will have to concede one part of the prosecution's case. Owing to the unfortunate practices of a few "bad apple" managers, investors' attention is inevitably concentrated by industry advertising on those few funds that have had the best results in recent years. Of course, firms that manage 100 or more funds—most of which underperform—will wisely focus their ads on the few that happen to perform well. As industry insiders know, this practice leads almost invariably to money pouring into "five-star" funds *after* their best years and then pouring out after the nearly inevitable poor years, a process that destroys up to a third of what investors would have had if they had just left their investments alone. That five-star ratings are of virtually no use in estimating *future* returns is naturally not acknowledged by active managers, who have a responsibility to their employers and coworkers to "stay on message."

More recently, the attacks on active investing have focused on fees. Attackers maliciously call upon our mystic chords of memory with such clever and evocative imitations as, "Never in the course of human history have so many paid so much to so few for so little." The usual definition of fees—"only 1%"—is being reexamined. And fees are increasingly being reframed, *not* as a percentage of the assets investors already have or even as a percentage of returns—which would result in 1% of assets ballooning to about 15% of returns—but, rather (and correctly), as *incremental* fees relative to *incremental* returns, compared with the indexers who persistently deliver the "commodity" market rate of return at the market level of risk. In this particularly odious comparison, the average active manager is shown to be charging incremental fees that amount to more than 100% of the incremental returns—before taxes. (Fortunately for active managers, this dreadful reality—a specter stalking the world of active investing—has not yet caught the attention of most investors.)

Although the cost and fees part of the attack against active investing may appear compelling, this narrow focus on benefits (or lack thereof) to investors—and only to investors—is obviously unfair to active investing. It leaves out all the many important social and economic *indirect* benefits enjoyed every day by everyone in the broader community. As an example of only one of the numerous benefits to millions of people, the costs of active investing (including investors' persistent losses relative to indexing) are quite small. That active investing has *not* worked out especially well for investors is not a sufficient reason to declare active investing a *failure*. To see why, let's look at the record of indirect benefits. They are both many and mighty.

Nobody doubts that efficient markets are a major social good in many ways. By enabling "outsiders" to participate with confidence, knowing that security prices are fair for both buyers and sellers and that transaction costs are low, efficient markets encourage millions of investors to trust the capital markets with their savings. Efficient markets thus enable growing companies—particularly new companies with great promise—to raise substantial amounts of capital at low cost. They also enable stronger companies to acquire weaker companies and to redeploy assets in ways that are more socially productive. A more dynamic corporate sector has been of great benefit to the economies and societies of the world.

As active investors have searched for, found, and arbitraged away market inefficiencies, the many local and national markets of the world have been increasingly combined into one global megamarket. Local companies are obliged by international investors to rise to the global standards of corporate discipline in law, accounting, governance, and many aspects of operating management as petty corruption declines, transaction costs shrink, and access to important information expands.

Aided by computers and theories of value, active investing has been integrating the world's stock and bond markets *and* incorporating the markets for commodities, currencies, real estate, auto and credit card debt, and even several sorts of insurance. The increasingly unified global market has produced faster growth, more and better jobs, more democracy, and better prospects for world peace. Massive market integration has increased access to capital, lowered the cost of capital, distributed risk, reduced uncertainty, and raised confidence in saving and investing.

The best long-term benefit of active investing—and of all its many benefits—is not just economic but also spiritual. With the release of the energies and talents of millions of people created by the shift from closed to open societies, we see greater access to education and interesting careers; better food, shelter, and health care; and more free choice in the overall "pursuit of happiness." Although active investing has not been the *only* reason for *all* this great success—lifting over 1 billion people out of poverty in just one generation—these changes could not have occurred without the impact of active investing at the macro level.

At the micro level, the benefits of active investing's success in making markets efficient have been comparably impressive. Malicious "active attackers" narrowly focus their vision and their analysis on the inability of active managers to achieve consistently superior returns—because the markets are made so efficient by active investors, but the reciprocal is also true. Not only is it hard to win; it's also hard to lose.

Not losing—or at least not losing decisively—means that many investors, both individual and institutional, can continue to hope that they too will eventually be among the winners. This hope keeps them and their active managers in the game, which, of course, is crucial to the breadth and depth of our megamarkets. If it costs investors a little in lower returns, isn't it clearly for the betterment of society at large? Since active investing is exciting and fun, investors who are losing a bit in purely economic terms surely enjoy a significant social good by being part of the action. (We all know that the players at the world's famous casinos are, on average, "losers" if calibrated in purely financial terms, but since they keep coming back, those nonfinancial benefits must surely enhance the players' overall experience.)

Some who attack active investors and their self-rewarding business practices seem uncomfortable with practitioners' ample compensation. Unrelenting attackers, apparently driven by the "green grievance" of jealousy, curiously ignore the enormous benefits to everyone in our society that come directly from active investors' generous philanthropy. We should be more appreciative of active investors' services to society as leading patrons of the performing arts and as core benefactors of colleges, universities, museums, hospitals, and orchestras and as major donors to political campaigns, which are so important to our democracy.

Although it may be temptingly easy for casual observers to fault active managers by focusing all too narrowly on the disappointing results and high fees experienced by naive but ever-hopeful investors, the splendid benefits rendered directly and indirectly by active managers clearly deserve much more of our collective recognition, respect, admiration, and even adulation.

★★★★

Thinking about the benefits flowing into so many parts of the world's economies and societies gave me a warm, contented feeling until I was roused by a flight attendant's instruction to sit up and tighten my seat belt. I had enjoyed contemplating the satisfaction that professional investors could take in doing good, however indirect it might be, in the world as we see it.

Although my reverie could be easily dismissed as mere fantasy, my observations over many years—of the worldwide explosion in IT and communications and the proliferation of research on companies, industries, economies, currencies, commodities, and every aspect of the investment process, as seen through my work on a dozen distinguished investment committees at leading institutions—have convinced me that very few investment managers are able to match or beat the market, particularly after adjusting for risk and after deducting costs and fees. Fortunately, all investors have access, through low-cost indexing, to funds that match the market returns at no more than the market level of risk. And this access enables investors to concentrate on the winners' game of defining their own unique objectives and designing long-term investment portfolios that are most likely to meet those objectives. To the extent investment experts continue to do the important work of advising clients on investment policies to achieve their true objectives and values *and* sustain their commitments through various markets, our profession will be appropriately admired and well rewarded.

12

Murder on the Orient Express: The Mystery of Underperformance

Evidence increasingly shows that a "crime" of extensive underperformance has been committed in mutual funds, pension funds, and endowments. In a pattern reminiscent of Agatha Christie's famous novel, Murder on the Orient Express, *an investigation leads to a surprising, if inevitable, conclusion: The usual suspects—investment managers, fund executives, investment consultants, and investment committees—are all guilty.*

A gatha Christie, for many years, the world's favorite mystery writer, perfected her guessing game by creating a "can you solve it?" puzzle in *Murder on the Orient Express.* Clues pointed in many directions but gave no certainty. As the plot thickened, Hercule Poirot, the wily Belgian investigator, deftly guided readers to an eventually obvious conclusion: No one suspect was guilty—*all* the suspects were guilty.

The same reality may explain the persistent failure of institutional investors to achieve their ubiquitous but evanescent investment goal of superior results, or "beating the market." The results are consistently disappointing; clues to the causes and leads to suspects abound; and suspicions and evidence implicate a full array of possible culprits, any one of whom could be the perpetrator. However, unintentionally, the "failure to perform" problem is made even worse by many funds that aim very high, set inherently unrealistic expectations, and then take on higher-volatility managers because their recent investment performance looks "better."

Despite the statistical impossibility of more than one in four funds achieving Top Quartile results, a majority of funds—more than twice the Top Quartile objective's capacity—solemnly declare this goal as their objective. (Lake Wobegon fans would not be surprised. Nor would behavioral economists whose research shows the famous 80/20 Rule at work in many self-evaluations. About 80% of people in group after group rate themselves "above average" as friends, conversationalists, drivers, or dancers *and* in having a good sense of humor and good judgment and being trustworthy.)

Maybe it is just human nature to be qualitatively optimistic about ourselves. But the investment results can always be quantified for objective analysis. Extensive and readily available data show that in a random 12-month period, about 60% of mutual fund managers underperform. Lengthen the period to 10 years and the proportion of managers who fall behind the market for this longer period is about 80%. At least as concerning, equity managers who underperform do so by roughly twice as much as the "outperforming" funds beat their chosen benchmarks. So, the underperformers' "slugging average" is doubly daunting. New research on the performance of institutional portfolios shows that after risk adjustment, 24% of funds fall significantly short of their chosen market benchmark and have a negative alpha, 75% of funds roughly match the market and have zero alpha, and well under 1% achieve superior results after costs—a number not statistically significantly different from zero.

If our profession fails to deliver on its promises, negative consequences could be in the offing for us as well as for our patient, long-suffering clients. So, let's look at the evidence to see why institutional funds have been underperforming.

The Evidence

Institutional funds underperform because their managers underperform—certainly not always and certainly not all managers, but by enough managers enough of the time to make the aggregate evidence undeniable.

Data from over 35 years of behavioral research on individual managers at institutional funds show that large numbers of new accounts go to managers who have produced superior recent results—mostly after their best-performance years—and away from underperforming managers after their worst-performance years. Another oft-repeated negative factor is moving into asset classes or subclasses after prices have risen and out of asset classes or subclasses after prices have fallen—moving assets in the wrong direction at the wrong time. This "buy high, sell low" pattern of behavior, so familiar to students of mutual fund ownership, also burdens institutional investors with billions of dollars in costs.

Forensic evidence in Figure 12.1 shows that institutional investors (pension funds, endowments, etc.)—despite their many "competitive

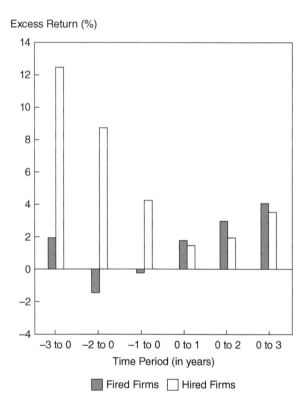

Figure 12.1 Excess Returns for Fired and Hired Investment Managers
Notes: All the differences between fired and hired managers before the firing are significant. The differences between fired and hired managers after the change are clearly indicative but not statistically significant. All data are for U.S. funds.

Source: Amit Goyal and Sunil Wahal, "The Selection and Termination of Investment Management Firms by Plan Sponsors," *Journal of Finance*, vol. 63, no. 4 (August 2008): 1805–1847.

advantages," including full-time staff, consultants, and the ability to change managers and select those they consider the very best managers—typically under-perform their chosen benchmarks. In a recent study of more than 1,000 institutional funds, the managers who were hired had achieved over the three years *before* their hiring significantly higher returns than the managers who were fired. (The to-be-hired managers produced substantial excess returns on domestic equities over the prior three years.) However, for the three years *after* the new managers were hired, the fired managers achieved slightly higher returns than the new managers. This difference—repeated over and over—incurs two kinds of costs that accumulate through repetition. What matters most is not the cost of the trivial underperformance of the new managers versus the fired managers after the change, but the substantial underperformance of the soon-to-be-fired managers over the years before the change.

Ironically, once the hiring is done, almost nobody involved studies the process of hiring managers who later disappoint. Managers tell themselves that their poor runs were just "anomalies" and look forward, often with remarkable optimism, to better times ahead—and better results. Meanwhile, clients tell themselves that they got rid of the bad managers. As Emerson so wisely observed, "The unexamined life is not worth living." Social scientists have observed that people with motivations to believe in their efficacy repeatedly "see what they believe in"—the illusion of validity—and so do not recognize even persistent shortfalls or failures. Although everybody knows that patrons of gambling casinos are, as a group, significant losers, the tables and slots stay busy. So, if neither clients nor managers examine or learn from their actual experience, the problem will continue.

If participants did examine their experience, they would see that one serious cost is the negative performance incurred by funds before they are finally provoked into taking action. This cost comes from the risks taken when trying to identify managers that might achieve superior future performance and actually increase the odds of future disappointment because recent past performance, however compelling it may appear, seldom predicts future performance.

Costs also matter far more than most investors realize. Investment management fees are not "low." Viewed correctly, such fees are actually very high. Over the past several decades, fees for institutional investors have risen from less than 1/10 of 1% to nearly ½ of 1% of assets for equity investments (less for fixed income and more for such "alternatives" as private equity and hedge funds). Because the client already has the assets and is thus looking only for returns, those same fees are actually more than 5% of likely *returns*—a more accurate recognition of reality.

But now, a new reality is stalking active managers. The very small commodity fees charged for index funds that consistently provide market-matching returns at market-matching risk. This means that active managers can only hope to deliver real value when they actually beat the market—which, we now know, most do not do, particularly over the long term. As a consequence, for active management, true fees—incremental fees as a percentage of incremental added value—are more than 50% of the value delivered by the more successful active managers and are far higher, even infinitely higher, for the many less successful active managers. Here's why: The real marginal cost of active management is the incremental fee that active managers charge versus the incremental returns they deliver after fees and costs of operations.

Seen correctly, active management may be the only service ever offered—and widely accepted—that costs more than the value delivered. (Students of real versus apparent cost will remind us that the true cost of a puppy is not the cost of a dog nor is the payment to the boat broker the true cost of a yacht. On the latter, J.P. Morgan famously observed, "If you have to ask what it costs, you cannot afford it.") Increasingly, clients are realizing that costs are at least a major part of the problem of underperformance—particularly in today's intensely professionalized market. The cruel irony is that so many active managers are so skillful, hardworking, and capable that they collectively dominate the market and so very few, if any, can beat the crowd. Judging by overall investment performance, the record is not comforting.

So, institutional underperformance—in addition to the high fees and the costs of manager switching—involves three "murder weapons": hiring managers late, firing managers late, and investing with managers and in asset classes that underperform. We are still left with the question that Agatha Christie fans must try to figure out: who dunnit?

The Suspects

The investment profession is not lacking in possible suspects for the crime of systematic underperformance.

Investment Managers

After almost three decades of working on business strategy with major investment management firms in Europe, Asia, Australia, New Zealand, and North America, it became clear that the main culprit had to be investment managers. Managers—knowing they are talented, hard-working, well trained, and dedicated—still sometimes believe deeply in the value of their work (behavioral economists call this familiarity bias). The circumstantial evidence was substantial. During new-business presentations and in quarterly review meetings, virtually all managers gave in to the understandable temptation to present their performance records in the most favorable light. Their records were almost always "enhanced." For example, the years included in historical "performance" charts were often chosen mainly to make the best impression. In addition, the benchmarks against which the managers' results were compared were often selected for similar reasons. Looking back, both the inconsistency of "relevant time periods" and the variety of benchmarks used were impressive. Even more disturbing is how many institutional managers still present their results before deducting fees.

Another "clue": Investment philosophies and decision-making processes—no matter how complex they might be to implement—were all too often oversimplified, documented with selected data, and then crisply articulated as convincing universal truths. Both prospects and clients were led to believe that each manager had developed a compelling conceptual competitive advantage in the "battle for performance." One aspect of client-manager meetings had an intriguing reality: Virtually every such meeting was actually a sales meeting. Of course, new-business presentations were also sales meetings. But so were the quarterly review meetings. The managers' unstated objective at every meeting was less about building a shared understanding of the uncertainties and difficulties of investing and more about "winning"—winning the account in a new-business competition or winning additional business when performance had been strong or winning a reprieve and retaining the account for a few more quarters when performance had been disappointing. No manager talked candidly with clients about how difficult investment management had become as company information and rigorous analyses proliferated, competitors multiplied, and information that had once been seen as a competitive advantage become increasingly "commoditized."

Realists would suspect that as much as investment managers might want to build their firms on the basis on superior performance, the more compelling motivation had become economic: to win new accounts and to keep old accounts while worrying about performance tomorrow. After nearly three decades of "behind the scenes" experience with over 100 investment organizations of various sizes in several nations, I was increasingly drawn toward the suspicions of the realists.

A close examination of the competitive rankings of investment managers makes a compelling case: Over and over again—even when they had to know that continuing to produce such superior results would be terribly hard—managers made special efforts to go out and sell their services and win new accounts when their recent annual performance numbers were particularly favorable. Well, they would, wouldn't they? Realists recognized that those managers who worked hard to get new accounts when their results looked best won more business, and those who temporized skillfully during patches of underperformance kept more business. So, if investors were asked, "Who dunnit?," the evidence would point to the investment managers as being guilty of causing institutional underperformance.

Investment Consultants

On reflection, however, another group of suspects had to be considered: investment consultants. They are paid fees, usually on retainer, to monitor an institution's current managers and to help select new managers after, of course, first helping clients decide to terminate underperforming managers. In the view of most institutions' busy investment committees, it has made sense to use an outside consultant who specializes in evaluating hundreds of potential investment managers, systematically evaluating their "performance" numbers, regularly interviewing their key people, and rigorously comparing actual behavior with projections and promises. The outside expert, ostensibly dedicated solely to the client's best interest, is independent and also able to do a more extensive and intensive evaluation. Moreover, the stated cost of retaining a consultant is low compared with having internal staff do the work.

A realist would note that investment consulting is a business. Although consultants would like to achieve great results for their clients, business economics almost inevitably dominate aspirations toward professionalism. Once the research costs of evaluating managers and compiling the database at an investment consulting firm are covered, the annual profitability of an incremental account is over 90%. And because well-managed relationships continue for many years into the future, their economic value is not just this year's fee but, rather, the net present value of many future years' fees. Equally, over 90% of the net present value of any lost account's fees is lost to the firm's profits. So, the owners of consulting firms pay close attention to their firms' business relationships, and the main priority of relationship managers is clear: Never lose an account. Eventually, as consulting firms get larger, this business priority naturally dominates compensation and promotion for every on-the-line consultant.

Given the great difficulty of the task, it would be naive to assume that any investment consulting firm could somehow consistently identify managers with superior future capabilities and skillfully terminate those about to disappoint. It would be far better for the consulting firm to build a strong defensive position by encouraging each institutional client to diversify its fund across various asset classes and to have multiple managers in each category. On both dimensions, "the more, the merrier" diversification protects the consultant's business by diversifying against the risk of any particular manager's performance difficulties doing harm to the consultant's relationship with his clients and future fees.

Of course, this hyperdiversification portfolio strategy has led to client institutions paying higher fees and having a large number of different managers, which increased the chances of one or more managers producing disappointing results. It also made the institution's fund executive and its investment committee all the more dependent on the consultant monitoring those numerous managers—plus the alternative managers who might be brought in when some of the current managers faltered or failed. Monitoring all those managers not only made the institution dependent on the consultant for information, but it also meant that no one manager was all that important to the total fund. The traditionally limited time of investment committee meetings—typically three hours once a quarter—was fully booked with reviewing the overall performance of the portfolio and reporting on a long list of specific managers, particularly those who were seriously underperforming. Keeping to the agenda left too little time for thorough evaluation of both the committee's own management of the manager selection process and the consultant's true added value.

Many consultants learned long ago the wisdom of following two practices with each client's investment committee. First, develop a particularly close, personal service relationship with the chair of the committee. This is easily done by increasing the frequency of research reports, report updates, e-mails, and phone calls to render impressively caring service. (A supplemental objective might be to develop nearly as close a relationship with the most likely next committee chair.) Second, invest-ment consultants learned to present at selection finals only those manag-ers who had compelling recent annual performance records and not to lose points by defending a "disappointing" investment manager. (Has any consultant ever presented a manager by saying, "While this manager's recent performance record certainly does not look favorable, our profes-sional opinion is that this manager has weathered storms in a market that was not hospitable to its style and has a particularly strong team that we believe will achieve superior results in the future"?.)

Consultants' agency interests—compensation for both consulting firm owners and individual consultants—are economically focused on keeping the largest number of accounts for as many years as possible. These agency interests are not well aligned with the long-term principal interests of the client institution. Although neither consultant nor com-mittee really wants it to be that way, a separation of agency versus prin-cipal behavior should have been anticipated.

Finally, after tracking which managers win accounts and which lose accounts each year—and then subdividing the records by consulting firm—the behavioral record indicates that consulting firms' clients have been hiring managers after their best years and firing managers after their worst years. So, the evidence points to this conclusion: The consult-ants did it! They are guilty of—or at least complicit in—the crime of causing institutional investors to underperform.

Fund Executives

Suspicion points in yet another direction—the institutions' own fund executives. One cause for suspicion is a curiosity: Fund executives fre-quently insist on having a separate account rather than investing in a pooled fund at a significantly lower fee—even though managed by the same firm using the same research and usually the same or similar port-folio managers. Separate accounts often make sense when investing in illiquid "alternatives," but the preference for separate accounts for "long-only" stock investing is a mystery. Although there are much-admired exceptions—in particular, several endowment CIOs with extensive experience and strong professional staffs—many fund executives are dis-advantaged. Often not deeply experienced in the complexities of invest-ing, they are not highly paid, especially when compared with the front-line "socially dominating" representatives of investment managers.

Investment managers learned long ago to be represented always by socially dominant people—hunters—who are highly skilled at closing transactions and are paid many multiples of what fund executives are paid. Disparagingly called "gatekeepers," fund executives are almost always staff-minded processing people who must often feel "caught in the middle" between investment committees with too little time and investment managers with too much skill and experience at selling—and an absolute determination to win. Through no fault of their own, fund executives and their staffs are set up to be overwhelmed. Rather than carefully buying investment services, they are *sold* those services. And the easiest time is at the peak of an investment firms' performance. So, a realist would be drawn, however reluctantly, to the grim conclusion that it is the fund executives who dunnit.

Investment Committees

During the past decade, a new kind of experience has provided me with another, better perspective on why institutional funds underperform. Having served on a dozen investment committees—in Asia, North America, and the Middle East—with funds ranging in size from $10 million to $300 billion, I can confidently state that the evidence points with remarkable consistency to yet another surprising culprit. With all their best intentions—both individually and collectively—the perpetrators of the crime of underperformance must be the funds' investment committees.

Consider the evidence. First, many investment committees are operating in ways that do not reflect the substantial changes in investment markets that have made obsolete many of the traditional beliefs about investing—particularly those outdated beliefs still often held by senior people who serve on investment committees. However unintentionally, many investment committees have misdefined their objectives and are organized in ways that are counterproductive. As Shakespeare put it, "The fault, dear Brutus, lies not in the stars, but in ourselves."

Certain internal factors that inhibit fund committees "come with the territory." Many are not helpful. Most investment committees devote up to 10% of their limited time to administrative matters: reviewing minutes of past meetings, setting dates for future meetings, and so on. Some 15–20% of their time is devoted to discussing the economic outlook and covering regulatory issues. Another 15–20% is spent reviewing managers' "performance" and comparing their fund's results with those of a peer group of funds. Usually, another 20% of the meeting time is devoted to presentations by two or three current managers who discuss the economy, the markets' outlook, their organizations' various perspectives on performance, their more interesting recent investments, and their look-ahead portfolio strategies. Always interesting and thoroughly documented, in combination, a series of these presentations by different managers can blend together in the memories of most committee members into one large "disassembled jigsaw puzzle" of data, concepts, opinions, and projections. What had seemed quite persuasive when first articulated can, in retrospect, seem confusingly jumbled together.

The committee then turns to the "real" work, often with the guidance of an investment consultant: considering the firing of one or two poorly performing managers among the dozens employed and then hiring one or more among the three or four "finalist" managers evaluated and selected by the consulting firm from the dozens of managers monitored. Usually, the selected managers have had the most apparently compelling recent performance and have made the most persuasive presentations. Each finalist manager's team enters the room; its members thank everyone, often individually, for "this important opportunity." They pass out binders of 40–60 pages loaded with "gee whiz" charts of past performance, extensive statistics on the economy and the major investment markets, several sheets of "bullets" outlining the managers' core beliefs and investment concepts, a few compelling examples of their recent investment triumphs, and short "credential" biographies of several key professionals. Although sardonic humorists might point out that it is like trying to select a spouse via speed dating, committee members dutifully strive to do their best to keep up with the main themes of the presentations, try to remember specific points made, and then make a judicious appraisal of the capabilities of the complex organizations being presented, all before the meeting time has run out.

Committees tend to differ somewhat from one type of institution to another. For example, most endowment investment committees comprise experienced seniors who devote their time without compensation to impart their wisdom and experience because they care deeply about their institutions. Often, although they are important patriots of the institution and feel honored to serve, they are not always experts in contemporary investing. As distinguished seniors, participants are reserved in demeanor, strive to avoid disagreement or confrontation, and, to ensure harmony, usually place their spoken views near the center of an emerging consensus. In addition to these challenging qualitative characteristics, endowment committees are often similar in such quantitative factors as meeting four times a year for three or four hours per meeting with little contact between meetings. Committee members are aware of the reality that the meeting time is fixed, the agenda is at least "full," and the chair is determined to complete all items by a pre-agreed time for adjournment.

Corporate pension committees tend to differ in several ways: Most are staffed entirely by internal executives representing such important parts of the sponsoring corporation as human resources, benefits administration, finance, and treasury. One or two investment staffers—typically young and serving on rotation for a few years for training purposes, but not extensively experienced in the complexities of investing—often hope to rotate to a divisional controller's or assistant treasurer's position. Usually chaired by the vice president for finance, meetings are disciplined, and the protocols of corporate deference to hierarchy are well understood. Committee meetings are shorter and more frequent than those for endowments. Open discussions on such theoretical subjects as how to evaluate investment managers or the reasons for skepticism about performance data are rare. Each agenda item has an explicit time limit, and the pace of meetings is expeditiously business-like.

Public pension fund committees have their own set of characteristics. They are large—often very large—to accommodate union representatives of such disparate employee groups as teachers, firefighters, police, and sanitation workers, as well as representatives of the government's budget office and treasury and of the mayor or governor. Many committee members are new to investing and its many complexities and to the importance of managing risk as well as returns. Some also have two or three "public" representatives or are required by law to be open to the public, and some even broadcast their meetings on radio or television.

Almost all investment committees labor under an array of handicaps, including the following:

- Believing performance data can provide useful information for evaluating active investment managers even though studies of past performance show that past results have no predictive power—except for the bottom decile. (High fees and limited capabilities tend to persist, so seriously disappointing results tend to repeat.)
- Believing the primary mission of their investment committee is to select top quartile managers who will significantly outperform even though the evidence shows that a majority of managers fall short of the market and almost none have outperformed by very much for very long.
- Staying with historically valid policies when circumstances have changed fundamentally.

- Being prone to the constraints of both "groupthink" and such aspects of behavioral economics as overreacting to recent events, being confirmation biased, and tending to ignore long-term norms.
- Being guided by an investment consultant whose advice may suffer from the very real agency problems discussed earlier.
- Making the double error of attempting to do too much of what they shouldn't do (making investment management decisions) and thus having too little time for the important work they should do (providing good governance).

Governance should include the following: evaluating the supervisory capabilities of the fund's internal management, understanding the real costs of actively managing investments, clarifying long-term objectives and short-term risk tolerance, developing realistic investment policies, determining the consistency with which actions fulfill agreed policies, and asking searching questions about the process followed by the fund's operating management and its investment committee. The best committees help bring stabilizing, rational consistency to the emotionally draining work of managing long-term investments in volatile markets and staying with chosen policies through periods of turbulence.

Conclusion

No matter how tempted investment committees may be—after objectively examining the accumulated evidence—to confess to causing underperformance, they are not entirely responsible. Investment committees are guilty, but they are not alone. They have accomplices. Investment managers, investment consultants, and fund executives are also guilty. No one suspect is guilty; they are all guilty.

But, in the "end-of-story" ironic twist so often enjoyed by Agatha Christie's many readers, none of the four guilty parties is ready to recognize its own role in the crime. Each participant knows that it is working conscientiously, knows it is working hard, and believes sincerely in its own innocence. Indeed, nobody seems to even recognize that a crime has been committed—nor to realize that until they examine the evidence and recognize their own active roles, however unintentionally performed, the crime of underperformance will continue to be committed.

13

Best Practice Investment Committees

Good governance by investment committees is the best and only reliable way to achieve superior long-term results for endowments and pension funds. Far more care should be given to investment committee design, membership, and leadership. Serving on the investment committees of Yale, Exeter, Singapore's GIC, the New Zealand Future Fund, and King Abdullah University in Saudi Arabia (one of the five largest endowments in the world) and several others, the importance of good governance has been made clear to me. Unfortunately, all too many institutions and families do not enjoy the benefits they could have had with more attention to organizing for good governance.

Thoughtful observers are increasingly in agreement that endowment and pension investment committees have important governance responsibilities in assuring the successful management of the pensions and endowments supporting the retirement security of workers in states, municipalities, and corporations as well as of many of our nation's most treasured educational, cultural, and philanthropic institutions.

While the full board of trustees has the ultimate institutional responsibility, the center of active good governance is the investment committee. The available evidence indicates that our nation's institutional funds (while assuming generous returns—usually by assuming they can and will outperform the markets in which they invest) are falling short of the market averages. Some will argue over the data, some will blame consultants, and some will blame the managers. All will be able to find examples that confirm their concerns about institutional investment management.

I share their concerns with *management but* believe there are comparably serious problems with *governance*. Unless the systematic failure of governance is overcome, any improvements in fund management will be dominated by the larger, more insidious problems of governance. Since spendable income from endowments is the crucial factor in institutional excellence for our leading universities, schools, museums, hospitals, and scientific research organizations, we all have a significant interest in the long-term investment success of their endowments. Endowment success, in turn, depends on two functions working well together—skillful investment *management* and good *governance*—assuring the investing program is right for the particular institution. Investment committees cannot hope to succeed in operational management in today's fast-paced market, but they can add "House of Lords" wisdom and guidance by focusing on good governance, the focus of modern Best Practices investment committees.

Committee Structure

Who should serve on a Best Practice investment committee? In investing, as in most professions, experience is not only the best teacher, it's the only good teacher. That's why investment committees need thoughtful and informed members ready and able to make good judgments based on the kind of wisdom that can only come from experience in investing. At least a strong a majority of each investment committee should have substantial experience as investors. (Note: Stockbrokers and bankers seldom are also experienced as investors.) A minority of committee members may be chosen for other reasons: executive positions, experience as business leaders, political stature and knowledge, expertise and understanding of a philanthropic institution and its finances or demonstrated philanthropic generosity.

The most effective committees range in size from 5 to 9 members—large enough to have diverse experience, expertise, and opinions and small enough so everyone gets heard and understood.

A senior organizational leader should always serve on or meet regularly with the committee to assure two-way communications and understanding by the investment committee of the financial management challenges *and* appreciation of the sponsoring corporation's or state's or municipality's resources or a charitable institution's long-term program strategy and its plans for fundraising. And, vice versa, financial managers setting the plans and budgets need to understand the unpredictable, market-driven realities of investment management and the long-term limits on an endowment's ability to produce spendable annual "income." As in any superior relationship, success depends on good two-way communication.

Endowment governance should be both coordinated with and integrated into overall governance of the institution's operating budgets, its capital and programmatic strategies, and its fundraising. Wise and effective integration of endowment investing, institutional finance, and fundraising is, of course, the central responsibility of the full board of trustees, but this important "macro" strategy work can be best initiated and even led by the investment committee.

Committee Mission

Clearly separating the work of *management* from the work of *governance*, the Best Practice investment committees understand that good governance provides the long-term policy framework and assures the working environment that enables operating managers to do their work both efficiently and effectively. As Peter Drucker famously explained, "Efficiency is doing things the right way; effectiveness is doing the right things."

Investment committees, usually meeting four or six times each year, have two reasons for concentrating on governance and for not attempting management. The first reason is a non-negative: In today's intensely managed, fast-changing capital markets, committees meeting quarterly are ill-designed and ill-timed for taking up operational decisions. They know they can't do it well.

The second reason for concentrating on good governance is positive: Even the best-organized and best-led committees will find themselves fully challenged by the responsibilities of good governance: setting appropriate limits on risk, setting optimal investment policies and objectives, agreeing on portfolio structure, assuring wise selection of investment managers, staying on a steady course during periods of market euphoria or despair, formulating sensible spending rules, and coordinating with the finance committee and the full board on overall governance so the fund's investment management organization performs its full and appropriate role in the context of the overall fiscal governance.

The best investment committees make sure investment managers are skillful, diligent, and cost-effective in investment management *operations,* but their primary focus and responsibility are on getting it really right on organizational governance and investment *policy.* In setting long-term investment objectives, Best Practice investment committees know that risk controls come first, long-term strategic portfolio and rate of return second, and spending policy third. Every organization is unique and each deserves its own custom-tailored set of governance policies on all three dimensions. Best Practice investment committees search continuously and diligently for the right balance between risk and reward. For them, boldly cautious is no oxymoron. Separately, Best Practice investment committees will make sure that external managers' compensation incentives are reasonably aligned with achieving the long-term investment results the pension fund or endowment looks for.

Investment Objectives

While risk management is the investment committee's first priority, this most definitely does not mean overly conservative "caution." As Robert Barker's committee famously reported to the Ford Foundation for endowments long ago, the opportunity cost of excessive caution can be very great. Over the past 50 years, public and private pension funds have also been too cautious and all too conventionally over-invested in bonds. The sad history of failures and shortfalls in endowment investing has more examples of too little courage than of too much boldness in asset allocation. Best Practice investment committees will insist on taking and managing sensible short-term market risks *and* insist on avoiding unnecessary long-term risks of real loss due to either over-reaching or through the silent opportunity cost of not really striving.

Where should investment committees turn for advice? First, every committee member should read the wisest and most useful book on institutional investing, David Swensen's *Pioneering Portfolio Management.* This thoughtful and explicit explanation of the reasoning behind each aspect of Yale's endowment management invites every institution to develop its own answers to each of the core questions: What is our strategic portfolio structure and *why?* What is our time horizon for investing and *why?* How do we select investment managers and *why?* What is our Spending Rule or rate of return assumption and *why?* What are our investment committee's particular governance functions and responsibilities and *why?*

Best Practice investment committees make certain that they secure the defensive perimeter via "active reconnaissance" with specific individuals responsible for keeping well informed about each investment manager's organization, its professional capacities, and its business commitments; actively engaging in "scuttlebutt" networks; rebalancing regularly; and regularly revisiting each manager at his office to watch for changes that might be early warning signals.

Best Practice investment committees revisit and reevaluate their central beliefs and the resulting policy guidelines in a rigorous "back to basics" way on a regular basis. This work is best done at a dedicated annual meeting for which all participants are expected to specify their best questions well in advance. If staff work will be required to gather data, ample lead time is assured. Best Practice committees will also evaluate their own performance to determine whether or not they have added value.

Risk evaluations by Best Practice investment committees will have three dimensions: income risk, asset risk, and liquidity risk. Assuring a predictable flow of income to support the institution's budget is usually the highest priority. The financial crisis showed many endowments how important liquidity can suddenly be.

The central governance decision will be deciding the degree of emphasis on equity investment and the need for portfolio liquidity. For long-term returns, the equity emphasis should be substantial *and* balanced with a discipline that recognizes both long-term investing advantages and short-term problems of market fluctuations. This is not easy disciplining, but it is vital for good governance.

Investment committees can make a major contribution to good governance by assuring the establishment of clear policies on the selection of managers. This does not mean that the committees will actually select or terminate managers. In fact, the best evidence of a committee confusing governance versus management—if it has an internal management—is that the committee hires and fires investment managers. But *governing* committees can and should require explicit statements of the policies and practices that will be used in selecting or terminating investment managers to be sure the *management* process is well thought out. For example . . .

- How many managers will be used—and why? Retaining numerous managers may appear sensible at first. Best Practice committees are finding that fewer and closer relationships often work better.

- What will be the maximum and minimum size of each manager's mandate—and why?
- What selection criteria and "due diligence" process will be followed—and why?
- What criteria will be used for manager terminations—and why?

Good governance centers on assuring that investment operations are within the skill set and risk capacity of the managers. The easiest investment operation uses index funds. If active management is considered, Best Practice committees will start with a rigorous review of long-term results—over at *least* the past ten years. (Such a review will show that most managers fail to match, let alone beat, the market *and* that the average shortfall is larger than the average value added.) Committees should also examine objectively the probability that their organization will be able to select managers who will outperform the index in the future, knowing that while many have tried, most have not succeeded. A sensible humility is an invaluable characteristic of good governance in investment management but pulling back from responsibility imperatives is certainly not.

If active managers are to be used, most small and midsize funds should consider using one manager with many different demonstrated skills. By concentrating its assets with one multi-capability firm, even a small fund makes itself an important client. This will justify the manager giving it "blue ribbon" attention and the benefit of the manager's best investment counsel *and* make it easy to rebalance or change portfolio structure if and when appropriate.

Self-Evaluation: Key Questions

Investment committees that want to be Best Practitioners will benefit from careful self-study to see if any of these signs of trouble are part of their problem:

- *Over-diversification and having too many managers.*
  Having many managers may be a virtual necessity for the largest funds when they also specialize in using small specialist managers. But smaller funds—$2 billion or less—should seriously consider working with just one or two major managers that have developed strong capabilities in advising on optimal asset mix *and* have demonstrated superior professional competence in each of the major asset classes.

(Rarely is a manager skilled at both investing in conventional asset classes and in "alternatives," such as private equity, real estate, hedge funds, etc., so those committees that want both types of investing will usually need both types of managers.)

While there are potential benefits in diversifying managers and having experts in each asset class or specialty, history teaches that the benefits of "diversification" by having multiple managers with the same basic mandate are maddeningly modest, particularly in the long run. After all, most equity managers already diversify portfolios across 60–80 different stocks.

With numerous managers, the committee will never develop with its managers the deep shared understanding that is needed to develop superb trust-based and open communications and relationships that enable client and manager to work well together to add value. With a dozen or more managers, at least one will be "on watch" or "in the penalty box," so the committee's limited time will get focused on solving problems rather than adding positive value. Not really knowing each manager well enough to weather stormy passages, committees will be sorely tempted to "bury mistakes" and "throw the bums out," incurring the cost of changing managers *and* repeating the sad cycle again—and again. It's easy for committees that meet only periodically, to get caught in "groupthink" and terminate managers that have recently performed poorly and hire managers who have recently performed well.

The expected duration of each manager relationship is long— ideally *forever*—because the cost of changing managers can be far greater than the 3–5% transaction costs usually cited. The all-in cost includes the cost of hiring "hot" managers *high* and firing "failed" disappointing managers *low*. Quickly chosen managers all too often disappoint.

Add to these visible costs the hidden costs of distracting the management away from working more rigorously on developing superb, long-term working relationships with their best managers. Candidly, there's far too much "dating" and not enough "marital" relationships in endowment and pension management. While committees typically blame the turnover on the investment managers, the real culprits are usually the committees who tolerate a "transactional" approach. The worst offenders are committees that hire impatiently—often on only one-hour "speed-dating" presentations—and then, because the main consideration is "good performance" rather than a well-developed, shared understanding with each manager, they repeat the costly in-and-out, in-and-out transactional sequence.

- *Rotating committee members too quickly.*
Some regular turnover is good and helps keep the committee and its discussions fresh. But if members come on and go off too quickly, they will not learn how best to listen carefully to each other and will miss the privilege of learning how best to work together *and* the group will lose the stabilizing benefits of institutional memory. Nor should committee members stay too long. They'll get stale and will stop listening closely to each other. Tenure on Best Practice committees will average six or seven years because for all sorts of working groups, this proves to be optimal.

    Service on committees should be staggered and planned so no one member or small group of members will ever be "essential." Terms of five or six years—renewable once or even twice—help committees quietly remove those who are not effective or are not enjoying service. Members should differ in background, age, and skills.

- *Allowing one or two committee members to dominate.*
The chairs of Best Practice investment committees are servant-leaders who take as their top priority facilitating the collective contributions of *all* committee members. This facilitation begins with selecting members who "play well with others" *and* have expertise to contribute. It extends through thoughtful preparation of the agenda and ample documentation—ideally from several different perspectives—so important policy issues are given time for full and open discussion *and* rigorous resolution. And it includes attending to the climate of meetings so they are interesting, enjoyable, give everyone the chance to be heard, and operate at "due deliberate speed."

- *Over-reliance on investment consultants.*
The best investment consultants have earned fine reputations for being helpful. Still, investment consulting is a *business,* particularly for the larger consulting organizations. The business strategy of many of these firms often involves guiding clients into extensive asset class diversification which leads directly to having so many different investment managers—none of which are really well known to the committee—that the committee becomes inevitably dependent on the consultant for monitoring and managing the managers. Instead of concentrating on long-term investment policy and other dimensions of good governance, available time at meetings gets taken up with the interesting and entertaining, but eventually fruitless business of firing the "poor performers" and hiring promising "winners" in a repetitive

cycle that, at its worst, could only please a Las Vegas marriage parlor. Consultants' performance should be evaluated regularly.

- *Selecting Top Quartile managers as an explicit policy.*
  Of course, if you did hire Top Quartile managers, your investment experience would be highly favorable, but the recorded data are overwhelming: Almost nobody has done it and nobody has done it for very long. The mean irony is that those committee members who harbor such aspirations are deluding themselves and sooner or later, damage their funds. The "Icarus irony" is that pressing to have the "best" managers all too often leads to hiring "hot" managers at the peak of their performance records and then getting sub-par results as peaks are followed by troughs.

  Good governance will avoid trying too hard to increase returns; will assure that only "all-weather" managers with strong professional cultures are selected; and will set long-term return expectations that can be sustained indefinitely. Achieving strong long-term rates of return will require being "bold, but not too bold" and "modern, but not too modern." Investment professionals learn through painful experience not to follow the crowd, particularly when a crowd is enamored of the view out the rearview window of recent experience with the recent past projected as easy glories still to come or as an inalienable right by those who join the parade late in the day.

- *Having too many investment managers.*
  Having too many managers is costly. The obvious cost is that when your total fund is divided into many small accounts, your fund gets charged the high end of the managers' fee structures. Other costs are hidden, but far more consequential. They include not knowing each manager well enough to establish a strong "shared understanding" relationship; not knowing how to interpret intermediate-term investment results; not understanding managers well enough to stay the course when performance falters; and not being well understood by the investment managers.

- *Excessive turnover of investment managers.*
  The Best Practitioners have an *average* tenure or duration of manager relationship of more than ten years. While an average relationship duration of less than ten years can be "acceptable," an average of only five years is not. The Best Practitioners will focus on selecting and working with managers so well that their average tenure will be more than 15 years.

  One exception to staying the course with managers is clear: When one of your managers brings the "good" news that they have joined forces with—code for sold out to—a major organization (usually a giant bank or insurance company, often domiciled in a different country) who will somehow provide all the resources they need to do great things, do not wait or seek to understand. Terminate immediately.

If this view seems too categorical, offer to stay in touch during the next two or three years and, if you are thrilled by the results of the combination—sure to be a great rarity—consider rehiring the previously terminated manager. But when first told, do not compromise or hesitate. (By the way, you will surely receive a brilliantly articulate and often quite moving explication of all the benefits and advantages to come, but the long history of such acquisitions is not at all encouraging. So be guided by history not friendship and terminate promptly.)

A second exception requires particular vigilance: When a manager changes his tune—moving away from the investment philosophy and decision-making process by which he earned the mandate to manage your fund *or* when it outgrows the asset size he had declared was its "sweet spot" or maximum assets aspiration, beware! Experience says that that manager has probably shifted his real focus from professional investing to the asset gathering business. Such a shift can be remarkably profitable for the managers, but all too costly for the clients.

- *Not measuring results by asset class versus peers.*
  Best Practice committees know to interpret performance data over time and in the context of reasonable expectations. They use annual and quarterly comparisons to peers primarily to encourage the manager to explain the real reasons for results that differ from expectation. Of course, any major difference from expectation may signal a major problem. If so, Best Practice committees will address it directly and rigorously. (Managers or custodians or investment consultants can provide the relevant data as part of their standard service.)
- *Staff turnover.*
  Pension or endowment management is a calling—a way of making a life, not just making a living—and depends on a strong understanding of the often subtle realities of the particular institution and its leadership. This takes care and time and they both require long-term continuity. Long-serving capable staff can make important contributions to good investment results and Best Practice committees make sure they have able, committed staff *and* make sure the staff are "career."
- *Not investing sufficiently internationally.*
  Diversification *is* the one "free lunch" for investors and diversification across economies and markets makes sense. However, most funds in most countries are over-concentrated in their "home" market.

- *Not considering indexing.*

  The obvious advantage of indexing is lower costs, but that's not as important over the long run as the better investment results. And that's not nearly as important as this: indexing keeps the committee focused on what really matters, getting it right on the strategic asset mix.

- *Policies not clear and decisive—and in writing.*

  The ideal set of investment policies—in writing—could be given to a group of "competent strangers" with confidence that they could follow the stated policies faithfully and return the portfolio in good condition with fine interim results ten years later.

  For pension funds, a central policy is the chosen rate of return assumption. Best Practices committees will not accept a rate of return that is not well documented as expected returns future and rigorously ask *why* for each asset class. If "active management" is expected for any class or for the overall fund, document *why*.

Spending Rule

While all investment committees are, of course, interested in good long-term rates of return, the Best Practitioners know that their first priority must always be—particularly in buoyant times when risks are easily overlooked—managing risk. (Of course, taking astute risks in a disciplined way is the key to earning superior returns over the longer run.) The short-term risk of market fluctuations can be reduced through an appropriate smoothing or spending rule to avoid disruptions in support provided to the institution's mission.

Wise spending and wise investing are "two hands clapping" in support of well-governed, well-managed institutions. Note that actuarial return and spending rules should conform to and be determined by investment results, not the other way around. Committees should never let spending wishes or "needs" influence, let alone determine, investment objectives. Making sure of this fiscal sequence is clearly the governance responsibility of the investment committee.

Best Practice committees evaluate their own members and their own operation as a committee. What are we doing right? Where can we improve? What should we add to our agenda? Where can we cut? Some Best Practice committees also evaluate each member, usually annually, using scale ratings on half a dozen agreed-upon key criteria—such as comes well prepared, stays focused on topic, adds value on substance, adds value on process, inspires confidence in judgment, speaks briefly and to the point, etc.—survey results can then be reported to each member by the Chair in comparison to the group's high-median-low scores.

Best Practice committees focus on policies. Similarly, the Spending Rule is the principal connection between an endowment and the budget of the institution it helps support. Deciding how much to draw from an endowment for current expenses and how much to continue investing for the future—and future spending—is one of the most important decision responsibilities of any investment committee. Most institutions' payouts cluster around 4.5–5% of assets.

While a variety of choices continues to be used at different institutions, Best Practice increasingly centers on the work of Yale's Nobel economist James Tobin, who formulated a sophisticated process to achieve what he wisely called "intergenerational equity."[1] Tobin described this objective eloquently:

The trustees of an endowed institution are the guardians of the future against the claims of the present. Their task is to preserve equity among generations. The trustees of an endowed university [or other major institution] . . . assume the institution to be immortal. They want to know, therefore, the rate of consumption from endowment that can be sustained indefinitely. . . In formal terms, the trustees are supposed to have a zero rate of time preference.

Consuming endowment income so defined means in principle that the existing endowment can continue to support the same set of activities that it is now supporting.

Committees should be careful of three temptations. One is to believe that the current budgetary priorities are so urgent that it's OK to make an exception and increase spending above the long-term norm "on this watch." Another is to become so optimistic after a long, favorable market with high returns as to say, "this time, it's different" and ramp up assumptions or spending to what may prove to be an unsustainably high level that will be painful to bring down.

The third temptation is to decide during a long bear market that the needs of the present are so strong that heavy drains on the fund—selling

---

[1] In Tobin's formulation, 70% of this year's draw is determined by last year's draw (inflated by HEPI or "Higher Education Price Inflation") and 30% is determined by the institution's long-term policy on the rate of spending—usually 4.5–5% of current endowment value. Over time, actual spending rises and falls with the market—but more gradually.

low in a seriously adverse market—have somehow become an imperative. Note that the best time to prevent this problem is to retard endowment spending or return assumptions for pensions when markets have been *favorable* and the idea of increasing the expected returns seems easiest and most tempting.

As J.P. Morgan famously warned, "Markets fluctuate" and so do endowments. That's why investment committees and trustees need to have a long-term focus when making decisions on the self-discipline of their actuarial rate of return assumption or spending rule. These rules only really matter when they are accepted as binding even when that discipline is most difficult to accept.

The Endowment Model

Many investment committees have been advised to make major commitments to "alternative" investments in hedge funds of various types, styles and kinds; private equity; real estate; venture capital; etc.[2] For leading endowments, the "endowment model" brought a truly marvelous record of strong rates of return over the very long term, but it would be a shame if this great work were misunderstood or misinterpreted and converted into a simplistic "anyone can do it" proposition that could lead some investment committees into unwise practices. As might be expected, the past record seems compelling, but wise committees will be alert to four different factors:

1. Strong past returns have attracted huge new inflows, creating what practitioners (rather like Hawaiian surfboarders) correctly call a "wall of money." While the supply of great ideas may increase, the inevitable reality is that overall returns have and will be reduced as increases in the asset denominator outpace the potential of returns numerator.
2. Demand creates supply. Recognizing the large profits to managers, new firms continue to be formed to capitalize on the major opportunities. Some will prove to be great firms and will deliver strong returns. But some may prove to be selfish predators feeding on hopeful investment committees. As supply responds to demand and new firms come into the field, the probabilities are great of either or both

---

[2]Typically, a few pioneering endowment funds' investment records are the best.

a decline in average professional skill and commitment and a rise in business profit motivation. *Caveat emptor*, particularly those coming late to the party.

3. Consultants sometimes overemphasize their roles at the leading universities that were early investors in "alternative" asset classes. While consultants may have been "present at the creation" and provided comparative data, historical market information, and sometimes even acted as facilitators, they were seldom the concept originators nor the crucial implementers.

    It's at least possible that some consultants' enthusiasm for replication is influenced, if not driven, by their firms' own economic interest in making the process of supervising numerous different kinds of managers so complex that committees will cede effective control of quarterly meetings and the overall investment process to the consultants. While committee members come and go, shrewd consultants will make themselves "permanent party."

    Profit-centered consulting firms compensate their individual consultants for not losing their clients and keep raising the fees as more and more managers and more and more services are used. Once the substantial costs of research are covered, the incremental costs to deliver reports or manager recommendations to additional clients are very small, so the incremental profits can be truly compelling. So again, *caveat emptor*.

4. As in any skill-based line of work, good concepts are necessary, but success is 99% skill, experience, and disciplined execution. The leading universities have strong, tough-minded, and hard-working teams focused on finding and working with the very best "alternative" managers—often at very early stages in their development. In addition, the leading universities are deep into the best part of the "scuttlebutt" network, exchanging leads, views, and information with other thought leaders. Reproducing all these advantages is difficult and takes many years of work.

In 2008, investors saw the worst market disruption in a very long time. Two obvious questions came to everyone's mind. First, what should be done? Second, what enduring lessons could be drawn from that dreadful experience?

The realistic and sensible answers to the first question come in two parts. First, if any inappropriate risks were being taken—bank balances over the FDIC insured $100,000 being a simple and familiar illustration—those bank balances should be divided among more banks. Similarly, securities should not be left in Street name with stockbrokerage firms.

The second part of the answer to the first question is for most investment committees both more useful and more important. As we all now
know, black swans—unexpected "outlier" events—do occur. And bell-
shaped probability curves do have "fat tails," meaning that the least probable events occur more frequently and with far greater impact than a
perfectly normal distribution of probabilities would indicate.

The enduring lessons to be drawn from experience are clear. Just as
precision is not the same as accuracy and risk is not the same as uncertainty, wise investment committee members will not go "too close to the
edge." That's why Ben Graham and David Dodd never invest without
having an adequate "margin of safety" or capacity to absorb error. In
investing, if precise calculation is required, a commitment is not an
investment, it's a speculation. Staying power—particularly the staying
power of the investment committee—is crucial to deciding how much
market risk can be taken. Long-Term Capital Management's computer
models did prove to be correct—in the long run—but the firm went
bankrupt in the short run anyway.

The Endowment Model—originated by institutions with over
300 years of institutional history—is a *long-term* model. Institutions and
investment committees that are not well prepared to maintain a very
long-term perspective on short-term experience will be wise to study
the endowment model carefully *and* adopt the model only to the extent
that they have the necessary staff capabilities, financial disciplines, and
internal understanding.

A final word: Serving on an investment committee should be interesting, enjoyable, and fulfilling. Best Practice committees are designed to
be successful on all three dimensions. If your committee does not measure up on all three criteria, change it. There's no reason *not* to be a Best
Practice investment committee that concentrates on excelling in *governance*. Sure, it takes thoughtful determination and strong leadership, but
it's also more fun—and for more personally and professionally rewarding.

Source: *Association of Governing Boards,* 2016.

14

Levels of the Game

One way to reach past the daunting complexity of investment management as a whole would be to break it into parts and concentrate on "solving" the complex puzzle one part at a time.

In the past quarter century, investors and investment managers have enjoyed a long bull market and splendid absolute performance, but relative performance has become worse and worse—and worse. That's why the Money Game ('Adam Smith's' delightful title for the adventures of performance investors in the 1960s) has become increasingly the Loser's Game (my less sanguine article title in 1975).

A large majority of professionally managed funds underperform the market index, particularly when cumulative performance is measured over longer periods of time. Over the past 50 years, mutual funds in the aggregate have lost 180 basis points compounded annually to the S&P index, returning 11.8% versus 13.6% for the index. Over the past decade, S&P 500 returns have been better than the results of 89% of all U.S. mutual funds. The average "underperformance" of mutual funds is reported to be 340 basis points. And the "professional shortfall" is found in international markets as well.

Of course, there is the possibility, even probability, of some "end-period dominance," since fewer than a dozen large stocks with high P/E multiples have given the S&P index an extra lift, and most active managers fare better when the stock market broadens out. Serious students of investing, though, would be wise not to dismiss the evidence too quickly.

Relative to the market averages, investment managers' long-term performance highs have been lower and their lows lower than they were a generation ago.

Why are the results of the efforts of so many hard-working, experienced, and talented professionals with so much data, information, and expert advice available to them so disappointing? Partly, in recent years, the shortfall has been magnified by the poor performance of and the overweighting of small-cap stocks in most professionals' portfolios. Partly, it has been due to strong price appreciation and the underweighting of a few large-cap stocks. (These parts of the shortfall can be expected to reverse as market returns revert toward average long-term experience.) And partly it's due to cash drag because managers, rightly or wrongly, carry cash positions. But these partial explanations should not distract us from recognizing the grim realities of the active investor's position.

The main reason managers' results are so very disappointing is that the competitive environment within which they work has changed from quite favorable to seriously adverse and it is getting worse and worse. Those inclined to dismiss dinosaurs should remember that those beasts roamed the Earth for over 100 million years before their climate changed from favorable to adverse. Professional investment management is now in a very different climate from that of just 30 years ago.

Before examining the change in climate, let's remind ourselves that active investing is at the margin always a zero-sum game. To achieve superior results through active management, you depend directly on the mistakes and blunders of others. Others must be acting as though they are willing to lose so you can win, after covering all your costs of operation.

In the 1960s, when institutions did only 10% of the public trading on the NYSE, and individual investors did 90%, large numbers of amateurs were, realistically, bound to lose to the professionals.

Individual investors usually buy for reasons outside the stock market: They inherit money, get a special bonus, sell a house, or have money as a result of something else that has no connection to the stock market. They sell because a child is going off to college, or they have decided to buy a home—again, for reasons outside the stock market. Individual investors typically do not do extensive comparison shopping across the many alternatives within the stock market. Most individual investors are not experts on even a few companies. Many rely on retail stockbrokers who are seldom experts either.

Individuals may think they know something when they invest, but almost always, what they think they know is either not true or not relevant or is already known by the professionals in the market. Their activity is not driven by investment information that comes out of market analysis or company research or rigorous valuation. The activity of most individual investors is what academics correctly call informationless "noise" trading.

So, it is little wonder that professional investors—who are always working inside the market, making rigorous comparisons of price-to-value across hundreds and hundreds of different stocks on which they can command extensive, up-to-the-minute information—thought they would outperform the individual investors who used to dominate the stock market and do 90% of all the trading. The professionals could and did outperform the amateurs.

But that was a generation ago. The picture is profoundly different now. After just 30 years, the former 90:10 ratio has been completely reversed—and the consequences are profound. Today, 90% of all NYSE trading is by professionals. In fact, 75% of all the trading is by the professionals at the 100 largest and most active institutions—and 50% is by the professionals at the 50 largest and most active institutions. And what a crowd of professionals they are! Top of their class in college and at graduate school, they are "the best and the brightest," supplied with extraordinary information, disciplined and rational; they are very highly motivated. They make errors, but they will make fewer and fewer of them—less and less often. And the errors they make are corrected more and more quickly.

Think about it further: most professionals are not beating the market because such skilled and unrelenting professionals *are* the market and they cannot beat themselves. The professionals' big problem is that they are no longer buying from and selling to the amateurs. There are not enough amateurs around. The professionals have to buy from and sell to other professionals—usually the most active and aggressive institutions. They all play to win.

The result is that active investing almost always either produces too little reward or costs too much, or both. (And this ignores the cost of taxes paid by shareholders in high-turnover mutual funds.) The overall climate for active investors has changed from hospitable to hostile and it won't go back.

To put all this into a different perspective, investment management can be divided into two parts. One part is the profession and the other part is the business. We all know the business part: business is booming. Fee schedules are up threefold in one generation, and assets have mushroomed as much as tenfold—and we all know how to multiply. (Public valuations further multiply the multiples of earnings.) "Too much of a good thing," to quote Mae West, "is wunnerful."

But performance on the professional dimension is not nearly so encouraging. As a profession, investment management can be further divided into two realms: one micro, and one macro. On the micro or craft level of analyzing securities, the profession clearly continues to progress remarkably. Analysts and fund managers at investing institutions enjoy and know how to use their extraordinary electronic access to extensive data and sophisticated interpretations by industry experts who are on call virtually all the time with detailed knowledge they organize and explain within a global context. Practitioners of the craft are well paid and highly skilled. Research and portfolio management have never been better.

Then there is the macro level of investment counseling. Working efficiently, as Peter Drucker has explained, means knowing how to do things the right way, but working effectively means doing the right things. Investment counseling helps investors do the right things. The investment counselor's main professional work is to help each client identify, understand, and commit consistently and continually to long-term investment objectives that are both realistic in the capital markets and appropriate to the objectives of the particular client.

The hardest work is not figuring out the optimal investment policy; the hardest work is staying committed to sound investment policy and to maintaining what Disraeli called "constancy to purpose." Being rational in an emotional environment ain't easy. Holding on to sound policy through thick and thin is extraordinarily difficult *and* extraordinarily important work. The cost of infidelity can be very high.

One example of the danger of emotion—driven by short-term misunderstanding and misinterpretation of stock market price data—has been quite costly for mutual fund investors. In the past 15-year, very favorable stock market, the average mutual fund gained 15% annually, but the average mutual fund investor gained only 10%. Fully one-third of investors' available return was lost by switching from one fund to another fund and all too often selling low and buying high.

Sustaining a long-term focus at either market highs or market lows is notoriously hard. In either case emotions are strong, and current market action appears most demanding of change, because the apparent "facts" seem most compelling at market highs and at market lows. This is why there is enduring truth to Pogo's statement: "We have met the enemy. and it is us." This is why investors can benefit so much from sound investment counseling.

★★★

While most investors take investment services offered in a conventionally blended form, it is possible to unbundle services into separate levels. There are five levels of decisions for each investor to make:

Level One: Asset mix—the optimal proportion of equities, bonds, private equity, or whatever, for the "policy normal" of the investor's portfolio. This is where investment counseling usually concentrates.

Level Two: Equity mix—"policy normal" proportions in various types of stocks: growth versus value; large-cap versus small-cap; domestic versus international, and so on.

Level Three: Active versus passive management—the appropriate method of operational implementation of the "policy normal" mix of investments.

Level Four: Specific manager selection (where most investors and most investment committees concentrate their time and effort)—in which investment firms will manage each component of the overall portfolio, firing the most disappointing and hiring the most promising.

Level Five: Active portfolio management—changing portfolio strategy, security selection, and executing transactions.

The least costly and the most surely valuable service the profession can offer is the very first level: getting it basically right on long-term goals and basic asset mix, often helped by wise investment counseling. The last two levels—the active management of managers (through hiring and firing) and the active management of portfolios (through buying and selling)—are simultaneously the most expensive and the least assured of success.

At Level One—setting realistic long-term investment objectives—every investor can be a winner, but as the accumulation of evidence makes increasingly clear, very few can or will win in the increasingly hyperactive and counterproductive pursuit of competitive advantage on Level Five.

That's the ultimate irony of the Loser's Game: We can be dazzled by the excitement and the action, and striving to win on Level Five where the costs to play are so high and the rewards so small. Even worse, the search for ways to beat the market distracts us from focus on Level One, where the costs are low and the rewards can be quite large.

As a profession, shouldn't we be encouraging our clients to focus less of their attention on Levels Four and Five, where the 90:10 shift to 10:90 has so profoundly and adversely changed the environment; and more on Level One, where the changed environment does no harm and actually makes strategy and policy both easier to implement and more sure to produce the expected or intended results?

Source: *Journal of Portfolio Management,* Winter, 2000.

15

An Invitation to Winning

Would you, like most investors, be glad to know—in advance—that your investment fund will be comfortably in the Top Quartile over the long term? Here, based on the evidence, is a sensible, confident way to get there. And it's easy!

Accepting reality is not always easy. And when acceptance would oblige giving up on a long-held set of beliefs, particularly when many others are apparently holding onto those same beliefs, accepting reality can be hard—very hard.

While Darwinian evolution enjoys extensive scientific confirmation, over 40% of Americans still profess belief in creationism. And over 40% doubt global warming. Although serious students of reality may find it hard to understand why so many resist indexing and exchange-traded funds (ETFs) or somehow believe in creationism or disbelieve in global warming, we should not be surprised. As Thomas Kuhn explained in his classic, *Scientific Revolutions*, change can be hard for those who have built their careers on developing the particulars of a theory to change to a new concept.

So it is with global warming skeptics who seized on major snowfalls in Washington last winter as "proof" against global warming without checking to see if the data might actually confirm rather than deny global warming. (The snow was, in fact, strong *confirmation* of global warming.) As biology probes ever more deeply into the way life really works, Darwinian evolution gets more and more confirmation. And so it is with indexing and ETFs. But "old school" skeptics persist.

Study after study adds to the accumulation of evidence that, with rare exceptions and very rare exceptions that could have been discovered in advance, active management costs more than it produces in value added. And no systematic studies support an alternate view. So what can we sensibly expect of the way people with strong economic or social or emotional interests in continuing to favor active management will behave?

The pattern by which innovations win acceptance is well known. The short description is simple: slowly, but inevitably. The process is one of resistance being overcome one person at a time. Resistance to innovation—or the viscosity of acceptance—differs by society: farmers were slow to accept the innovation of hybrid seed for corn; doctors were less slow to accept new kinds of pharmaceuticals; and teenage girls are quick to take up the new, new anything.

Two groups are key players in the diffusion of innovation:

- *Innovators* are always trying new things: Their experiments often fail, but they delight in the newness and little mind the failures because they do not overinvest in their experiments and they don't take it personally if the new thing fails.
- *Influentials* are widely respected for their ability to pick new ways with high rates of success and almost never fail. That's why many, many people watch what they do and follow them with confidence. Interestingly, Influentials monitor Innovators closely, and when they see an experiment succeed with Investors, they will then try it too. Because the Influentials only try what has worked for the Innovators, their success rates are very high. And this explains why so many others will follow them and why they are Influentials.

Use of ETFs and indexing are—albeit at a remarkably slow pace—moving up the familiar curve of innovation and are doing so at a slowly accelerating rate. Why? Because more and more investors are realizing that ETFs and indexing have been more successful—after fees and after adjusting for risk—than active management.

Is this a slam on active managers? No! Certainly not! In fact, it is only because active managers are so talented, hard-working, and well-armed with databases, computers, Bloomberg terminals, CFAs, and other advances, *and* so clearly dominate stock market activity.

Fifty years ago, professional investors' trading was less than 10% of the market; today, professional trading is well over 95% *and* derivatives are even larger in value traded and are 100% professional. (And trading volume is over 2,000 *times* greater.)

In reality, the supreme compliment to active management is ironic: Only because so many are so good is their market—while certainly not "perfect"—so efficient due to so much talent working so hard and so skillfully to get it right that almost no active managers are able to do better than the expert consensus—particularly after fees and costs of opportunities. Active manager fees may be 1% of *assets,* but they are about 15% of *returns* and over 100% of incremental returns when restated as incremental fees as a percent of incremental returns over the widely available indexing alternative. Increasingly, the unhappy results of active management are causing clients to have serious questions about the cost:benefit value of active investment management.

Given the persistent accumulation of evidence, there should be no wonder that individuals and institutions now using ETFs and indexing are steadily increasing their allocations. The real wonder is why the two rates of increase are not even greater.

As all grandparents and most parents know—and as most grandchildren will come to know—the real test of a good driver is simple: No serious accidents. And as all flyers know, safe, dull—even boring—is the essence of a good flight. The secret to success in investing is *not* in beating the market any more than success in driving is going 20 MPH over the posted speed limit. Success in driving starts with being on the right road. And success in investing comes from having clearly defined objectives and the right asset mix *and* staying with it.

ETFs and indexing make it easier for investors to focus on what really matters: setting the right goals on risk, designing the portfolio most likely to achieve sensible objectives, rebalancing as appropriate, and staying the course. Indexing and ETFs simplify implementation (while improving results versus active management) freeing the investor to focus on the really important work of getting it right on investment policy. That's why ETFs and indexing are increasingly important for individuals and institutions that are correctly interested in winning the Winner's Game and *not* losing the Loser's Game.

Source: *Wealthfront,* Summer, 2012.

16

Small Slam!

For most active investment managers, the benefits of portfolio diversification can have two "performance-retarding" problems. One is the danger of diluting the expertise that could be devoted to each investment and is needed to outperform the expert competition. Another is not investing enough in the very best opportunities to make a major difference. My long-term interest in fees—and how to see them accurately—are both on display in this short piece.

My father loved bridge and played often and well, usually for serious money. He was impressed one evening when his bridge partner—an acquaintance he had not played with before—opened with a preemptive bid: "Small slam in hearts!" He was astonished when his happy partner said, "It's a laydown!" Dad was astounded as his partner showed his hand: It was all hearts! Aghast, Dad asked the obvious question, "Why didn't you bid grand slam?"

He was not amused by the reply: "Because I wasn't sure how much support your hand would give me." Dad never fully recovered.

Bridge is a more even-handed game than investing. In tournament bridge, the penalty for underbidding is as severe as the penalty for overbidding, because both are equally "not right." Both are equally wrong. The same should be true in measuring a portfolio manager's investment performance. For a client, the "opportunity cost" of a gain not made will be just as much a loss, over the long term, as any "real" loss. Inappropriate caution should be at least as concerning in investing as in bridge.

As investment managers, wouldn't we be more successful in achieving good results for our clients if we would force ourselves to act boldly on some strong convictions? For example, why not begin by forcing ourselves to put at least 50% of the portfolio in 10 or fewer "compelling opportunity" stocks? (Note that a client with several investment managers already has lots of diversification, including diversification of information gathering and decision making. Having each individual manager "fully diversified" surely results in an excessive number of holdings in the client's combined portfolio.)

So, our first question is the pervasive "unmentionable": To what extent are we "closet indexers"? How much do our actual portfolios truly differ from the index? An even harder question is, what fees are we charging relative to the assets composing this differentiating portfolio—or even to the incremental return earned from this differential portfolio?

The publicly available data on institutional managers' investment results are not encouraging. On average, as we are all recurringly reminded, active managers do not beat the index, so the industry's average differentiating portfolio is *not* beating the market. It is getting beaten. Why? One answer may be "taking too much risk." A better answer may be "being too cautious." The traditional answer to the inherent difficulty in investing is to diversify. I'm not so sure. Remember H.L. Mencken's admonition: "For every complicated problem, there is a simple answer. And it's wrong!"

We know investing is a complicated problem. Is diversification a too simple answer? Diversification is widely regarded as providing a defense against uncertainty. But does it? Let's take another careful look. First, a long list of holdings is no more "portfolio diversification" than a huge pile of stones is Chartres Cathedral. Both need deliberate design and skillful construction.

Second, increasing the number of holdings dilutes our knowledge, disperses our research efforts, distracts our attention, and diminishes our determination to act—when really called for decisively and with dispatch. If you work hard enough and think deeply enough to know all about a very few investments, that knowledge can, at least theoretically, enable you to make and sustain each of your major investments with confidence. The more you "diversify" by increasing the number of different investments you must understand, the more you risk increasing your *not* knowing as much about each of your investments as do your best competitor investors, particularly the most expert and thus the quickest to take preemptive action.

Only a surprisingly small number of well-chosen different positions are needed to provide diversification's protection against major errors of commission. Usually, this protection against disaster can be achieved with fewer than a dozen different positions. After that, increasing the number of different investments in a portfolio can increase uncertainty more rapidly than it reduces risk.

Meanwhile, investors who are preoccupied elsewhere—or whose attention is too dispersed for them to be sufficiently attentive to "first warnings"—are not ready or able to take prompt action. Disturbingly, the very portfolio diversification intended, in theory, to protect us from risk may, in practice, actually be increasing our true uncertainty. This greater uncertainty can cause investors to make errors of commission or of omission that might have been avoided if they had been able to devote enough time to each investment.

The stock market may be a continuous demonstration of "economic democracy," but the decisions of the most successful investors are not democratic. Investing is necessarily—as are all sports, all arts, and all sciences—a meritocracy. Philip Fisher continued to champion in writings and in practice over more than half a century owning the stocks of a few truly outstanding companies and concentrating on becoming sufficiently expert in each of them to stay serenely committed for the very long term. Mies van der Rohe, understanding the distractions of too much detail, admonished his fellow architects that "less is more."

That is why Warren Buffett, the Great American Investor, advises investors to visualize themselves as having a lifetime "decision ticket" with only 20 numbers to punch. Each time you make a decision, punch your ticket. After 20 punches, you must leave the game. You are played out. Buffett has gone so far as to declare four of Berkshire Hathaway's investments permanent: Coca-Cola, Disney, GEICO, and the Washington Post Company. Buffett's exemplary results—from a very concentrated portfolio of very long-term holdings based on very thorough homework—give an encouraging indicator of our opportunity.

As investors, we will make better decisions if we concentrate our skills and energies on making fewer and better investments, deliberately searching for the Great Decisions. When turnover is as high as it is today, we are doing so many things that we do not make enough time to think through and do the *best* things in a very big way. That is what makes Warren Buffett and Phil Fisher so special. Larry Tisch is no slouch either. John Neff turned in his generation's best risk-adjusted return for large mutual funds by making astute and courageous long-term portfolio strategy decisions that were concentrated on his best, most rigorously reasoned opportunities. Consider life. How many truly important decisions do we make in our own private lives?

As investors, how many of us truly understand the importance of our "slugging average" making our best investments our very biggest? Are we doing sufficient analysis to make fewer, larger, and longer-lasting investments? Are we just "playing to play," or are we "playing to win"? The difference is decisive. Dad would want to know whether, as investors, we are seriously looking for and truly ready to bid "Grand Slam"!

Source: Charles D. Ellis (1997) Small Slam!, *Financial Analysts Journal*, 53:1, 6 8, copyright © CFA Institute reprinted by permission of Taylor & Francis Ltd, **http://www.tandfonline.com** on behalf of CFA Institute.

17

A Lesson from Seaside Cemetery

The importance of not following the crowd and, instead, developing your own independent plan is certainly true in investing where so many investors seem to follow others and seem to find comfort in "conventional wisdom." Of course, it always helps to be blessed with good luck!

At Seaside Cemetery in Marblehead, Massachusetts, over 70 years ago, I was given a lifelong lesson in the advantages of not following the crowd, particularly when the crowd was most sure of the rightness of their collective view on what to do and why.

We were Boy Scouts, chosen to march right behind the Veterans of Foreign Wars and the American Legion color guard on Memorial Day in the parade that began downtown at the Historical Society and wound up at Seaside Cemetery. We were to stand at attention as the men—who had outgrown their uniforms horizontally even more than we had outgrown ours vertically—aimed their rifles into the sky and fired the traditional 21-gun salute of remembrance.

We may have been chosen to show support for the VFW and the Legion, but as boys our real reason for being where we were was, to us, obvious. We were hoping to get some of the 21 cartridge shells. "Boys," said the Commander,

You will all stay behind this line because this is a solemn occasion. We are here to remember those who made the supreme sacrifice.

Now, I know you're interested in the cartridges as souvenirs, so here's what we'll do. After firing the salute is completed, I will pick up all the spent shells. You will stay right where you are. On my command, One, Two, Three, I will roll the shells toward you. As my hand lets go the shells on Three!—and *not* before then—you boys can come run an' get 'em.

We understood. We were "obedient Scouts"—*and* sure hoping to get some of those shells!

The salute was fired. The shells were collected. The Commander faced us. We all knew what to do: Be first! We jockeyed anxiously for position, just behind the line, each determined to dash out faster than all the others. The Commander was ten feet away. We were *ready*.

Then it hit me. If everyone was determined to be *first*, it *might* be smart to be *last*. I decided to be different.

The Commander's hand swung back. "One!" Every boy was ready to pounce. "Two!" The Commander smiled and then, his hand swept forward "Three!" and the boys were off! The shells were bowled perfectly. The boys were fast, all trying to be *first* to those shells. All the boys but one: me. Being different worked well—very well.

In one minute, having hung back, I'd picked up four shells that had rolled right under all the other boys and into the space where I was the only one looking. Into my pocket they went—and then I piled in with the others. After all, I might find another.

But that's not the point. The point is that when the opinions and behavior of others dominate a situation and its probable outcome, making your own plan is frequently wise, always worth considering, and often quite rewarding.

Making your own plan is the best, and probably the only, way to *win* The Winner's Game. And it's so easy *if* you can ignore that rascal, Mr. Market, and stay apart from the crowd that follows him to the Loser's Game. But this requires the kind of learning and experience with data that only professionals can be expected to have, particularly when either the opportunities to get it right or the dangers of getting it wrong are large.

Thoughtful and effective investment counseling is centered on helping investors specify realistic long-term investment objectives and properly structure their strategic portfolio or asset mix. Such counseling is both the opportunity and the challenge facing the investment management profession.

Source: Charles D. Ellis (2011) The Winners' Game, *Financial Analysts Journal*, 67:4, 11–17, copyright © CFA Institute reprinted by permission of Taylor & Francis Ltd, on behalf of CFA Institute.

18

Tommy Armour on Investing

Borrowing lessons from other fields is often a good way to reflect on our own accustomed ways of thinking and acting. Golf is a major source of important lessons on life—and for investors.

Tommy Armour was, during his era, the greatest teaching pro in golf. After turning pro in 1925, he won every major golf championship. Then, starting in 1929, he taught golf at Boca Raton. His 1953 book—still in print—is one of the best books on playing golf. It certainly has the best, most encouraging title: *How to Play Your Best Golf All the Time*. For those who absorb its lessons, Armour's book fulfills the title's promise.

As everyone who has ever played the Great Game knows, golf is life. So is investing. The great challenge in golf is not how to hit the ball or how to line up a putt or come out of a sand trap. The great challenge is to control the golfer—yourself. It's the same in investing: Know your capabilities and resources and play within them.

An obvious opportunity for investors would be to study with a great teacher like Armour and learn his "golf" lessons that are so applicable to investing, including this great overall summary: "Simplicity, concentration, and economy of effort have been the distinguishing features of every great player's methods, [while others] lost their way to glory by wandering in a mass of detail."

Observers of Berkshire Hathaway, where so few investments are made in a typical year and investments are held so long, can be forgiven if they feel an urge to shout out, "Yes! Keep it up, Warren!" And investors in the American Funds would not be unjust to point out that this family of mutual funds—with the best long-term investment results—has low portfolio turnover. Index funds, which outperform most active managers, are designed to concentrate successfully on simplicity and economy of effort. All too many investors suffer the penalties of too much turnover.

As Armour says, "Action before thought is the ruination of most of your shots." There is at least a good chance that institutional investors, with an astonishing high portfolio turnover, would benefit from more careful consideration before taking action and slowing the whole process down.

Indeed, Armour summarizes his years as a competitor, teacher, and student of the Great Game with a simple fact that undoubtedly will improve your scoring: "It is not solely the capacity to make great shots that makes champions, but the essential quality of making very few bad shots." Imagine how investment performance could be improved by deleting any fund's three or four worst stocks. Like all great teachers, Armour repeats himself: "The way to win is by making fewer bad shots." Fund managers might wisely devote more time and effort to removing their "stinker" stocks and to not losing.

Armour goes on to explain his meaning with somewhat different words: "Play the shot you've got the greatest chance of playing well and make the next shot easy." Armour might change this advice a bit for investors to: Make the investment decision today that makes holding on for the long term easy.

Active investing by institutional investors where over 90% of "public transactions" are by institutions and a full 50% are by the 50 largest institutions, all of whom are well informed and competitive—leaves little margin for error. As Armour explains, "In major championship golf, the margin of error is narrow. It's wide in the club competitions between higher handicap players, but there, as well as in expert competitions, you'll note that what distinguishes the winner is that he made fewer bad strokes than the rest."

We all know, even though public confessions are quite rare, that the main reason for selling stocks is inadequate research and judgment at the time of purchase, just as the principal cause of divorce is inadequate consideration before the wedding. Wouldn't we do better as investors if we concentrated our investments on those stocks that we have good reason to conclude from thorough research have the greatest chance of doing well over many, many years?

Armour may not have included the "money game" in the set of alternatives he had in mind when—half a century ago—he said of golf, "No other game is as exacting as golf in that so many specifications must be met to make a precision fit of implement and player," but if he were revising his great book today, Armour might well include investing.

Investors continuously chasing "big winners" while repetitively underperforming the markets fit Armour's observation: "The fact that at least ninety percent of the millions of golfers score in the 90s or more than a stroke a hole over par is highly significant. It is a plain indication of their inherent limitations. Few of them are reconciled to their limitations." (The last sentence may be particularly important for the "best and brightest" who have been streaming into investment management.) Armour goes on to say, "Fortunately, practically all of them can learn to reduce many of the faults that are preventing them from getting as close to par as nature will allow them."

In golf, we play against ourselves. But in investing, we play against ourselves *and* against all comers. And the competitors coming after us are getting better and better all the time. So, now is a good time to learn Armour's immortal lessons over again. Competence in investing is not an absolute but a relative measure. And the relevant competition is getting so much stronger that most investment managers should recognize that, even if their absolute skills are improving, the grim reality of their own relative competence is surely and persistently fading.

Armour would want us to understand that the shrewd way to go forward is to take more time, have more knowledge and understanding, play to our strengths, invest in the ways we do best, and make investment decisions that make the next decision easy. As Armour said, "Every golfer scores better when he learns to play within the limits of his capabilities." And in investing, our capabilities are always relative capabilities.

Source: Charles D. Ellis (2004) Tommy Armour on Investing, *Financial Analysts Journal*, 60:5, 15–16, copyright © CFA Institute reprinted by permission of Taylor & Francis Ltd, http://www.tandfonline.com on behalf of CFA Institute.

19

Ted Williams' Great
Lessons for Investors

Ted Williams played professional baseball for the Boston Red Sox. Six times
American League batting champion, his career record would have been even
better had he not been called to active duty in Korea in 1951–1952, the
years in which, during the few months he played ball, he averaged over 400.

Ted Williams, gruff, aloof, and taciturn, produced a great batting
record over his 22 years of playing baseball and wrote one of
the best books on the sport, *The Science of Hitting*. Filled with
insights gained from intensive study, every analyst and portfolio manager
would benefit from reading this superb compilation of lessons learned
and how they can be applied to investing.

Expert investors know that hitting home runs in the stock market
is hard. So many complex judgments must be just right: estimation of
future earnings produced by the confluence of myriad factors inside and
outside the company; changes in other investors' perceptions and projections; and estimations of future market valuations. That's why investors are unusually well positioned to understand Ted Williams' assertion
about the difficulties of hitting in baseball. "Hitting a baseball—I've said
it a thousand times—is the single most difficult thing to do in sport."
That statement commands attention, particularly among competitive
people in the notoriously competitive and constantly measured field of
investment management.

Having caught our attention, Williams continues.

I get raised eyebrows and occasional arguments when I say that, but what is there that is harder to do? What is there that requires more natural ability, more physical dexterity, more mental alertness? That requires a greater finesse to go with physical strength, that has as many variables and as few constants, and that carries with it the continuing frustration of knowing that even if you are a .300 hitter—which is a rare item these days—you are going to fail at your job seven out of ten times? If Joe Namath or Roman Gabriel completed three of every ten passes they attempted, they would be <u>ex</u>-professional quarterbacks. If Oscar Robertson or Rick Barry made three of every ten shots they took, their coaches would take the basketball away from them.

As though he was talking about great stock pickers or portfolio strategists, Williams goes on, "Baseball is crying for good hitters . . . Hitting is the most important part of the game; it is where the big money is, where much of the status is, and the fan interest."

Know Thyself

Getting serious about getting better at hitting is not dissimilar to improving your skill as an investor. Williams explains: "Much of what I have to say about hitting is self-education. You, the hitter, are the greatest variable in this game of baseball. To know yourself takes dedication. That's a hard thing to have. Today, ballplayers have a dozen distractions." Every professional investor would agree with both points: we need to focus with dedication and we face too many distractions.

But, nodding our heads is one thing. Taking the right action is different. Williams had no patience with the concept of great "natural" hitters. He knew better. As a serious student of hitting, he worked hard at figuring out exactly what did or did not work well. Williams experimented with different stances, tried different bats before settling on 33 ounces as best for him, and got the Red Sox to put a scale in the club house so he could check every bat's weight. As he explained his attention to every detail that could affect his performance, Williams said, "Bats pick up condensation and dirt lying around on the ground."

Much of *The Science of Hitting* explains the "game theory" of interactions between pitchers and batters in different situations. But it is in this area of what a hitter can do on his own to increase success that Williams offers his best insights: How many investment analysts and fund managers could up their own games by careful, objective study of their past decisions in search of imperfections to reduce or remove?

As a serious student of hitting, Williams worked hard at figuring out exactly what did or did not work well. The traditional view in baseball had been that there was a single strike zone—an understanding which colored how players and their performance were assessed. Williams dismissed this, insisting instead that there were actually 77 different "mini zones"—seven columns of eleven little zones. And for each mini strike zone, he calculated his batting average. What a revelation! Williams' batting averages varied from a mere .230 in the low and outside "mini zone" to a mighty .400 in his "happy spot."

No wonder Williams' first rule for success is: "get a good ball to hit!" As he explains, "A good hitter can hit a pitch over the plate two or three *times* better than a questionable ball in a tough spot. Pitchers still have to make enough mistakes to give you some balls in your happy zone. All hitters have areas where they like to hit. But you can't beat the fact that you've got to get a good ball to hit!" Or as Warren Buffet often advises investors: "Wait for the fat pitch."

Do More of What You're Good At

Williams offers a series of tips on hitting that investors can readily convert to investing. As a serious student of his nearly 8,000 times at bat, Williams believed "every trip to the plate was an adventure—one I could remember and store up as information." How many of us have the same joyful approach to our times at bat as investors? How many of us collect, categorize, and carefully analyze all our many decisions? And Williams not only studied with diligence his own many experiences, he studied other hitters. And he was committed to "practice, practice, practice. I hit until the blisters bled. It was something I forced myself to do. Extra batting practice is how you learn."

Acknowledging that he had 20-10 vision—a most convenient advantage for a hitter—Williams sounds a lot like a winning investor reviewing his record of performance. "What I had more of wasn't eyesight. I had a higher percentage of game-winning home runs than Babe Ruth; was second only to Ruth in slugging and percentage combined; walked more frequently than Ruth and struck out much less."

Then Williams goes on to say what every great investor knows is the secret of success: "I had to be doing something right and the principal something was being selective."

Ted Williams was a very good batter. He made himself a great player by studying the game and, most of all, studying himself in unrelenting detail on every dimension. What a great lesson for anyone determined to excel—particularly in the major league of today's professional investment management.

Source: Essentra Conference on Behavioral Analytics, October, 2019.

20

Symptoms and Signs

While symptoms in investment management indicate serious problems for our profession, numerous signs are that most of us are not paying nearly enough attention to the potential value of investment counseling to our professional success on which, of course, our business depends to be successful over the long term.

Investment management is in trouble as a profession now, and prospectively as a business, because investment performance is in trouble and investment performance is at the core of both the profession and the business.

For anyone looking at the business dimensions such as profitability, growth or acquisitions, this alarm must seem quite false. After all, the *business* is booming. But on the professional dimensions, such as client satisfaction and loyalty, the evidence for concern is rising. The troubles are getting worse, and several of the causal factors of trouble are interrelated and reinforcing.

Eventually, if the industry falters and stumbles on the professional dimensions, the business dimensions will also be hurt. Just imagine the economic impact of a return to the low fee levels that prevailed before the general acceptance of "performance" investing!

Searches for Understanding

Analytic models from other disciplines can enable open-minded observers to see developments in their own disciplines anew and perhaps more clearly. Thus, navigators and medical doctors have had experience in their searches for understanding that can be useful for investment managers and their clients who seek to understand and manage investment performance.

Consider an analytic model from medicine. When they diagnose a disease, physicians differentiate quite strictly between two very different phenomena: symptoms and signs.

- *Symptoms* are those manifestations we can so readily identify ourselves: headaches, upset stomachs, muscular aches, and the like. We turn to our doctors, identify the location and nature of the discomfort we feel, and ask them to identify the illness we suffer and cure it. Our doctors sort through the symptoms we have noticed—and others we may not have noticed—somewhat like sorting the pieces of a jigsaw puzzle, looking for an informative pattern.

  As doctors know, not all symptoms are linked to disease, and many others are only indicative. Some are psychosomatic and some are ephemeral. Even when symptoms are real, our doctors can be genuinely challenged to diagnose and isolate the true cause of the illness and estimate its future pathology.
- *Signs*, like the evidence of a specific type of cancer, are quite different. Signs may not be evident to us as patients, but there is no doubt for the knowing doctor. You may feel and look just fine, but your doctor knows if you have a certain disease and what the disease is. In some cases, the signs are *pathognomonic*, and the diagnostician knows both the disease and its sequence of events and their pacing. This is the grim reality when, for example, your doctor discovers the signs that mean, despite your feeling fine, you are certainly doomed by a virulent cancer.

Most diagnostic work is quite difficult. Long years of hard studies and many years of professional experience are vital to your doctor's success in making the correct diagnosis. Access to such powerful diagnostic instruments as MRI scanners has been transforming medical diagnoses as doctors shift from estimation and interpolation to knowing. Technology continues to transform medicine. The great advances of science in medicine enabled Dr. Lewis Thomas to say that, by about 1960, so much scientific knowledge had been accumulated about the nature of disease that science had finally gained ascendance over iatrogenic or doctor-caused diseases such as infections caused by doctors moving from one to another patient without adequate scrubbing-up after the first patient. After 1960, that doctors' scientific knowledge had become ascendant.

Navigation at sea has gone through a similar great progression. John Harrison's invention of accurate timekeepers for use at sea enable sailors to determine their longitude. (They could already tell latitude by their sextants.) This enabled Captain James Cook to sail throughout the Pacific on his great voyages of discovery and know where he was and how to get where he intended to go. Under Mathew Fontaine Maury, sea captains of the maritime nations undertook in the mid-nineteenth century the systematic worldwide collection of data on such influential variables as water temperature, current, and wind speed and direction. The carefully collected data were plotted on charts, and their patterns were analyzed. Soon the best routes for sailing to catch the most favorable winds and currents were plotted. The happy result was that long ocean passages became both substantially shorter and more predictable *and* safer. (U.S. Navy charts 150 years later still carry a legend citing the innovative work of Mathew Fontaine Maury.)

Fifty years ago, radar again revolutionized navigation. Sailors could "see" the coastline and other vessels in thick fog or heavy rain or darkness. Then came SONAR for depth measurement, and then Loran. Today, global positioning satellite systems (GPS) take navigation even farther. Navigators can now locate their positions anywhere on the surface of the globe *and* at any level above or below the surface—with accuracy to within one square meter.

In addition to keeping sails trimmed, sea captains took responsibility for plotting optimal courses across the seas for safe passage, and eventually for on-time arrivals. In addition to relieving pains, medical doctors took responsibility for preventative medicine and for curing more and more diseases. In each case, the transformation in capability has converted the nature of expectation. We now expect doctors to diagnose a remarkable range of diseases, and we expect on-time arrivals.

The same transformation in ability to know where we are and to know how to get where we intend to go has been developing an investment management. The tools available are advancing rapidly in their ability to be specific. Just one generation ago, Longstreet Hinton, distinguished head of the Trust & Investment Division of Morgan Guaranty Trust, would respond with confidence in his warm Vicksburg, Mississippi, voice to General Motors' senior financial executive's question about how GM's large pension fund was doing, with the genial and clearly conversation-ending comment: "Everythin' is comin' along jes' fine."

With research led by economists at the Cowles Foundation at Yale, and the Merrill Lynch Center at Chicago, comparisons to the S&P 500 became widely available by the early 1960s. The 1970s experienced

A. G. Becker's ubiquitous comparisons of individual funds to dozens of other funds of similar size without, however, any regard for the important differences in asset mix, investment strategy, or objective. By the 1980s, numerous carefully defined and constructed indexes were available, and a particular fund's performance could be measured—asset class by asset class—relative to any of several benchmarks.

Today, rigorous and detailed analysis of beta, alpha, Sharpe ratios, and performance relative to virtually any specified benchmark is part of all careful studies of performance attribution. As a result, investment managers and their clients can now know exactly where a particular portfolio is positioned relative to the market. And they can know how that portfolio would be expected to perform, given any reasonable scenario of future market behavior.

This progress brings us to the central contemporary challenge. The tools of analysis now available to both managers and clients are so good that they convert the challenge from answering "Where are we now?" to asking instead, "Where do we want to be and exactly how do we plan to get there?" Since clients can now get what they ask for, explicit and exact definition of a manager's intention is all the more important today in evaluating the manager's actual achievements.

Investment managers and their clients need to differentiate between the investment equivalents of medicine's symptoms and signs and act always on the enduring, objective data. In defining and understanding investment objectives and in evaluating investment performance, investment managers and their clients need to know how to discriminate between data that convey real information and data that are only noise.

If clients focus on symptoms, managers may be tempted to manage the symptoms. The most common way managers manage the symptoms is by changing the period over which performance data are reported and discussed. (In ice hockey, every defense player soon learns the great lesson about covering skillful forwards: Don't watch the eyes or the head or the puck or the stick—or even the hands. Watch the hips, because skaters have to go where their hips go.) Dominance of performance data, as we all know, is very powerful when skillfully manipulated. (Examples are sadly abundant in reports of mutual fund "performance" in advertisements. In the early 1970s when pollution was fast becoming a public concern, the jets taking off from LaGuardia came under pressure to stop dumping the thick exhaust spewing out of their engines, seen as a blatant disregard of the public. The problem was quickly solved by chemistry—no more black exhaust smoke. Yet the real polluting was not eliminated at all because the chemicals that were added to make the exhaust invisible actually increased the pollution. But the symptom was "solved," and consumers stopped protesting because they thought they'd won, when actually they'd lost.)

Good Investment Performance

Of course, symptoms are inherently evident, or they wouldn't be symptoms at all, but they are not necessarily useful information. When we discuss performance, we must ask the classic vaudeville question: "Compared to what?" We now know it's crucial to specify the relevant peer group or standard and compare results to that standard. Being ahead of or behind the S&P 500—which 25 years ago was an attention-grabbing major revelation—is now recognized as nothing more than an artifact. The real question is whether the manager is ahead of or behind the specific agreed upon benchmark.

Good investment performance is not simply having favorable outcomes; it's at least as important to have achieved those results in a deliberate, predictable, repeatable way so the favorable outcome is expectable in the future. That's why conformance to intention is at least as important as performance. As the great sports coaches tell their teams: "Plan your play, and play your plan."

Conformance means diligently playing with the investment manager's known field of competence, adhering to the manager's chosen discipline, and conscientiously avoiding what tennis players call unforced errors which cause players to lose to opponents whose playing is more steady and consistent. Conformance also helps eliminate the vagueness that so often confuses the discussion at investment review meetings. Conformance obliges managers and clients to focus on developing and specifying investment objectives and investment policies.

Fund executives' informed evaluations of an investment manager's ability to produce expectable and predictable operational investment results depend upon collecting and using large enough or long enough samples for statistical validity. (An equal concern is with appraisal periods that are too long, such as mutual funds that create their "performance records" *before* their assets ballooned.) Realistically, quarterly and annual performance results are only very small samples from the continuous process of managing portfolios over the long, long term. Small samples are notoriously unreliable. (My favorite illustration is the story of the English anthropologist returning from his eighteenth-century expedition to study the natives of America. At the Royal Society's annual dinner at London's Mansion House, he rose and began his personal report with the solemn declaration that, "In North America, *all* Indians always walk in a single file." (Pause.) "At least the one I saw did.")

As any Bayesian statistician would gladly explain, hyperactive clients who make decisions to hire and fire managers on short-interval performance data are taking a big risk of sampling error. Too many fund executives and investment consultants appear to compromise the validity of their performance data by relying on periods of time that are far too short.

Experience confirms the concern. For all too many funds and for all too many consultants, the average manager they fire outperforms the average manager they hire as a replacement. It's all about the dangers of underestimating the powerful tendency toward regression to the mean. The "data" most investors use to evaluate investment managers are not sufficiently robust—and so are not very helpful. Institutional investors know from experience, and the data confirm the same or worse for individual investors in mutual funds. Recent years' performance simply does not accurately or reliably predict future performance.

The secret for success in evaluating investment managers is for fund executives (and their consultants) to be careful not to pay too much attention to *symptoms*, useful as they can sometimes be and instead, to focus on *signs* and the real causes of underperformance.

In evaluating investment managers, here are some of the serious symptoms we all know to watch for:

- Organizational change: Turnover in key people; changes in decision process or structure; or key investors not working constructively together, particularly if one result is the symptom of increased dispersion of results.
- Change in ownership can lead to changes in the organization's leadership or internal discipline or motivation. (A sudden gain in the personal wealth of key investors can be quite distracting.)
- Asset growth can overburden the capacity of an investment manager's decision-making process. (This has been a particular concern for small cap fund managers.)
- Recently experienced super success . Leaving before the ball is over can be particularly difficult for the investor who has enjoyed a great party. The technology growth stock manager who rode the tide of the market's increasingly intensive love affair with technology growth stocks to an all-time peak level of valuation was sure to have a tough follow-on period relative to the overall market. The same sort of bub-

ble occurred in the two-tier market of the Nifty Fifty in the 1970s; and the elevation to super-valuation of insurance and electric utility stocks in the 1960s; in Japanese shares in the 1980s; or in telecoms in the 1990s. As Yogi Berra so wisely said, "It's déjà vu all over again."

- Dispersion of results. The most effective way for clients to evaluate a manager's investment performance realistically is to require each manager to report the results achieved for *all* the portfolios he or she manages, categorized, of course, by investment policy and objective. Such full disclosure substantially reduces the risk of sampling error that always comes with a review of a single portfolio (a small sample) over a relatively short period (an even smaller sample). More significantly, one of the most important symptoms of real trouble is the dispersion of results between portfolios that share the same mission and so should achieve the similar results.
- Drift in investment philosophy or poor decision-making process that can take the manager into unfamiliar territory and away from a proven zone of competence. Fund executives know that the structure of their portfolio allocations matters: growth versus value stocks or large cap versus small cap or international versus domestic, and all their combinations.

It really makes no difference whether the manager's results are more or less favorable than the benchmark: If the manager is out of zone, that's what matters. For a driver, being off the road on the left is as bad as off the road on the right, just as too far is as bad as too short in a game of ring toss. The agreement between manager and client has been broken. Infidelity *is* infidelity.

Wise clients note that investment performance, like learning languages or negotiating peace agreements, does not come in smooth, steady, consistent increments, but in irregular surges, followed by periods with no visible gains. Similarly, the stock market makes more than 80% of its gains in fewer than 20% of its trading days. And most superior managers achieve the great majority of their superiority over benchmark performance with a small minority of their investments during just a few quarters.

So, too much attention to the current performance numbers or to passing *symptoms* can be very misleading. (That's what political powerhouse Mark Hanna had in mind when dismissing a contemporary politician by saying, "He had his ear so close to the ground it was full of grasshoppers!") If the symptoms persist, however, they will in aggregate be equivalent to *signs*.

Investment Management

In investment management, some of the signs are external or environmental, and some are internal to individual managers. As the period over which results are measured is extended, more managers will fall short, and the persistence and magnitude of the average shortfall will be greater.

Without dwelling on the sobering realities, here are some of the signs that indicate not a universal inevitability but an increasingly high probability that increasing numbers of clients will see their managers produce results that fall short of the overall market. (Note that the larger the manager, the more numerous the clients *and* the greater the probability of underperformance. As a result, the experience of clients, on average, will be worse than the experience of managers.)

Consider that in a single generation the market has been transformed. The market now reflects the well-informed judgment of professionals. The old 10:90 ratio of institutional trading versus individual trading has been completely turned upside down. Today, institutions control 90% of NYSE public trading. This is why market makers have grown more cautious and more disciplined about risk management and hedging with derivatives. And with 50% of all New York Stock exchange transactions executed by the 50 largest and most active professional investors, the natural spreads in the stock market are getting tighter and tighter.

The margin for error has steadily become smaller *and* is still shrinking; the penalties for error are greater, and they hit faster. With institutions dominating the market, the market becomes more and more efficient. So, errors in pricing and in valuation are fewer and briefer in duration because more and more information is known faster and faster to more and more active investors.

Extensive, expert, and well-crafted as it is, the dominating information and analysis coming from Wall Street is shared so broadly and so rapidly that within hours of its discovery, most research has already become the "ultimate value-free commodity" because everyone knows it, it is already in the market price.

Managers with high turnover are particularly affected by tighter markets, so playing the "money game" is less rewarding, and staying out of harm's way is increasingly important. As we're all advised when playing poker: "If after 20 minutes you don't know who the game sucker is, chances are you are."

As the years go by, active funds have become less and less likely to be rewarded by getting a jump ahead of competitor funds just by acting more quickly on fast-breaking information when so many institutional investors know what can be known and are equally swift to take action.

Hugging the index leads managers to overdiversify portfolios, and hold too many different stocks to be able to have superior insight or make better decisions than their peers who now dominate market activity and prices. In addition, dutifully matching the index can make portfolio managers replicate the index willy-nilly. When a few very large companies' stocks selling at very high price/earnings multiples dominate the overall index (as was the case in 2000), this infuses extraordinary unintended price speculation into the index.

Excessive activity runs up the annual operating expense of executing transactions. Not only does this impose significant frictional costs on portfolio results (plus short-term taxes on taxable funds), but it also raises the specter that institutional investors are scrambling to outwit or outguess the other institutional investors who all share most of the same information and dominate the quick response price-setting of the stock market.

Who would argue that such a quick-on-the-trigger activity is *investing*—and not speculation? And if it is speculation, it's a risky kind of speculation: not on corporate developments, but on the probable market reactions of other institutions as they anticipate each other. The transaction costs of high-turnover portfolio operations can easily exceed the net benefits of all that activity, the recognized cause of the Loser's Game.

Fees and costs have doubled over the past 30 years for mutual funds and institutional funds. In a 15% annual rate of return "cornucopia market" environment, the steady increase in the rates charged by investment managers may not have been given particular notice, but if annual returns were to fade to an average of 6–8%, who would not notice the large fraction of that average return going as fees to the managers?

The real costs of portfolio management will be better understood when clients learn to compare fees not to asset managed or even to total returns, but to incremental, risk-adjusted returns. Very few managers add so much value over a decade that their fees on this basis are under 50%. For most managers, their real fees on real value-added are in excess of 100%.

What Signs Mean

The aggregation of these several signs leaves little mystery as to the general trend of the investment management industry. While varying considerably from firm to firm, the overall trend is toward both increasing difficulty for investment managers and increasing disappointment for clients.

The investment management profession needs to recognize the risk of courting an inevitable shortfall in results and client dissatisfaction, by continuing to claim to clients that "our mission is to achieve superior operational performance," which a majority of managers over and over again confirm to do. We can and should be concentrating on the classic, but all too neglected mission of astute investment counseling—where we can surely succeed with major benefit for our clients.

Investment counseling on long-term goals and appropriate investment policy and asset mix is our true professional calling. When the right goals and objectives have been defined for each particular investor, and appropriate investing policies have been worked out, operational implementation via indexing is both inexpensive and achievable *and* beneficial.

The genius of this past generation has, ironically, transformed the challenge for investment managers and their clients from finding ways to "beat the market" to learning to accept market realities as a given and to make the best of this by making explicit the important choices about long-term objectives and asset mix.

Those who accept the challenge and the opportunity will be shifting from the craft of money management to the profession of investment counseling, and from nearly inevitable losing to assured winning.

Source: *The Journal of Portfolio Management,* Summer, 2002.

21

Lessons from the Warwick and Château Chambord

Dad gave good lessons on how to understand costs and pricing and how to make more informed decisions as a customer. Fees in investment management are far, far higher, when correctly seen, than most investors recognize. "Only 1%" is an extraordinary self-deception. Taken as a percentage of superior results, fees for active investing (before taxes) average over 100%.

Dad taught lessons in a memorable way. We children came home at the end of a winter's Saturday afternoon of movies at the Warwick Theater on Pleasant Street in Marblehead, Massachusetts, and Dad asked, "Enjoy the movies?"

"Yes," we replied. "John Wayne."

Then Dad asked one of those questions that starts a lifetime of pondering: "Why? Why do they charge so little for tickets?" The easy answer was easy: "Because we're kids, Dad. And they charge only 12¢ so lots of kids will come." But easy answers would not do, and Dad persisted, "Why does the Warwick charge only 12¢ when the truth is they don't make any money showing movies?"

"Dad, is this a trick question?"

"No, it's not a trick question, but getting the right answer will take some careful thinking."

And that is how Dad got us to work it out with him that the folks at the Warwick were willing to show John Wayne movies at a loss because they were making a real profit selling cokes and popcorn at very high prices. Dad wanted us to learn to separate appearances from realities.

Several years later, Mom and Dad invited us to join them in New York City for dinner at a very special French restaurant named Château Chambord. As we examined the enormous menu, we could not help commenting on how wonderful the dinner would be *and* how very expensive it was.

Then Dad asked another of his probing questions, "How would you explain the fact that this fine restaurant continues in business if I told you something I happen to know: They don't make *any* profit selling this wonderful food?"

"Dad, is this a trick question?"

"No, it's not a trick question, but getting the right answer will take some careful thinking." And that is when we learned that the profits at a great restaurant are not from gourmet food, but from drinks, cocktails, and wine. Dad was again teaching us to think about the salient differences between appearance and reality. (J.P. Morgan had the same idea in mind when he said that for every important business decision, there are almost always two reasons: One is readily recognizable as a very good reason; the other is the *real* reason!) Dad's philosophy was simple and profound: Whatever you are doing, be sure you recognize what is really going on. Do not get confused.

In investing, we are learning that the best way to achieve long-term success is *not* in stock picking and *not* in market timing and *not* even in changing portfolio strategy. Sure, these approaches all have their current heroes and "war stories," but few hero investors last for long and not all war stories are entirely true. The great pathway to long-term success comes via sound, sustained investment policy: setting the right asset mix and holding on to it.

A Brief History

Most of the most important developments in the macro-environment of investment management within which we practice our profession and build our businesses can, with only moderate outrage to the data, be described by using one all-purpose chart, which summarizes our apparent "reality"—ever upward over many years. This one chart can be used to support *each* of these 10 key propositions:

- Institutional assets have grown substantially.
- Market valuations, particularly of equities, are up substantially.
- Trading volumes are up substantially.
- Hiring of investment managers by institutional clients has increased substantially.
- Information access has certainly increased substantially. Count the Bloomberg terminals.
- The numbers of M.B.A.'s, Ph.D.'s, and CFA charter holders have increased substantially.
- Use of investment consultants has increased substantially.
- Fee schedules for both mutual funds and institutional accounts have increased—over 50 years substantially.
- Profitability of investment firms and compensation of investment professionals have increased substantially.
- The valuations at which investment firms are bought and sold have increased substantially.

Current Reality

The realities *are* different. Professional investment managers are not "beating the market." Annual data are increasingly confirming the grim reality: The professionals are lagging.[1]

The data are even more disappointing when the length of time for which results are reported is extended to cumulative 10- or 15-year evaluation periods. In these rather more important time periods, even fewer professionals can keep up with the market averages.

Equally disconcerting, the overarching reality of performance data is that it is not predictive. The past is not prologue. So, even the manager with a "good" record is often not a good bet to outperform in the future. Results are closer to random than we would like to believe. The long-term experience of investors with the active portion of their portfolios—*after* deducting the index-fund equivalent so we can examine just the incremental consequences of active management, is grim.

Do you recall Fred Shwed's wonderful story about the innocent out-of-towner being driven past the yacht basin on the East Side of Manhattan? With pride and enthusiasm, his host and guide pointed out

---

[1]And the data we use are moderately "favorably biased" because of the familiar problem of survivorship.

the largest boats: "Look, those are the bankers' and brokers' yachts." His guest asked, "But, wh-wh-where are the customers' yachts?"[2]

So far, clients have not focused on the inability of professionals to add value through active management because they have been looking at the overall experience. "A rising tide lifts all the boats," and the tide in our market has been rising very favorably. Our clients' views might be very different if we did not have the rising tide. So, now is the time for our profession to be asking Dad's kind of questions: Why is our profession so generously rewarded when unable to add value? Why are the results of the efforts of so many hard-working and talented professionals with so much data and such advanced tools so disappointing?

Down Side Up

The answer is simple: One great environmental change appears to have up-ended—in just one generation—the central assumption on which active investment management is based. The cheerful ratio of 10:90 has been converted to a glum 90:10. Let me explain.

To achieve superior or better-than-average results through active management, you depend directly on the mistakes and blunders of others. Others must be acting as though they are "willing to lose" so you can "win." In the 1960s, when institutions did only 10% of the public trading on the NYSE and 90% was done by individual investors, the amateurs were set up to lose to the professionals.

Here are some of the characteristics of individual investors that are worth keeping in mind: Individual investors typically do not do extensive "comparison shopping." Most individual investors are not expert on even a few companies. They rely on retail brokers who are seldom experts either. They buy because they inherit money, get a special bonus, sell a house, or something else equally *outside the stock market*. They sell because their child is going off to college or they have decided to buy a home—again, for reasons *outside the stock market*. The activity of most individual investors is not driven by investment information based on market analysis or company research or rigorous valuations. The activity of most individual investors is what academics correctly call "informationless trading."

---

[2]Fred Schwed Jr, *Where Are the Customers' Yachts? Or, a Good Hard Look at Wall Street* (New York: John Wiley & Sons, 1995), p. 16.

So, it is little wonder that professional investors—who are always in the market, making rigorous comparisons of price to value across hundreds of different stocks on which they can command extensive, up-to-the-minute information—would have thought they were able to "outperform" the individual investors who did 90% of all the trading done on the NYSE. They could and did—a generation ago.[3] But not today.

Today, after 50 years, the old 90:10 ratio has been completely reversed. The tables have been turned all the way around—and the consequences are profound. Now, 90% of all NYSE trades are done by the "professional" crowd.[4] And what a crowd of professionals they are. Top of the class at graduate school, they are "the best and the brightest," and they are highly motivated. They do not "play to play"—they play to *win*.

But hard as they try, the grim reality is that the professionals are not beating the market. The simple reason is that these skilled and unrelenting professionals *are* the market. Sure, the professionals will not always get it right, but they will just as certainly be trying very hard—all the time and with every resource they can muster. Yes, they do and will make errors, but they will make fewer and fewer errors less and less often and the errors they do make will be corrected more and more quickly. Their "only" problem is that there are not enough amateur patsies around. So, active investing produces too little reward or costs too much or both.[5]

The cumulative genius of the past generation has transformed the challenge—for both investment managers and clients—from finding ways to beat the market to learning to accept the semi-efficient market reality as a given and to make the best of this reality by making explicit the important choices about long-term objectives and policies. This challenge means shifting from investment *craft* to the true investment *profession* of informed, skillful investment counseling.

To advise on asset mix, investment counselors will do well to have skills in managing portfolios in each asset class—so they can help implement what they recommend—and to have open channels of communication with clients. Communication is important because both parties

---

[3]The way it *used* to be reminds me of the two Drill Sergeants in the movie, *Full Metal Jacket*, observing their recruits double-timing information to their graduation exercises at the end of basic training. "One out of ten of these boys is *real* soldiers. The rest are just . . . *targets*."

[4]In fact, nearly 75% of all the trading is done by the 100 largest and most active institutions, and 50% is done by the 50 largest and most active institutions.

[5]This grim, grinding reality was described in my article "The Loser's Game," *Financial Analysts Journal* (July–August 1975): 19–26. Since then, the reality has gotten worse because professional practitioners have gotten better and better.

have important work to do in the process of determining appropriate long-term investment objectives and defining the investment policies most able to achieve those long-term objectives.

The trusted investment counselor's main professional work is to help each client identify, understand, and commit consistently to long-term investment objectives that are both realistic in the capital markets and appropriate to the particular client. The hardest work is not figuring out the optimal investment policy; the hardest work is helping clients stay committed to sound investment policy and maintain what Disraeli called "constancy to purpose." Sustaining a long-term focus at either market highs or market lows is notoriously hard. In either case, emotions are strongest and current market realities are most demanding of change because the facts seem most compelling which is why there is enduring truth to what Pogo so wisely explained: "We have met the enemy and he is us."

Holding onto sound policy through thick and thin is extraordinarily difficult and extraordinarily important work. The cost of infidelity can be very high. For example, during the past 15 years' very favorable stock market, the average mutual fund gained 15% annually, but the average mutual fund investor gained only 10%. Fully one-third of the available return was lost by mutual fund investors switching from one fund to another fund—all too often selling low and buying high.

Dad would have challenged the perceptions of investors—and of most investment professionals—with what we kids found a familiar series of inquiries, but with an interesting difference. Instead of asking why the sellers are selling their services, Dad's questions would drill down into why buyers are buying. Here's the way the inquiry might go:

"Why do investors pay such handsome fees for investment management?"

"Because, Dad, folks want to make money and they expect to make more money when they pay up for the best managers."

"Did you know that it actually works the other way around?"

"Dad, is this a trick question?"

"No, it's not a trick question, but getting the right answer will take some careful thinking."

And before long, Dad would have us understanding that there are three levels of decision for the investor to make and that, whereas most investors take investment services as a blended package, services can be unbundled into three separable components or levels:

- Level One—the optimal proportion of equities as the "policy normal" for the investor's portfolio.

- Level Two—equity mix, policy normal proportions in various types of stocks growth versus value, large capitalization versus small capitalization, domestic versus international.
- Level Three—active management versus indexing.

Dad would then explain that investment counseling on asset mix (a Level One decision) and on equity mix (a Level Two decision) is inexpensive and needed only once every few years. (An individual investor with $1 million can buy this service from an expert for less than $5,000 once every 5 or 10 years. An institution with $10 billion might pay $50,000.) Active management (a Level Three decision) can cost—for the management and the transactions—about 1% of the $1 million individual investor's assets, or $10,000 each year and $50,000 over five years.

The irony, Dad would point out, is that the most value-adding service available to investors—investment counseling—although demonstrably inexpensive, is in very little demand. Active management, although usually not successful at adding value, comes at a high cost.

Dad would want us, as investors *and* as investment professionals, to at least consider thinking independently enough to realize that the three levels of service can be obtained separately and that we can limit what we pay to the added value of the results we can reasonably expect. Dad would want us to think carefully about the real challenges we face. As Warren Buffett has said about poker: "If after 20 minutes you don't know who the patsy is, *you* are the patsy!" Let us not fool ourselves.

22

Investment Management Fees Are Higher Than We Think

High fees and long-term growth in asset management have made investment management one of the highest-paid major industries in the world. Twenty years ago, only a few investors had recognized that fees are really high. This would change.

Although some critics grouse about them, most investors have long thought that investment management fees can best be described in one word: low. Indeed, fees are seen as so low that they are almost inconsequential when choosing an investment manager. This view, however, is a delusion. Seen for what they really are, fees for active management are high—and much higher than even many critics have recognized.

When stated as a percentage of *assets*, average fees do look low—a little over 1% of assets for individuals and a little less than one-half of 1% for institutional investors. But the investors already own those assets, so investment management fees should really be based on what investors are getting in the returns that managers produce. Calculated as a percentage of returns, fees no longer look low. Do the math. If returns average, say, 8% a year, then those same fees are not 1% or one-half of 1%. They are much higher—over 12% for individuals and 6% for institutions.

But even this recalculation substantially understates the real cost of active "beat the market" investment management. Here's why: Index funds reliably produce a "commodity product" that ensures the market rate of return with no more than market risk. Index funds are now available at fees that are very small: 5 basic points (bps) (0.05%) or less for institutions and 10–20 bps or less for individuals. Therefore, investors should consider fees charged by active managers not as a percentage of total returns but as *incremental* fees versus risk-adjusted *incremental* returns above the relevant index.

Thus, correctly stated, management fees for active management are remarkably *high*. Incremental fees are somewhere between 50% of incremental returns and, because a majority of active managers fall short of their chosen benchmarks, *infinity*.

Are any other services of any kind priced at such a high proportion of client-delivered value? Can active investment managers continue to thrive on the assumption that clients won't figure out the reality that, compared with the readily available indexing alternative, fees for active management are astonishingly high?

Fees for active management have a long and interesting history. Once upon a time, investment management was considered a "loss leader." When pension funds first mushroomed as "fringe benefits" after the World War II wage-and-price freeze, most major banks agreed to manage pension fund assets as a "customer accommodation" for little or no money—in explicit fees. With fixed-rate brokerage commissions, the banks exchanged commissions for cash balances in agreed proportions. The brokers got "reciprocal" commission business, and the banks got "free" balances they could lend out at prevailing interest rates. In the 1960s, a few institutional brokerage firms, including DLJ, Mitchell Hutchins, and Baker Weeks, had investment management units that charged full fees (usually 1%) but then offset those nominal fees entirely with brokerage commissions. Their actual fee was *zero*.

When the Morgan Bank took the lead in charging fees by announcing institutional fees of one quarter of 1% in the late 1960s, conventional Wall Street wisdom held that the move would cost the bank a ton of business. Actually, it lost only one small account. Thus began nearly a half century of persistent fee increases, facilitated by client perceptions that fees were comfortably exceeded by incremental returns—assuming the right manager was chosen. Even today, despite extensive evidence to the contrary, both individual and institutional investors typically expect their chosen managers to produce significantly higher-than-market returns. That's why fees can still seem "low."

A relatively minor anomaly is getting more attention: While asset-based fees have increased substantially over the past 50 years—more than fourfold for both institutional and individual investors—investment results have not improved for many reasons. Changes in the equity market have been substantial, particularly in aggregate. Over the past 50 years, trading volume has increased 2,000 times—from 3 million shares a day to 6 billion. Derivatives, in value traded, have gone from zero to far more than the "cash" market. Institutional activity on the stock exchanges has gone from under 10% of trading to over 90%. And a wide array of game changers—Bloomberg terminals, CFA charter holders, computer models, globalization, hedge funds, high-frequency trading, the Internet, and so on—have become major factors in the changing market.

Most important, the worldwide increase in the number of highly trained professionals, working intensely to achieve *any* competitive advantage, has been phenomenal. Consequently, today's stock market is an aggregation of all the expert estimates of price-to-value coming every day from extraordinary numbers of hard-working, experienced, well-informed, professional decision makers. The result is the world's largest ever "prediction market." Against this consensus of experts, managers of diversified portfolios of publicly traded securities who strive to beat the market—after fees and operating costs—are sorely challenged.

If the upward trend of fees and the downward trend of prospects for beat-the-market performance wave a warning flag for investors—as they certainly should—objective reality should cause all investors who believe investment management fees are low to reconsider. Seen from the right perspective, active management fees are not low—they are high, *very* high.

Extensive, undeniable data show that identifying in advance any particular investment manager who will—after operations costs, taxes, and fees—achieve the holy grail of beating the market is highly improbable. Yes, Virginia, some managers will always beat the market, but we have no reliable way of determining in advance which managers will be the lucky ones.

Price is surely not everything, but just as surely, when analyzed as incremental fees for incremental returns, investment management fees are not "almost nothing." No wonder increasing numbers of individual and institutional investors are turning to exchange-traded funds and index funds—and those experienced with either or both are steadily increasing their use.

Meanwhile, those hard-working and happy souls immersed in the fascinating complexities of active investment management might well wonder, Are we and our industry-wide compensation in a great global bubble of our own creation? Does a specter of declining fees haunt our industry's future? I believe it does, particularly for those who continue to define their mission as beat-the-market performance.

Source: Charles D. Ellis (2012) Investment Management Fees Are (Much) Higher Than You Think, *Financial Analysts Journal*, 68:3, 4–6, copyright © CFA Institute reprinted by permission of Taylor & Francis Ltd, http://www.tandfonline.com on behalf of CFA Institute.

23

Computer People May Be Planning a Revolution

While both culture and structure clearly subordinated computer "techies" to investment professionals in every investment organization when this piece was written over 50 years ago, it was possible to ponder a revolution even though the term Artificial Intelligence had only just been coined.

C.P. Snow found this some years ago and wrote about it in his book, The Two Cultures: and a Second Look, *from which came: "There have been plenty of days when I have spent working hours with scientists and then gone off at night with some literary colleagues . . . It was through living among both of these groups—and much more, I think, through moving regularly from one to the other and back again—that I got occupied with the problem of the 'two cultures.'"*

There's been a lot of fancy talk over the years about the tremendous impact computers were going to have on the investment management business. The fruits of multimillion dollar investments by senior executives at banks, brokers, mutual funds, and the like would be harvested and the rewards would be abundant.

Maybe so. But what's holding it all up is the fact that Computer People and Investment People usually don't work well together.

They may well be employed by the same companies and go to the same office buildings, but they don't work together. This is particularly true among the nation's investment institutions where Computer People and Investment People work on very different kinds of problems, have wholly different ways of defining what they are trying to accomplish, and go about their work almost oblivious to their economic coexistence.

Computer People develop sophisticated programs to identify any repetitive patterns of behavior in stock prices and offer elaborate and extensive testing of many hypothetical patterns. They conclude that the stock market is like a random walk. Prices have no pattern. Nothing that is past is predictive of future prices. Meanwhile, Investment People draw lines with oyster forks on the damask tablecloths at Oscar's to show themselves why Wigitronics looks like a breakout on the upside.

Computer People develop models to measure the real diversification in stock portfolios and graph on N-dimensional space the optimum mix of a particular group of stocks while Investment People tell one another: "You've got a good list" and a senior trust officer—axiomatically not a CP—admits to a pal that he had always thought Markowitz was a left-wing political columnist syndicated by the *Washington Post*.

CPs prove to their satisfaction that pershare earnings estimates have bimodal distributions and that their sample means do not meet the test of doing unbiased estimates, while IPs discourse with considerable erudition about the sociology of Avon Ladies and what a change in the selling cycle means for earnings in 1972.

Not only are they working in completely different worlds and with incompatible methods, when they do come together to work cooperatively on a problem, they speak different languages. The IPs will ask: "What stocks should we be buying?" And the CPs will answer in equations full of sigmas and primes and figure eights lying on their sides. In other words and terms, they are not all together. The IPs do not use what the Computer People do and the CPs do not do what the IPs can use. And they don't seem to care. In fact, they seem just as happy that they don't have to work together because they really don't want to work together.

As a result, Computer People have not had much impact on Wall Street. On the other hand, this unhappy experience is not really unique. For instance, here is a comment on the tangible results of six years of publishing articles in *Operations Research* magazine by C.W. Churchman in the *California Review* in 1964: "In no case was there sufficient evidence that the recommendations derived from O.R. projects were . . . carried out by management."

Certainly, the companies in the investment business are spending an awful lot of money on computers and computer people and the top people all talk about the future role of computers. And annual reports always show the newest computers. Why then don't the Investment People make more use of computers? The basic reason for this pervasive failure to use is that Investment People and Computer People come from two very different cultures. They are strangers to each other.

Optimists and skeptics will say it is nonsense to claim that Investment People do not and will not take full advantage of the concepts, techniques, programs and skills of Computer People. Yet those who believe this simply do not understand how truly different IPs and CPs really are. I am no anthropologist, but here are some of the more obvious differences which I have observed:

- CPs wear ties that are gray or gray-blue or gray-green or brown and have subtle patterns woven into the fabric or have a single decorative figure near the bottom and a Countess Mara label. IPs wear regimentals from Brooks Brothers, block prints or madras; IPs do not use double Windsor knots.
- CPs wear white shirts and blue shirts. IPs wear stripes, yellows, and occasional pinks; theirs button down.
- CPs studied mechanical engineering at Penn State or RPI. IPs took English Lit at Brown.
- IPs went to graduate school at Harvard, U.Va. and Stanford CPs went to MIT and Carnegie Tech.
- CPs live in New Jersey or Brooklyn; IPs live in Connecticut or Manhattan.
- IPs eat at expensive restaurants for lunch and are gaining weight. CPs do not and are not; they assume the Lunch Club is a generic term.
- IPs have friends and relatives "in the business" ahead of them. CPs make their friends after joining.
- IP offices are carpeted; CP offices are linoleum tiled.
- IPs are still Republicans; CPs are Independents or Democrats.
- IPs are best at ages between 40 and 60; CPs are best between 28 and 35.
- CPs are smarter. IPs wear longer and darker socks.
- CPs talk shop in sober and earnest tones; they are supportive in a professional-toprofessional sort of way. IPs like to gossip and only talk shop if they believe they will be amusing. Both groups like to knock the other.

- CPs drink Perfect Manhattans; IPs drink Negronis.
- CPs wear brown suits; IPs do not.

While not all my observations may jibe with yours, it is safe to conclude that noncommunication and cultural alienation have so far resulted in a social standoff that gives the false appearance of stability in the situation. Such is not the case. The technology of computer hardware and the techniques of advanced programming are being applied with increasing effectiveness both at the institutions of higher finance and at institutions of higher learning.

While Investment People are standing pat (and providing a fixed target), Computer People are doing three things to achieve ultimate primacy. First, they are systematically testing the statistical validity of every proposition that IPs have put forth to explain why they do what they do. So far, although only a few have been completely tested, no IP theory has survived the full testing process. So, CPs are learning what most of IPs do that doesn't make sense.

Second, the CPs are analyzing the actual results achieved over the years by IPs and have developed some very powerful; albeit preliminary, evidence that despite all their marvelous role-playing and their elaborate dramas and their dedicated efforts to make money for their clients, the Investment People as a group *and* individually have failed to contribute much of anything to higher profits. In other words, what IPs do doesn't work over the long term.

Third, some CPs are trying to develop entirely new approaches to solving the investment management problem. They talk quietly and earnestly together as revolutionaries always seem to do just before their movements really get going. They concede that the investment problem will not be easy to solve, but then note that it is not as difficult as a moon landing or a missile defense system. And they have plenty of time.

Computer People are beginning to be quite confident that, with time, they will succeed in their collective efforts to understand the stock market and that their programs will truly revolutionize the investment management field. Investment People maintain that this is surely not realistic, but they are beginning to be less and less confident that they can safely ignore the rumblings from below. And once in a while they ponder privately: "What would happen if one of those guys actually got a computer program that worked? Like, what would happen to all of *us*?"

Source: *Institutional Investor*, December, 1970.

24

Characteristics of Successful Investment Firms

Few topics are as interesting to most investment professionals as how best to organize an investment organization. Yet over the long term, most investment firms, despite their best intentions and good efforts, do not achieve superior results for their clients. They don't even keep up with market indexes. One reason is the cost of operations. Another reason is high fees. For individuals, another is taxes. But, the main reason appears to be the superb quality of the competition and the great "equalizer" because almost all institutional market participants have equally superb computer power, Bloomberg terminals, internet access and equally capable investment managers and almost everyone knows almost all the same information at the very same time.

It should, in theory, be quite easy to develop a first-rate professional firm. We all know the recipe. Get top people. Have a clear purpose. Have high professional standards. Take a long-term view. Always remember that clients come ahead of the firm. Always remember that the firm comes ahead of the individual. And always remember that as an individual, professional commitments come ahead of the financial rewards. Maintain discipline at all times, and you shall succeed. Or as Mr. Morgan put it, "Run a first-class business in a first-class way."

The recipe is the same one for successful management that Marvin Bower of McKinsey & Co. wrote about in his book, *The Will to Manage*. The title says it all. There wasn't anything unusual about what the management of any really good company was doing. They had the same recipe every other management had, *but they were doing it*. That made all the difference.

David Ogilvy has written a third book, *Ogilvy on Advertising*. It's fun to read, has lots of pictures—and a good deal of real insight. He discusses five great advertising agencies and comes to the conclusion that the principal factor required for success was and is persistence.

One of the problems with identifying great and successful investment management firms is that most organizations doing very well now will not still be doing very well 10 years from now. Most of the organizations we admired most 10 years ago are *not* those we would put on our shortest list of the great successful firms today. There is nothing quite so temporary as success in an intense, dynamic, "people" business like ours.

Professional Business Goals Conflict

Many observers believe there is a basic conflict between the professional goals and the business goals of an investment management organization, and that these two spheres work against each other. There's no doubt that they will be in direct conflict if either is mediocre. Any semi-good professional commitment or semi-good business goal will sooner or later corrode any organization.

But there is no conflict between really good business goals and really good professional goals if each strives for excellence and if the respect for both is sufficient. For example, it is only business strength that gives professionals the independence of mind and sureness of purpose that allow them to do first-rate professional work. Only professional independence is likely to result in the really good work that is needed to make a really good business. There is no conflict as long as each is truly strong. Most organizations, however, find it very hard to achieve and sustain excellence in both areas, a matter that requires attention. The culture or the climate of the organization must always favor the professional dimension. When in doubt, lean toward the professional side because there must be that kind of favoritism.

The Importance of Strategic Considerations

Fees are one of the most powerful forces in the success or failure of an investment management organization. The fee level you set determines the market you will serve. Once you have chosen the market you will serve—which you do indirectly when setting your fees—you can then identify the key factors for success and the rules of the game in that particular market.

In strategy, clarity and simplicity are critical. Most organizations are uncomfortable identifying what they will not do. It is not what you are willing to do, but what you will not do that most clearly defines who you really are. Peter Drucker has a lot to say on this. It can be easily summarized. Focus your attention on areas of excellence; as professionals, do those things that you do quite well and try not to waste time doing the other things in which you are only moderately good. The external focus should be on the major opportunities.

Identifying the Big Decisions

In the formation of business strategy, many organizations fail to recognize that it is a completely different line of work from their investment management activity or their routine business administration. Go to a different environment—in a different timeframe—taking two or three days away from your offices and clearly separated from your regular work. Otherwise, the time-urgent decisions will drain away the time you might have had for those things that might be more important.

We never take too much, or even sufficient, time for the big decisions: those soft, subtle, avoidable decisions on basic policy and strategy that can and will lead to very hard decisions later on if they are not attended to when "soft." The "soft" decisions are not easy. They are difficult because they are of basic value: the selection of young people and the training, coaching; the trust put in them; decisions on which areas of development to give special emphasis; on the quality of the commitment you will make to your clients. It is in these areas of "softness" that the really important decisions will be made, and they cannot be made wisely and well in the press of daily activity.

Strategy formation is not planning. Planning is a *negative* function in the sense that its whole intention is to eliminate errors, reduce uncertainty, and avoid mistakes. If we were so good that we could plan the right things two or three years ahead, wouldn't we simply do them now? Firms that are successful understand the value of a planning discipline, but it's a discipline against negatives.

Our People and Our Communications

The most important part of a very successful organization is first-rate, high-caliber people. However, most of us do not give enough time and attention to selecting or developing the truly first-rate young people in our organizations. It is difficult to give them the environment they need and the attention they want. First-rate people are so wonderfully rare that if we find them and bring them into our organizations, we should give them everything they need to flourish.

Successful firms have a tremendous consistency on basic values. The "really interesting" discussions seldom take place—because they are not needed. The organization that has deep agreement on the most important philosophical matters does not have "interesting" crisis discussions. The best firms have a consistent set of core values with a wonderful diversity of experience and orientation, ways of thinking and articulating, and personalities—all with deep mutual respect. It is out of that kind of common weal that an aristocracy of talent is likely to come forth.

The matter of size and market liquidity is a false issue for most investment management organizations. There are some for which it would be right to say that market considerations would put constraints on their ability to manage money. But most investment management organizations are not constrained externally. They are constrained, instead, by their internal difficulties, largely their difficulties of communication.

Consider, for a moment, the German U-boat fleet, which in the early part of the Second World War was dreadfully successful. Much as the American-British navies would like to say that they defeated the U-boats, the reality is that the U-boats defeated themselves. The reason is that the U-boat command was in Berlin. The original concept was that all U-boats would look for cargo ships, and if they found a ship they would radio back to Berlin, and Berlin would decide where every U-boat should go. When Germany had only 50 or 60 U-boats, that system worked well. When they got to 400 or 500 U-boats, the deluge of data piling in on Berlin so exceeded Berlin's capacity to process and organize the data that headquarters' decision-making could not keep up with the demand.

This same problem of data overload is characteristic of investment management firms that are in trouble. The enormous volume of data can overwhelm decision making and make it seem impossible to find time to think. Successful firms protect their decision makers from the tyranny of data and find ways to control the flow of information coming into their organizations. They make sure that the research is working for them—not the other way around. It does no good to "play the horse to someone else's Lady Godiva."

For internal communication, the great problem is adding people. As you add people arithmetically, their relationships go up geometrically. There is a rapid progression toward decisions that are social or political, rather than objective and fact-founded; decisions that are made with inadequate reflection because so much time is spent talking. Direct, simple, short lines of communication are wonderfully powerful. One of the great organizations in the history of the world, the Catholic Church, has only four levels of communication between God and the average parishioner. That's a model communication system. The closer we get to simple, clear, direct communication, the greater our chances to succeed.

Getting Bigger vs. Getting Better

Growth and expansion are entirely different from one another—even though in the investment field, we tend to talk about expansion as though it were growth. Expansion is getting bigger. Growth is getting better. Doing more difficult, more valuable things—often for more substantial and demanding clients.

The great enemy of growth is expansion. Peter Drucker, once again, says that the easiest way to get first-rate resources that can be put to work on first-rate opportunities is to stop doing things you don't do particularly well and devote the liberated resources to things with which you could succeed greatly.

Getting bigger almost necessarily means that you will have fewer wonderful people joining your organization in larger numbers. It almost necessarily means that you will be doing more things for more customers. As you expand the volume of work, there is a grim tendency to enter lines of work that are less value-adding and to serve smaller clients. As the margin of value-added declines, so does the margin of profit—but both are hidden in the short run by expansion's increase in total profits. Expansion is almost always linked to a decline in quality offset by a rise in quantity.

Tenure, Turnover, and Structure

Optimizing the balance between common commitment and diversity recommends average tenure of professionals of six and seven years. If it is less than that, people won't know each other well enough to work together most effectively. Beyond six and seven years, they'll know each other all too well and so be tempted stop listening carefully.

The great silent enemy of vibrant, effective strategy is structure. The strategy, created to meet a market's requirement, needs a structure for implementation. As soon as the structure is in place, however, it strives to wrest control of the organization away from strategy. Structure, over time, almost always wins. Structure resists change if it possibly can. It holds on to the familiar past and keeps us from advancing toward our future with a bold, contemporary strategy.

Beware the normal tendency toward the "Peter Principle." Don't take your best investment manager and make him a not-very-good organization manager. Keep the best investment achievers, if you are lucky enough to have them, free to invest. Try to make it possible for them to invest 100% of the time. There are many more good general managers than there are good investment managers. The basic talents that lead to great success in an investment manager are not likely to lead to great success in an *organization* manager.

Compensation Now and Later

Compensation is the great driving force in any organization's strategy. It is not just the financial compensation that's important; and, most particularly, it's not the current dollar compensation.

Do you have distributive justice? If everybody knew exactly what everybody was being paid, would it make good sense to them? The best test of that is one every organization ought seriously to consider: total disclosure of compensation policy. Fair play is the essential factor in compensation. Without fair play, no organization will be successful for long.

Beyond current compensation, there is a looming problem for the most successful of the independent investment management firms. In many of these firms, a great confrontation will come between three generational groups. One group will say, "We started this firm. We were here when there was almost no one here. We did the first pieces of business. We took all the risks. It should be ours." The next group will say,

"The first arrivals may have started this company, but it wasn't much of an organization or much or a business when we first got here. We are the ones who brought in the really big accounts. We are the ones that made the really important strategy moves. We are the ones that made it a really successful business, so it should be ours." And the third generation will say, "We are the future. We are moving into more and more client relationships. If you lose us, the future will be rough. The firm should be ours." Usually, those "generations" will not be more than 10–15 years apart.

Stature, respect, and recognized importance are vital aspects of compensation. There certainly ought to be no one in the investment management business inadequately compensated today. The pay is, frankly, spectacular. The prospects are even more charming. But there are people who will be unhappy because they are not treated with the respect as professionals that they are entitled to. In successful organizations there is a high level, even a surplus, of respect, recognition, and admiration among the professionals and collective pride in the organization and its commitment to professional excellence in serving clients.

The Power of Good Ideas and Good Clients

Knowledge is not a constant. Insight is certainly not a constant. Big ideas of real value seldom come along. The best investment management organizations seem to be good at pausing to see those good ideas and exploiting them.

An important dimension of successful investment management organizations—true of great organizations in many fields—is having great clients. If you have clients you do not enjoy or admire, or clients that do not expect much of you, you should seriously consider terminating your relationships with them. They will hold you back. If you have great clients, reach out to them, and ask them to demand even more of you, to challenge you to be the very best you can be.

Appraising "Success"

What makes for successful firms? Business success in investment management is not hard to come by. Fees are high. Costs are relatively modest. Technological risks are minimal. Foreign competition is not consequential. Growth comes easily. Customers are unusually loyal.

Competition is docile. Demand exceeds supply. It's a wonderfully easy place to have a business success.

In terms of professional success, however, I would ask some questions.

First, how many of the really important developments in investment management have come from within—from within your own organization or from within our profession—as opposed to coming from outside?

Have we, as a profession, truly contributed to our national society? Have we added net value? I confess to having some genuine doubts. If you took all the fees paid to all the investment managers, added up all the transaction costs incurred by these managers, and then compared the total to the risk adjusted incremental returns of the portfolios, which would be larger?

Have we truly advanced young people in their professional development? Have we succeeded in educating our clients, particularly with regard to the importance of setting long-term policies on asset mix and risk levels? Have we taught them how to avoid market timing? I suspect that, on those dimensions of professional success, we're not yet very successful. In the long run, however, satisfying the real and legitimate needs of clients will be the best part of our professional success.

Leadership is the final characteristic of successful firms. To become excellent, a firm needs strong leadership—not an individual, but ideally a group of leaders committed to concept of how to deliver real value and glad to make the time needed to pursue that idea with great and substantial vigor.

25

A New Paradigm of Investment Management

The managerial disciplines required to achieve organizational success—recruiting and rigorously training the most capable people, developing a strong culture centered on serving clients unusually well, etc.—have, in recent decades, been increasingly subordinated to the discipline of a specific kind of investing—growth versus value, etc. serving one kind of client: institutions vs individuals. Actually, organizational excellence can accommodate more than one investment specialty and enables an investment organization to serve major clients better over the long term.

A new paradigm is developing in investment management—a new organizational and "management" paradigm—that has the competitive strength to dominate the investment management business and the practice of the investment profession. The new paradigm is remarkably different from the paradigm that has, over the last quarter century, became the accepted and dominant norm in the field.

The presently dominant paradigm is a specialist manager with one investment "product" serving one market, usually pension funds. The developing new paradigm is a multimarket, multiproduct organization.

My thesis is that because the new multimarket, multiproduct organization—when properly led and managed—is more consistently capable of meeting the long-term needs of clients and investment professionals, it will be increasingly accepted and will become the norm. In fact, the evidence suggests the Darwinian process of one species displacing another—because it is even better matched to the situation—is progressing very rapidly now.

The Past

To put the current situation in perspective, recall the situation 50 years ago. It was simple: Insurance companies and insured plans dominated pension fund investing through the 1940s.

In the 1950s, with the proliferation of corporate pension funds symbolized by General Motors' agreements with the UAW to set up a separate fund and to provide "fringe" benefits during the Korean War price freeze, a new paradigm moved into ascendance—the large bank trust departments offering a narrow product line: balanced accounts. But their offering included a crucial difference: Equities could be 30% or even 40% of total assets, far greater than the 5% limit of the insurance companies. And in the postwar bull market, being in equities made all the difference.

By the mid-1960s, two key changes in the situation were increasingly significant. Pension fund assets had become quite large and having so much money with one manager was questionable. In addition, performance was being measured and compared, and some of the largest bank trust departments were seen to be underperforming another type of manager—investment counselors that explicitly sought "performance."

Five more changes were increasingly evident through the 1970s and into the 1980s. First, plan sponsors split up their funds among more and more investment managers in part because they sought specialist managers and in part because many of the most promising specialist managers were small, relatively new firms. The multimanager concept of pension fund investing further encouraged the formation of specialist managers.

Second, plan sponsors were clearly willing to pay higher fees to get the "performance" managers they believed could obtain higher rates of return that would more than cover the cost of higher fees. Third, investment managers learned that they could win substantially more business by engaging boldly in vigorous direct selling—and so they did. Fourth, the institutional brokerage industry developed considerable capabilities in research and the execution of block trades to meet the needs of "performance" managers. Finally, assets continued to grow, and more and more pension plans and endowments organized themselves to "manage the managers"—particularly, to be buyers that could meet the sellers of investment services and make a market.

And what a market it was, particularly for the specialist investment managers. They became so notoriously successful that the trust departments and the insurance companies abandoned their traditional organizational structures so they could try to replicate the new paradigm that is so familiar to us all—a group of experienced portfolio managers in their forties with strong analytical backgrounds, engaging personalities, high energy levels and considerable skill, who strive to achieve superior performance as a creative team, manage portfolios actively, seek to develop close professional relationships with clients, and are skillful in both direct selling and in working with consultants. They earn substantial compensation as individuals, charge high fees as firms, are exciting to be with, and have fun. They met the market on its own terms—and have proliferated.

The 1980s extended the developments of the 1970s. Asset classification became increasingly important. Manager classification became increasingly important. You were either a value manager or you were not; you were a growth manager or you were not; you were a sector rotator or you were not. You had to pick one and stay there. Product proliferation began, and the different kinds of specialization that investment managers might undertake multiplied.

One solution to the problem of proliferating managers was the emergence of a completely new industry: "consulting." At least 50 consultants now intermediate between plan sponsors and investment managers, trying to solve the problem of proliferating asset classification, proliferating managers, and product proliferation.

The Future

Managers are classified according to an ever-expanding set of specific categories. A manager is either a value manager or a growth manager and, within each of those categories, a large-capitalization, or a small-capitalization manager. He is a passive, quantitative or an active manager. He may operate with or without "technology." A global or international manager can concentrate on the Pacific Rim, on Europe or Latin America, on the emerging markets globally, or on any specific part of the world with or without currency overlays.

On the bond side of the business, a manager is immunized or dedicated, structured, or indexed or index-plussed. He could have GICs or BICs; be in the high-yield sector, with or without credit evaluations; deal with private placements or the extended market; avoid or concentrate in mortgages and asset-backed securities of all kinds. A bond manager could be international or global, with or without currency overrides; have a STIF or a medium-term note portfolio; be involved in bank loan packaging or convertibles, sector switching, arbitrage, constant yield, constant duration, and so on.

From the investment manager's point of view, the world is not particularly simple either. The large, medium, and small institutional funds have fundamentally different characteristics. Public funds are tremendously different from corporate funds, and endowment funds are different from both. The 401(k) plans are growing rapidly and have fundamentally changed the terms of the competition. Nuclear decommissioning could be an important market. Insurance companies are becoming interesting and, of course, there are large numbers of different kinds of offshore funds. The United Kingdom, Japan, Germany and Canada—each an important market opportunity for American managers—are very different from each other and from the American market.

All the complexity on the investment manager's side and all the complexity on the client's side are beyond the capacity of most of us. Some new way of being organized is needed, one that has the capacity to deal in many different markets. It must be effective for the client, and it must be productive for the investment manager. It must be capable of dealing successfully with multiple products. And it must be a multimarket organization, so it can access business from many sources.

The new form of organization must be reliable and sustainable both for the client and for the manager. It must allow individuals of considerable talent and pools of capital of large size to make long-term commitments such as the structure shown in Figure 25.1. The stars represent investment management capabilities, which can be defined as "products." Each is carefully, rigorously defined as to concept, specifications, and performance. The circles represent markets to which the organization sells its product capabilities. The interior space between products and markets will be dominated by superior capabilities in relationship management and development with particularly strong professional investment counseling—problem delineation and problem solving—servicing the specific needs of specific clients.

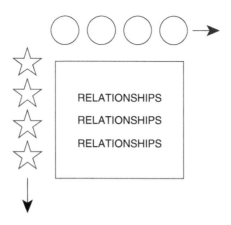

Figure 25.1 The New Paradigm

This multimarket, multiproduct investment management organization meets several needs of major clients: product specification and product conformance, product innovation to meet new needs or exploit new opportunities, the confidence and convenience that go with long-term professional relationships, possibly lower costs, and relationships that are "client-driven" rather than "product- driven." And this organization better meets the needs of many investment managers, for professional growth and creativity and financial security at high pay levels without betting their business careers as well as their professional reputations on a single way of investing in a single asset class.

These organizations can afford to invest in acquiring increasingly costly and essential systems, developing new products, and developing new markets—and they will. And as product specialization and market segmentation proliferate, an increasingly large share of new products and new markets will be developed by the organizations that master the new paradigm. In fact, these new organizations are already dominating new product development and new market development.

Three concluding observations seem important. First, the new paradigm will not overwhelm all the boutiques. The best specialist firms will continue to prosper—but it will be more and more important to be very, very good. Second, not all of the multiproduct, multimarket organizations will be assured of success. Only those that produce consistent product quality and service quality will succeed.

Finally, the new paradigm is certainly not "just" a return to the old "balanced manager." The old paradigm trust department or insured plan couldn't come close to competing with the new paradigm organization.

The new paradigm organization is profoundly different on every important variable: leading-edge investment innovation, strong client-centered
relationships, devotion to product excellence in design and conformance
in execution, strong business development, and exceptionally rewarding
careers for gifted, motivated professionals, with business strength the
foundation for professional excellence.

Source: Charles D. Ellis (1992) A New Paradigm of Investment
Management *Financial Analysts Journal*, 31: 2, 16–18, copyright © CFA
Institute reprinted by permission of Taylor & Francis Ltd, http://www.
tandfonline.com on behalf of CFA Institute.

26

Lessons on Grand Strategy

At Yale University, one of the most popular and most demanding courses—Grand Strategy—asks students to examine each of the major dimensions—military, political, social, technological, and economic—aspects of national strategy that combine into an overall strategy for each nation. Leaders of major investment organizations are comparably challenged to develop the best Grand Strategy for their organizations. It's not easy.

Grand Strategy, whereby all aspects of a nation's strength—military, economic, political, cultural, and organizational—are combined into an overall, long-term program to advance a nation's major interests, has important lessons for all leaders of investment management organizations. For long-term success, such leaders need a coherent, integrated combination of an inspiring purpose or mission and superior recruiting and training of investment managers who will excel in information technology, trading, risk controls, efficient and effective support operations, business development, customer service, and both research and portfolio management.

Given the multiple dimensions on which investment organizations compete and seek to excel, the present and future leaders of the world's many investment organizations would not be surprised to find that history's masters of Grand Strategy—Clausewitz, Sun Tzu, and Mahan—all have important lessons in leadership to share with the leaders of contemporary investment management firms.

Carl von Clausewitz understood the frustrating importance of the multiple uncertainties in his field, just as investors understand the frustrating uncertainties in their field. As he wrote in his great book, *On War*.[1] "War is the realm of uncertainty; three quarters of the facts on which action in war is based are wrapped in a fog of greater or lesser uncertainty . . . War is the realm of chance." And every experienced investor would appreciate the importance he attached to that proposition even if not agreeing to leave out investing, as Clausewitz did when he declared "no other field has such incessant and varied dealings with this intruder."

Clausewitz's observation that "everything is uncertain and calculations have to be made with variable quantities" must sound dreadfully similar to the views now held—180 years later—by most contemporary investors as they ponder the many variables in each of their investments. Still, although contemporary investors would appreciate his meaning when comparing his wars to their own dynamic world of work, they might differ with Clausewitz on his assertion about war that "no other human activity is so continuously bound up with chance." But every portfolio manager would say amen to Clausewitz's statement that "continual change and the need to respond to it compel the commander to carry the whole intellectual apparatus of his knowledge within him. He must always be ready to bring forth the appropriate decision."

Both portfolio managers and research analysts lament the many unexpected and unpredictable minor factors that can cause disappointment, particularly when their results fall short of their expectations. Similarly, as Clausewitz observed, "Countless minor incidents of the kind one can never foresee combine to lower the general level of performance, so that one always falls short of the intended goal."

"Tactics and strategy are two activities that permeate one another in time and space, but are nonetheless essentially different," said Clausewitz. "Their inherent laws and mutual relationship cannot be understood without a total comprehension of both." And so it is in portfolio management as macro investment policy and portfolio strategy intersect with micro tactical actions in managing every portfolio all the time.

---

[1] The standard translation today is the indexed edition, edited and translated by Michael Howard and Peter Paret (Princeton, NJ: Princeton University Press, 1989).

Clausewitz's famous dictum that "war is the continuation of [political] policy by other means" can easily be translated by investment professionals into a comparably central proposition: "Investing is the continuation of an investor's overall financial strategy by other means." Great investment success depends on understanding each particular investor's objectives and overall financial situation with respect to resources, income, spending, time horizon, and risk tolerance.

For Clausewitz, as for most professional investors, the role of theory was to help the serious practitioner understand and take advantage of the evidence of history. Clausewitz defined the term genius in the military as a mix of originality and creativity raised to the highest power, which is close to the admiring way we use the term today when describing repeatedly outstanding investors.

"Investing is simple—but not easy," warns Warren Buffett, and Clausewitz said much the same thing: "Everything in war is very simple, but the simplest thing is difficult." Clausewitz concluded his description of whether war is more art than science—anticipating today's running dialogue about art versus science in investing—by saying that the term *art of war* was more suitable than *science of war* because success in war so often depends on creativity. Even as quantitative techniques, increasingly efficient markets, and indexing gain stature, active investment managers still make a similar argument in favor of art over science in investing and emphasize the importance of creativity to great investment success.

Reflecting on their own field of endeavor, professional investors would surely agree with Clausewitz as he reflected on this:

War is no pastime; it is no mere joy in daring and winning; no place for irresponsible enthusiasts. It is a serious means to a serious end, and all its colorful resemblances to a game of chance, all the vicissitudes of passion, courage, imagination, and enthusiasm it includes are merely its special characteristics.

Experienced investors always try to separate having the courage of one's convictions from just being stubborn. Similarly, Clausewitz feared the distortion of strong character into simplistic obstinacy:

"Obstinacy is a fault of temperament. Stubbornness and intolerance of contradiction result from a special kind of egotism which elevates [itself] above everything else [and] to which others must bow."

"Friction, as we choose to call it," said Clausewitz, "is the force that makes the apparently easy thing difficult." The institutional investor with experience in trading might respond, "If I could execute all my orders instantly and without cost, my results would be better too!"

Centuries before Clausewitz developed his strategic concepts, the great Chinese general Sun Tzu memorably declared in his seminal work, *The Art of War*, "The supreme art of war is to achieve important objectives without fighting."[2] As Sun Tzu also said, "The skillful commander takes up a position so he cannot be defeated. Thus, a victorious army wins its victories before the battle." Likewise, today's best investment strategists deploy their portfolios in ways that will achieve superior long-term results and can withstand the severe interim tests of disruptive markets without the need to depend on clever portfolio tactics.

Sun Tzu said, "Skillful warriors first make themselves invincible. Invincibility lies in the defense; the only possibility of victory [lies] in the attack." Similarly, skillful institutional investors make it a top priority to structure a robust portfolio that can withstand the stresses and strains of contemporary market disruptions.

Investors might see trading as the equivalent of fighting. Both activities involve battling for competitive advantage in the struggle to achieve superiority, but an ideal investment would be held forever with no trading or battle for advantage. As Sun Tzu said, "When those experienced in war move, they make no mistakes. Therefore, I say: Know yourself and know your enemy, and your victory will never be endangered." Likewise, the best investment managers study to understand themselves; their skills and weaknesses and where they have comparative limits or advantages; their clients' objectives; and their competitors. In this way, they reduce the costs and distractions of excessive portfolio change or turnover and avoid the mistakes that so often come from reacting to others instead of following their own well-conceived strategies.

Avoiding the costs and distractions of tactics—fighting specific battles—explained Sun Tzu, enables the wise military leader to concentrate on defining priorities and pursuing wise strategies to achieve long-term military-political objectives. Similarly, avoiding the costs, mistakes, and distractions of trading in a portfolio of 60–80 stocks with 100% turnover, which involves several hundred decisions—some to buy, some to sell, many not to buy, many not to sell—being made every year, the fewer the number of decisions, the more an investor could focus instead

---

[2]The popular 1910 translation by Lionel Giles was recently reprinted (New Orleans: Megalodon Entertainment, 2010).

on major policy decisions.[3] The best investors have low turnover in part because they have a superior understanding of the long-term investment value of each position and are thus less affected by interim changes in market price.

Sun Tzu recognized how difficult it can be for a general who has deployed his troops and made commitments to his senior officers and his ruler to change his battle plans as combat circumstances change. What portfolio manager has not found the same kind of difficulty in explaining to supervisors, colleagues, or clients a major portfolio restructuring only a few months after explaining, with some conviction, the superior investment logic of the prior portfolio?

Technology, then as now, can change the nature of the contest. In Sun Tzu's time, technology offered weapons of high-grade iron that could hold a sharp cutting edge, as well as the crossbow, which fired heavy arrows long distances. These new weapons brought compelling change. Today, derivatives, the Internet, Bloomberg terminals, and computers bring change to investment management. In our era, as in Sun Tzu's, change can produce serious consequences for those unable to understand how to take advantage of that change.

Alfred Thayer Mahan[4]—through his monumental text, *The Influence of Sea Power upon History*,[5] and through his personal friendships with Theodore Roosevelt[6] and Senator Henry Cabot Lodge—became the world's most influential naval strategist. Mahan's principles of naval strategy came to dominate the policies and strategies of all the leading nations' navies, much as Warren Buffett's and David Swensen's principles have come to dominate institutional investors' portfolio strategies today.[7] Contemporary investment strategists can profit from studying the lessons of Captain (later Admiral) Mahan and the reasoning behind them.

---

[3]One of Sun Tzu's more recent students was Mao Tse-tung, who studied his own failures far more than his successes—a practice that investors might find beneficial if they would take the time.

[4]Just as contemporary investment managers are often celebrated royally, Mahan dined with Queen Victoria and the prime minister and received honorary degrees from both the University of Oxford and the University of Cambridge when he visited England in 1893–1894.

[5]A.T. Mahan, *The Influence of Sea Power upon History: 1660–1783* (Boston: Little, Brown and Company, 1890).

[6]Mahan had long advocated building the Panama Canal and having a navy indisputably strong enough to protect it; Roosevelt joined the campaign while Assistant Secretary of the Navy and put it into action as president.

[7]Mahan acknowledged his intellectual debt to Jomini, just as Buffett and Swensen would acknowledge Keynes and Graham.

A navy is by nature an attacking arm, and so is an investment portfolio. There is no hiding place on the open seas or in the stock and bond markets. Thus, a leader in either realm must accept the sea and weather or the market as they are and always be thinking about the offense. Mahan advocated concentration of forces, just as active investment managers advocate concentrating an investment portfolio on a few dominating concepts or themes. But the creative offense in investing needs a strong defensive base. Sun Tzu emphasized the importance of taking a readily defendable position, and Mahan's first dictum was always to maintain a "shield of defensive power." Wise investors appreciate how important it is, as a first priority, to establish a vigorous defense that is assertive, not "defensive." Only with a robustly defendable portfolio structure can an investor hold on for the long term despite the inevitable major disruptions when market prices seem to go crazy.

Just as portfolio managers treasure close communication with expert analysts, Mahan was clear about the importance of good connections between supplies and the forces that depend on them and saw communication between units as "the most important single element in strategy."

Mahan, quite unintentionally, provided another lesson for today's investment managers. By not recognizing the power shift driven by phenomenal improvements in the number and quality of railroads which reduced the primacy of seaborne movement, Mahan missed a major and transformative change. He also failed to anticipate that such synthetics as rubber, fiber, and plastics—which can be made anywhere—would change trade patterns and make naval blockades far less confining.

Similarly, portfolio managers have had to look sharply for such changes as globalization, derivatives, and the overwhelming dominance of markets by professional investors—and the shift from defined benefit to defined contribution retirement plans and the accelerating acceptance of index funds and exchange-traded funds—to protect themselves from the classic problem of history's admirals and generals: fighting the last war.

Source: Charles D. Ellis (2013) Lessons on Grand Strategy, *Financial Analysts Journal*, 69:4, 6–9, copyright © CFA Institute reprinted by permission of Taylor & Francis Ltd, http://www.tandfonline.com on behalf of CFA Institute.

27

Pension Funds Need MORE Management MANAGEMENT

Retirement plan sponsors abdicated most policy decisions to investment managers over 40 years ago. In too many cases they get the "same old" Procrustean policies. As clients, endowments and pension sponsors have had important contributions to make and should have asserted them because each individual or institution investor is different from others, so their investment policies should be different, too.

With so very much at stake, the apparent modesty of senior executive time and attention devoted to the strategic management of employee benefit fund assets and liabilities—even at large and sophisticated corporations—is disturbing. Recent comprehensive research shows that corporate pension executives delegate most of the responsibility for both asset management policy and portfolio operations to investment managers. The wisdom of this conventional practice deserves searching re-examination, particularly in view of the massive amount of money involved.

In terms of both assets and contributions, employee benefit funds are becoming increasingly important in corporate finance. Employee benefit fund assets of large corporations now total more than $200 billion, including about $160 billion in pension funds, $26 billion in savings and

**Table 27.1 Corporations Delegate Broad Policy Discretion
to Investment Managers**

Policies and practices	Company specifies policies (%)	Company provides guidelines (%)	Manager has full discretion (%)
Amount invested in real estate	54	3	21
Amount invested in foreign securities	46	8	30
Amount invested in private placements	10	32	32
Ratio of stocks to bonds	38	25	29
Maximum amount invested in any one security	26	8	47
Minimum quality ratings for bonds	22	27	44
Maximum amount invested in any one industry	20	20	55
Minimum total rate of return	16	39	36
Minimum income that must be earned on portfolio	11	33	45
Diversification of equity portfolio	7	24	61
Short-term cash reserves	7	25	61
Volatility or "beta" of equity portfolio	6	23	61

thrift plans and $16 billion in profit sharing plans. Another $74 billion of pension obligations are not yet funded, although 38% of this amount represents already vested benefits.

To put these gargantuan sums into perspective, consider that total pension obligations of large corporations equal 32% of stockholders' equity; and annual employee benefit plan contributions averaged 20% of corporate profits in 1977—up from only 5% in 1950, 11% in 1960 and 17% in 1970. Not only are the amounts large, they are different. They represent a new financial phenomenon—*growth liabilities*. Pension fund assets, contributions, and obligations continue to grow more rapidly than the companies that sponsor them.

ERISA vests the primary fiduciary responsibility for managing these assets in the corporation sponsoring the plan. Yet, over 60% of the 1,000 companies surveyed by Greenwich Associates delegate to managers policy control over such basic dimensions as cash reserves, equity portfolio diversification, portfolio turnover, and bond maturity schedules (see Table 27.1).[1] And the trend is toward more delegation of these basic

[1]All data are taken from annual research on corporate pension management conducted each year by Greenwich Associates.

Table 27.2 How Policies Specified by Executives Are Changing

Policies and practices	1975 Research (%)	1976 Research (%)	1977 Research (%)
Amount invested in real estate	34	38	54
Amount invested in foreign securities	19	31	46
Amount invested in private placements	n/a	n/a	43
Ratio of stocks to bonds	43	46	38
Maximum amount invested in any one security	n/a	n/a	26
Minimum quality ratings for bonds	26	26	22
Maximum amount invested in any one industry	n/a	16	20
Minimum total rate of return	25	23	16
Minimum income that must be earned on portfolio	n/a	n/a	11
Diversification of equity portfolio	n/a	20	7
Short-term cash reserves	20	7	7
Volatility or "beta" of equity portfolio	7	4	6

powers of portfolio policy to investment managers. In fact, larger corporations, which are typically more assertive with suppliers, delegate more policy authority to managers than do smaller companies. Delegating operating authority, however, does not dispose of policy responsibility.

Executives say they are getting more actively involved in setting investment policy, but they say so in decreasing numbers. In 1975, 54% of the executives surveyed said they would get more actively involved; in 1976, the percentage dropped to 44% and by 1977 only 33% said they would get more actively involved. The executives' statements (summarized in Table 27.2) reveal only two areas in which an increasing percentage of executives specified the investment policy that managers were to follow—amounts invested in real estate and amounts invested in foreign securities.

The Challenge of Modern Capital Theory

A profound confrontation has developed between traditional concepts of investment management and a relatively new theory based on extensive capital market research. The debate between the advocates of the two schools of thought, "traditional" and "modern," covers each of the main dimensions of investing: whether to diversify broadly or to concentrate on selected investments, whether deliberately to minimize portfolio turnover as an unrewarding and largely unnecessary cost or to accept it as a minor cost necessary and incident to the pursuit of significant opportunity; whether to change portfolio risk or volatility over the market cycle or to hold it constant, whether to change the stock-bond ratio or cash reserves or to hold them constant throughout the ups and downs of the market, whether the objective of investing is to manage *reward* or to manage *risk*.

The dispute may occasionally seem academic and at other times almost polemic but, despite such distractions, modern capital theory and its practical application will be of great and basic importance to corporate employee benefit funds and their effective management in the decades ahead. Corporate executives must decide for their own funds where they stand in this debate. (Of course, *not* to decide *is* to decide.)

Among the broad cross-section of senior investment officers of major investing institutions 59% felt that it was unrealistic to expect most institutions to beat the market averages, while only 16% agreed that index funds—designed to replicate the market averages—would outperform the institutions. The two views do not square—except with the impressive 59% of the institutional investors who say they would oppose considering the use of index funds for pension funds. (An interesting challenge to pension executives is the resistance of senior corporate management to indexing. Of the pension executives surveyed, 62% said senior management would be reluctant to index, and 61% said senior management is less interested now than it was a year ago.)

Perhaps it is unfair to expect practitioners of the established school of investment management to sponsor the new contender, but it is disconcerting to see these professionals so antagonized by the relatively innocuous idea of using index funds for a portion of pension assets. After all, index funds are only the simplest technique making use of the splendid methods by which modern capital market theory enables investment managers—quite possibly for the first time—to control portfolios and to obtain reliably intended results. Realistically, the "debate" about index funds is already over. More than a third of the pension funds with assets of more than $250 million are already using index funds; most of these companies expect to use index funds more extensively in the future, and nearly half the companies not yet indexing expect to begin soon.

A far more comprehensive, and therefore threatening, prospect facing the traditionalists is the use of tools based on modern capital market theory to design portfolios deliberately differentiated from and carefully controlled in relation to the market averages. When it becomes more widely recognized that investment managers and their clients can obtain results that are highly predictable, given the investment environment, the importance of policy setting and the impact of explicit accountability will rise rapidly. Many investment managers are not well prepared to accept this accountability.

Contrary to conventional expectations that thoughtful investment counseling between managers and clients can lead to investment policies that meet the particular funding and financial characteristics of each employee benefit fund and each plan sponsor, research reveals *no* significant differences in portfolio composition due to *any* of the following, presumably basic, policy considerations—size of company, size of plan, percentage of plan participants now working versus retired, benefit formula, average age or length of service of participants, or actuarial interest rate assumption.

These considerations *can* matter, but only if corporate executives vigorously represent to their investment managers the special characteristics of their company and their plan at the time basic investment policies are being formulated. Corporate pension and profit-sharing funds are subject to too many differences of resources, constraints, and intentions to be treated in what appears to be such a Procrustean manner.

Conclusion

The competence most needed in the management of employee benefit funds is not more *investment* management, but more *management* management. It is hard work, but unlike portfolio management, which is apparently difficult to do well, it can be done well, and the rewards can be very large.

Source: Charles D. Ellis (1979) Pension Funds Need Management Management, *Financial Analysts Journal*, 35:3, 25–28, copyright © CFA Institute reprinted by permission of Taylor & Francis Ltd, **http://www.tandfonline.com** on behalf of CFA Institute.

28

The Significance of 65

Despite enormous changes in our society, belief in the "right" to retire at 65 has continued as a constant "given." Actually, 65 was a man-made pragmatic solution for a particular political problem—in Germany—over 150 years ago. Since then, major changes in healthcare have substantially changed how long (and how well) we live. Allocating all these extra years to retirement has profoundly changed the work/retirement balance with dark consequences for millions of individuals and for our society.

Numbers can be deceptive. They are *quantitative,* yet in the blink of a chameleon's eye they can convert into *qualitative* symbols when linked to the dynamic world of emotions, expectations, and beliefs.

Consider the deeper meanings that surge to mind as you ponder such numbers as 65, 9/11, 18, 16, 13, 1st or 99-and-44/100%. Do we *all* think of retirement, the World Trade Center, voting, driving, bad luck, that first kiss, or Ivory Soap that floats?

Context matters because an *objective* number can, as a symbol, have many *subjective* meanings. As we all know, the same numbers can have very different symbolic or emotional meanings: 5 minutes early vs. 5 minutes late for lunch with a friend versus 5 minutes late for a plane versus 5 minutes late for a wedding versus 5 minutes late for *your* wedding.

We expect numbers to remain constant—phone numbers, a lock combination, birthdays, and anniversaries or even our weight on the bathroom scale. The number 65 is one number that we must recognize as having changed significantly in its meaning; and if we don't, we could all be making huge mistakes.

Everyone knows 65 is "the age of retirement." Retiring at 65 has been around so long that most of us accept it as a fact and a right without question. But the meaning of 65 has been changing a lot over a long time.

In 1935, Social Security became law and 65 became the Full Retirement Age. But what did 65 really mean and where did it come from? The concept of a government-mandated retirement program for workers had already "originated" twice in the United States, once with disabled Civil War veterans in the late 1860s and once in the 1920s with the massive Federal move into regulating the nation's railroads. With a commitment to modernize as well as regulate our railroads, various groups studied everything about the railroads of other advanced nations, particularly in Europe and especially in Germany, which had the world's most advanced railroads at the time.

Bismarck's Germany: A Leader in Nineteenth-Century Tech

It was noted that Germany retired its railroad workers at 65 *and* that this was one reason their rail system had such an exemplary safety record. So retirement at 65 was put into the U.S. railroad legislation. But how had 65 been selected by the German railroads?

Originally, Chancellor Otto von Bismarck had established the retirement age of 70 in the 1880s. Having brought the numerous different Germanic states into one Pan-German empire Bismarck was looking for powerful symbols to demonstrate the advantages of a unified Germany. The telegraph was new and fast, so it was developed as part of the postal system to symbolize the technological benefit of a unified Germany. Similarly, the railroads were new too.

With a network of railroads, coal and iron could be moved great distances from the mines to the steel mills, while fresh food could be moved quickly from farms to cities. Passengers too could travel easily and at low cost whether for business or pleasure. The benefits were exciting evidence of Bismarck's political genius and a unified Germany's glorious prospects. Everything worked well—until the major train wrecks which were, of course, widely reported in major newspapers.

Talk about PR problems! The cause of these dreadful accidents had to be determined and stopped! As it turned out, the accidents were almost always due to the fellows at the switches literally "falling asleep at the switch." Why? Because they were so old. On further examination, it was learned that the work crews—worried that the oldest men couldn't keep up with the others in the hard, manual labor of laying heavy ties and rails—had assigned the old men to the light work of manning the switches. But, sitting alone for hours in the warm sun, the old workers sometimes dozed off.

This presented a dilemma. To get workers to leave their traditional farming jobs to work on the new-fangled railroads, Bismarck had promised to pay workers for life. So they could not just be laid off: that would have provoked a storm of protests. The only answer was to pay workers *not* to work and a new term "pension" was used to describe those payments.

To minimize the cost, retirement was set at 70, an age to which very few lived. Later, to be sure to eliminate all old-age accidents, this age was reduced in 1916, to 65. (Meanwhile in the United Kingdom, Neville Chamberlain, as Chancellor of the Exchequer, had introduced pensions at 70, which also were quickly reduced to 65 when he saw what the Germans were doing.) A few years later, retirement at 65 was picked up by the U.S. Congress in the Railroad Retirement Act. So it was that 65 was already a well-established precedent when Social Security was being formulated in 1935.

Living Longer Requires a Change in Thinking

At age 65, life expectancy for the male American worker in 1935 was less than 13 *years*. Today at 65, life expectancy is over 20 years (thanks to better diets and healthcare).

One of the results is that the average number of expected years in retirement is now much longer than in 1935. The ratio of working years to retirement years has changed dramatically—from over 3:1 to just 2:1. This 2:1 ratio is *not* sustainable! It's not sustainable because few workers will have the self-discipline to save the 12–14% of income during their working years that would be required to invest and sustain them through all those years in retirement.

But there is another way: Rebalance! We can rebalance by moving the fulcrum so our work and *save* years, are balanced with our retirement *spend* years. Once we understand the realities, most of us will each want to move the retirement age fulcrum from 65 to 70—or more.

So now let's look at how the *meaning* of 65 has changed. Obviously, the major change is in the number of retirement years that need to be financed by Social Security benefits and by savings, mostly in 401(k) plans (or IRA conversions from 401(k)s). The second big change is the increasing costs of the last few years of life, particularly when it comes to healthcare and assisted living. (One reason we live longer is major advances in healthcare technology—MRIs, pharmaceuticals, etc. are both wonderful *and* expensive.)

Working to 70 leads to another important number: If, instead of claiming Social Security benefits as early as possible—at age 62—we each decide to keep working until 70, we increase our Social Security benefits a lot. By working 8 more years—some 20% longer—we increase our annual Social Security benefits by a full 76%—payable for life and continuously adjusted to offset inflation.

And in addition, our 401(k) or IRA balances also go up a lot—in three ways: For each of those 8 years, we don't need to take money out to cover expenses (because we're still working); we continue contributing—ideally 14% each year; and our investments keep compounding *tax-free*. This troika should more than *double* our balances *and* our payouts.

Retirement *is* expensive. That's why an increasing number of workers are realizing that 65 is a very misleading number. Those who are well informed about their choices will want to continue working until 70, both to increase Social Security benefits and to increase 401(k) payout.

What folks don't know about the benefits of working longer and the even bigger gains in 401(k) payouts—because 65 does not mean today what 65 used to mean many long years ago *can* hurt us—can hurt us badly. The pain for individuals will also be pain for our society and our politics, particularly if a political demagog exploits the resulting dissatisfaction.

To borrow from Bishop Berkeley's philosophical question about the great tree falling in the forest when nobody was there to hear it; if workers don't know the facts about the 76% increase in Social Security benefits, does it matter? It sure does to me! Doesn't it matter to you?

Source: *Wealthfront*, Autumn, 2014.

29

Where Were We?

Investing for retirement security is, for most Americans, by far their most important financial challenge. Unfortunately, most people do not know how to make life's key investment decisions. Fortunately, we have many trained experts in our profession. Shouldn't investment professional organization take the lead on guiding our fellow citizens?

We admire politicians who are statesmen and show courage, but not those who can be bought. And we vote against those who do not understand or say they do not understand our core aspirations. We admire corporate leaders who build organizations that we know we can trust to produce great products at moderate prices (but certainly *not* executives like Enron Corporation's Jeffrey Skilling, Andrew Fastow, and Kenneth Lay). We admire—and enjoy admiring doctors like Marcus Welby, lawyers like Perry Mason, and investors like Warren Buffett because we know that they are looking out for our interests and that we do not have to watch over them.

In our complex society, we expect the professionals to be on watch and to tell us what we need to know when we need to know it. The essential factor in every profession is well-earned trust by laypeople, and the professions are distinguished most clearly by the way they fulfill their explicit and implicit responsibilities.

The investment profession has grown steadily in numbers of practitioners all around the world, in the richness of its body of knowledge, in the skills required, and most obviously, in the generous distribution of financial rewards to its members. Accepting that we have taken good care of ourselves, how well have we done by *our* laity—and as a result, how well have we done by our deepest values as true professionals? Different observers, having different perspectives, will focus on different dimensions of concern: Some argue that fees and costs are too high; other worry about hedge funds; and others focus on performance presentations being deceptive and research being compromised in firms dominated by investment banking. Take your choice.

My choice of concern is one that appears to receive little attention because it has developed slowly and indirectly. You do not have to be a behavioral economist, a Freudian psychologist, or a newspaper editor to know that surprise gets more attention than significance. Slow, steady stealth slips past us—until someone or something alerts us to pay attention.

How would we react—or want to react—if a politician or a corporate executive or an investment manager suddenly did the following?:

- Deprived 20 million workers (and their dependents) of *all* the retirement security their employers offered.
- Cut in half the amount of retirement benefits to be received after age 65 for another 20 million workers (and their dependents).
- Caused 10 million future retirees to concentrate the investments supporting their retirement security in one stock—and to make matters worse, in the stock of the company where they work and that they already depend on for job security.

"Am I my brother's keeper?" has come down through the centuries as one of history's most lame expressions of "not getting it." We owe it to ourselves to be sure that we in the investment management profession are never unaware of or indifferent to the largest investment problem faced by most Americans.

Would the investment management profession take action if we had a clear and compelling opportunity to speak up and show Congress that simple legislation is all that is needed to protect millions of innocent American workers from serious harm? Past harm is reversible. It has been caused by the notorious Law of Unintended Consequences and the compartmentalized thinking within the federal government that have combined to divert our citizens away from the road to retirement security and onto a path toward retirement poverty.

Let's take a closer look.

For more than half a century, the SEC has required those who would give investment advice to register, demonstrate their competence, and submit to supervision—all in the interest of protecting individual investors from the unscrupulous or incompetent. Ever cautious about precedent, the SEC has been reluctant to allow corporations to advise their employees about investing. This reluctance has been extended to advice on investing 401(k) retirement plans—even including advice on whether to sign up.

For more than a quarter century, the U.S. Department of Labor has been a faithful steward of ERISA and its famous "named fiduciary" provision. The DOL has been reluctant to absolve corporate plan sponsors of responsibility for the long-term consequences of investment decisions—unless those decisions were made by individual plan participants with no involvement by the plan sponsor.

The third factor in this troika was equally well intentioned. More than a quarter century ago, Congress authorized 401(k) defined-contribution (DC) plans as alternatives to defined-benefit (DB) pension plans. Initially, most 401(k) plans were simply conversions from the old supplemental savings plans of the Bell System and the "Standard Oil" companies (plus a few so-called profit-sharing plans), but as corporate financial executives saw the benefits of avoiding the long-term liabilities of DB plans and the attendant risk of quarterly EPS disruptions resulting from unanticipated changes in interest rates (or major changes in stock market process), the inexorable forces of financial reality pushed increasing numbers of corporations to switch from DB plans to DC plans.

And, of course, such switching was encouraged by some employees who preferred to make their own investment decisions during a long bull market and by some who were attracted by the opportunity to borrow "their" balances to make down payments on homes, pay college tuitions, or pay off credit card debt. The 401(k) plan seemed to provide a grand win-win opportunity. With everyone seeing benefits, switching from DB pensions to 401(k) plans has continued, and 401(k) plans now dominate private sector retirement plans. Corporate DB plans are fast disappearing.

Behind the happy talk, there is a dark side. At companies with 401(k) plans, employees who asked, "Should I sign up?" were told "That's up to you. According to our lawyers, we can't advise you on that." As investment professionals, we know that young workers are unlikely to focus on retirement security that is three or four decades away. Older people may recognize that time is crucial to compounding returns, but young people—particularly those with large, 18% credit card debts—have much more compelling concerns *today*. So, we know many will decide not to sign up—at least, not yet. And we know "not yet" usually leads on to future "not yets," and eventually, it can become, "not ever."

Those who asked, "How should I invest?" were told, "You decide. We're not allowed to advise you on that." But as investment professionals, we know that most workers have little knowledge of and little self-confidence in making long-term investments. And the data show that large numbers of people, particularly at lower income levels, opt for the "Safe" choice of a money market fund—which is fine for *savings* but not for long-term *investment*. With experience, we now know that large numbers of plan participants, having made one decision on asset allocation and then never change it, so many of those who sign up for money market funds, however temporary they may have intended their decision to be, stay in "savings" and never convert to "investments."

Another substantial problem with DC plans can cause grievous harm, as shown by Enron, Lucent Technologies, Polaroid Corporation, and so on. Employees often know and trust one company above all others: their employer. And employers often like to encourage workers to invest in "their" company. The result is that way too much of many 401(k) plans is invested in the plan sponsor's stock, even though all investment professionals know that diversification is the only "free lunch" in investing. And we know that if your *income* depends on one company, you already have a large concentration. Adding to that concentration another concentration of 401(k) investments is very unwise.

Data are available on these macro dimensions of DC plans: non-participation, inadequate levels of participation, commitment to savings rather than investments, and inadequate diversification. It is not a pretty story. And it is getting worse as more and more plan sponsors switch to 401(k) plans. Moreover, given recent Congressional "toughening up" on the rules of DB plan funding and the increasing charges for Pension Benefit Guaranty Corporation coverage, the rate of switching will surely accelerate.

With the shift from DB pension funds to 401(k) plans, what did employees lose? Several quite wonderful benefits: automatic enrollment, professional asset allocation, insurance against the risk of living "too long," the guarantee of the sponsoring corporation, professional selection of investment managers, a guaranteed level of monthly retirement benefits—and freedom from anxieties about "having enough" no matter how long you live and "doing the right thing."

So, what can and should our profession do? Until several months ago, our profession had a splendid opportunity to be the leaders in sounding the alarm to warn Congress and in calling for legislation authorizing plan sponsors to urge employees to participate fully, and to invest (not save) in appropriate investment vehicles. We could have urged all DC plan sponsors to adopt the following policies:

- Employees are strongly encouraged to participate, and participation is automatic unless employees choose to opt out.
- Nonparticipants are urged—perhaps annually—to reconsider participating.
- Those who participate at low levels are encouraged to increase their percentage participation automatically each time they get a raise.
- Participants are encouraged to invest in life-cycle funds.
- Life-cycle funds—not money market funds—are the "default" investment.
- Plan participants with large—greater than 10%—percentages invested in the plan sponsor's stock are encouraged to diversify.
- All participants are given easy-to-understand and engaging information —via booklets and the Internet—about the high cost of retirement security and the great importance of using time, compounding, and benign neglect to achieve good investment results.

The time has passed for us as a profession to advocate these changes. The good news is that Congress has taken actions on *all* these key points. But for our profession, the questions remain: Where were we? Why were we not boldly taking the lead years ago? And now that Congress has passed the necessary enabling legislation, will we take the lead in urging plan sponsors to take advantage of the opportunity they now have to encourage individual workers to participate and to do so in the new easy way so they will enjoy retirement security?

We missed one major opportunity, but we already have another— maximizing use of the enabling legislation. And more opportunities will arise in the years ahead. Hasn't the time come for our profession to go on active alert and look for ways to serve millions of nonprofessionals by speaking up? Here is what we can do now to accelerate and broaden use of the opportunities Congress has given our fellow citizens:

- Urge each company we cover as analysts or invest in as portfolio managers to take bold action to enroll all employees in 401(k) plans and with employees' participating at the maximum.
- Do the same with our colleges and universities.
- Urge our employers to provide life-cycle funds.
- Celebrate plan sponsors who take the lead.

Let those of us work together in the investment profession to help millions of workers catch up on providing the financial security they *will* need. Action does matter.

30

Hard Choices: Where Are We Now?

As a profession, investment management seems to be an important source of the expertise and experience needed to determine the full scope of the retirement security problem looming ahead and to figure out the appropriate solution. Time is running out.

Investing for retirement is increasingly recognized as the central investment problem for most Americas and is increasingly recognized as one of our nation's most important and dangerous challenges.

At the center of every discussion or debate on Social Security and retirement policy are questions of fairness and justice. As so often in debates over public policy, "where you stand is where you sit." Each of us has a different personal story and thus a different personal situation and different assumptions, expectations, and understandings of promises made or promises heard or believed. And our specific vantage point is a powerful determinant of how we see every aspect of this complex problem *and* the resolution each of us considers fair.

Demographers can know the future shape and scale of the problem by simply "aging" the present population. But because our personal experiences and perspectives differ, our beliefs about fairness differ—often greatly. That's why the choices we need to make—*before* choices are made for us or, for worse, are taken away from us—are so hard, particularly the choices that must be made through the political process of a large, pluricentric democracy.

As a society and nation, we need a "guided conversation" to explore the complex issues and questions and to clarify the main components in a wise and enduring resolution of our ballooning national retirement security problem. The longer we delay objective analysis, the more complex and entrenched our national problem will surely become *and* the harder, more painful the resolution. There is no happy solution; there is no magic answer. It may already be too late to achieve a good answer for this great question, but it's not too late to develop a "least bad" response.

To encourage the necessary—and necessarily constructive— "conversation" among the many policymakers who need to be engaged, this brief piece offers a sensible pathway to an overall resolution. Anyone who thinks a resolution now would be difficult must also believe that the longer we defer our decisions, the more difficult and painful resolution will be for all of us.

The Problem

A grim majority of Americans are in serious financial trouble—and most of us don't even know it. Financially, we are like boys and girls who are proud of their dark suntans without realizing that in 40–50 years, they will be patients of dermatologists checking for melanomas and other skin cancers—or like teenage smokers who, years later, will have a seriously elevated risk of lung cancer.

None of us wants the United States to be plagued by large numbers of impoverished elderly people who have outlived the retirement funds they once thought ample for a comfortable retirement. They can't go back to work because they won't know the people at their old company. They will have made their own investment and spending decisions, so nobody else will feel responsible for them. These former workers will be all alone, pleading to the gloom, "Why, oh why, didn't somebody tell me?"

If we do not make hard choices now, what pension experts call the "predictable surprise" will be no surprise at all *and* it will be nasty. Other nations—Australia, Chile, and Singapore in particular—have faced the same challenges and taken appropriate action. We can learn from their experiences. But will we?

One of our challenges is to find the appropriate balance between freedom of choice based on self-reliance and a social compact with regulations such as we now have from licensing drivers at 16 if they pass written and practice tests to unemployment taxes to product safety.

First, we need to define the central balance between work years and retirement years. When Social Security was introduced in 1935 and retirement was set at age 65, the rational "balance" was roughly 45 years of work and 15 years of retirement, a ratio of 3 to 1. With the remarkable gains in healthcare, our actuarial life expectancy has been pushed *up* to 85 while our average age at retirement has *declined* to 63. So, the overall ratio has fallen to below 2 to 1. Our present rate of saving for our present years of working and being realized results in too little to provide enough for all those years in retirement *and* assisted living.

Working longer—moving the fulcrum further out along the timeline—is an obvious answer. Although the case can easily be made that most of today's workers are not engaged in heavy physical or dangerous work and so could easily work until age 70 (or even 75), changing the retirement norm to 70 would run up against strong social and political resistance because such a change would conflict with the embedded belief that workers have a "right" to retire at 65 (or earlier). Retiring at 65 has long been seen as central to our national social contract, but the view that it is a "right" is a myth.

A retirement age of 65 was set over 130 years ago in Germany, primarily for reasons of politics and public relations. To attract workers to leave their family farms to work for the "newfangled" railroads that Chancellor Otto von Bismarck had made a symbol of the benefits of the German Empire—transporting fresh produce to cities and coal and iron to steel mills—Bismarck guaranteed lifetime employment. The oldest workers, assigned to the easy job of minding switches that were used only a few times a day, were literally "falling asleep at the switch" and causing accidents that threatened to make a mockery of Bismarck's symbol. So, he paid them *not* to work and chose age 70—and later dropped it to 65—because so few lived that long and the estimated cost was small.

Thinking clearly and objectively about the long term is hard for all of us, and in addition, most of us find thinking rationally about money very hard. Combining money *and* time and mixing in the political complexities of resolving questions about long-term financial fairness will be very, very hard. But the impact on millions of Americans and on our American way of life—our social compact—will be even worse if we do not agree on how to manage the major variables and do not have the national will to make the hard choices facing us.

State and municipal pension funds continue to be almost entirely defined benefit plans with three interested parties, only two of which negotiate the benefits: the government and the labor union. No genius is needed to predict the results. Mayors and governors want to avoid "labor troubles" that would interrupt public services *and* do not want to increase taxes because either could bring defeat at the next election. Union leaders know this and so agree to swap near-term "labor peace" for increased long-term pension benefits. Both parties agree to defer recognition of these pension benefit obligations by agreeing to use high "actuarial" assumptions about future rates of return so as *not* to accumulate explicit, realistic benefit commitments. The result is that required contributions to fund future pensions are seriously understated. Invisible or hidden, these obligations are contractual obligations.

For corporations facing hard choices as they set the terms and conditions of their retirement plans, one choice has been easy: switching from defined benefit plans to defined contribution 401(k) plans.

The United States has also had "difficulties" of its own making. For example, to protect the innocent from the unscrupulous, the SEC has a history of regulating individuals and organizations that offer investment advice. When ERISA was passed in 1974, plan sponsors were made explicitly responsible for acting as fiduciaries under the jurisdiction of the US Department of Labor. One result: Lawyers advised clients that it was unclear which policy precedents of which part of the US government—the Department of Labor or the SEC—would govern if a plan sponsor advised its employees on how to invest 401(k) assets; so, lawyers advised their corporate clients to offer no advice. This outcome almost always left each inexperienced individual "free to choose" in an area where decisions are important and mistakes due to action or inaction are numerous *and* can have serious adverse consequences, particularly over the long term. Examples include all the well-known mistakes made by individual investors—buying at or near market highs, selling at or near market lows, selecting or dropping specific funds on the basis of their past performance (which seldom works). In addition, many 401(k) participants begin their employment with tiny assets—too small for "investment"—and so they opt for a safe savings account and then, as the years go by, never change that decision.

However unintentionally, what we say collectively to the average worker is harsh in long-term consequences: "You're on your own now." Will that average worker with no experience in long-term investing have enough funds for retirement? It's up to the individual—and grimly unlikely.

After you stop working, your financial security will depend on five factors:

- How long you work.
- How much you save.
- How well you invest.
- How much you spend each year.
- How long you are retired.

The first factor matters greatly. Most of us should work longer—to at least 70—so we can save more for retirement. The next two factors determine how much money you'll have in retirement. If you worry that you'll find these decisions—like the decision to lose weight—difficult to make *and stick with*, you are not alone. They *are* hard decisions that are very hard to stick with day after day, year after year.

For many people, the secret is to recognize and embrace the "obvious": You are saving and investing for *you*. So, it all begins with saving. Here's something you can do for yourself within your employer's retirement plan. If your employer offers to match all or part of your contributions to the plan, be sure to *match the match* 100%. Your employer is doing the right thing for you and your coworkers, so take advantage of this benefit and recognize that your employer's matching contributions are really "found" money that goes into your account tax-free. Even better, all contributions—yours and your employer's—accumulate and compound, year after year, tax-free.

The last two factors determine how much money you'll need. Although regular exercise, healthy eating, and not smoking can extend your life by a year or so, your gene pool will leave you little choice about the length of your life. The average life expectancy for all Americans is now 85. For Hispanics, African Americans, and poor people, life expectancy is less; for the affluent, life expectancy is somewhat more. And if 85 is the average, 20% will likely die before 82 and another 20% will likely live past 90.

Because most of us do not choose when we die, our real choice regarding how long we are retired centers on our decision about how long we work, either full- or part-time. Increasing numbers of people not only find their work interesting and fulfilling but also enjoy the social context of their work because that's where most of our best friendships are.

To some extent, you can decide how much you'll spend in your retirement years in much the same way you decide how much to save during your work years. Examples of economizing include downsizing your home and reviewing your spending to see where you can cut back without feeling a real loss. (Although some of us spend somewhat less in retirement, some of us spend more.) Be careful to avoid the mistake many people make of not anticipating a major increase in the cost of healthcare. The *average* person spends 60% of her total lifetime healthcare expenditures in the last six months of life.

The easiest way to understand the great power of compounding is to use the Rule of 72. Simple and effective, the Rule of 72 goes like this: At X%, it takes Y years to *double* your money, and X times Y always equals 72. So, let's try an example or "test run" and see how it works. If your investments are returning 6%, your money will double in 12 years ($6 \times 12 = 72$). If your investments grow at only 4%, they'll take 18 years to double ($4 \times 18 = 72$). If your investments earn 8%, your money will double in 9 years ($8 \times 9 = 72$), double again in another 9 years, and double yet again to *eight times* as much as the original amount after the next 9 years!

That's why *time* is the Archimedes lever of investing. A dollar saved at age 25 and invested at 6% will be $2 at age 37, $4 at age 49, $8 at 61, and $16 at 73 (and $32 at 85). But getting that $16 or $32 depends on saving $1 at 25 *and* investing it sensibly over the long term. This, of course, takes self-discipline, but the necessary self-discipline is a lot easier to muster when we focus on the multiplied benefits that we all would want to enjoy. Where retirement is decided by each individual, many people continue working into their mid-70s. Those who do not have this option should consider working part-time.

The Rule of 72 works just as easily and effectively with debts as it does with investments. That's why banks want everyone to "take advantage" of credit card debt. Behold the Rule of 72 again! At 18%, the debt doubles in just 4 years, doubles again in another 4 years, and doubles yet again in another 4; so in only 12 years, $100 increases to $800 of debt.

When you spend today, instead of having multiples more to spend tomorrow, be careful to make your decisions as objectively as possible. The easiest (or least *hard*) way to act rationally is to make your decisions long before the "moment of decision," when you are calm and in the mood to set personal financial policies you believe you can stick with.

As we all know, the opposite of saving is borrowing. The laws governing 401(k) and other defined contribution plans allow individual plan participants to borrow from their accumulating savings for "hard-ship" reasons. These laws sound compassionate and that's the intention, but the definition of hardship is so generous that it unintentionally encourages people to divert their much-needed retirement funds into nonretirement spending instead of working harder on their self-discipline.

How your retirement funds are invested is important because many of those dollars are invested for a very long time—20, 40, even 60 years. So, although the day-to-day and year-to-year market prices, economic inflation, profits, and politics will cause the stock and bond markets to fluctuate—and sometimes greatly—around their long-term trend lines, a few realities are virtually certain over the long term. The stock market will outperform the bond market and will fluctuate more. Money market investments will—not always, but usually—earn about 1% more than inflation; quality bonds will earn about 2% more than inflation; and a diversified portfolio of stocks will earn about 5% more than inflation.

Most of the time and over most periods—particularly over long periods—stocks outperform bonds. So, how much should a 401(k) investor commit to bonds? For a long-term investor, the answer depends on how calm the investor will be when the stock market is behaving most horribly. Investors who are experienced with markets, highly rational, and able to maintain calm and *take no action* when the markets are causing others great distress—a remarkable and lucky few—will be able to focus on the very long term and sustain major commitments to stocks with an investment horizon of well over 20 years.

The conventional wisdom on asset mix (e.g., "invest your age in bonds") ignores an important reality and is seriously misleading. If people would take a "big picture" look at their overall finances—investments *and* earned income—they would invest less than the conventional amounts in bond at various ages. Many people own their home. While returns are non-financial—the pleasure of owning and living in your own home—a home is a "stable value"—part of your total portfolio and deserving full recognition. Most people with 401(k) plans are employed, and they can and should look at their savings from their salary as a "bond equivalent" in their total financial picture. If savings is capitalized at, say, 5%, then $10,000 of annual savings would have substantial estimated future value, which would be huge in a total-picture portfolio of a 30- or 40-year-old. Social Security benefits are another substantial part of the total picture.

Conclusion

Thinking clearly about money is hard for most people. Most of us are far from expert about investing. We "know" money is important, but we don't talk about money objectively or regularly, even in our own families or with ourselves.

Thinking clearly about the long term is also hard. Most of the time, most of us do not think more than a few years ahead. How many of us have sat down and written out a savings and investing plan for the next 10 years that we could and would want to live by? Most of us would blush in recognition that we are "*not* ready for the question."

But the question won't wait. In fact, most of us are already facing serious trouble, trouble that we still do not recognize. We need to make hard choices on how much to save, how long to work, how to invest, and how much to draw from our savings for spending in retirement. Each of these important choices is hard; getting them all right is very hard. And waiting instead of making sensible choices *soon* will surely make every choice harder. Of course, *not* deciding will make our personal and national problem harder—much harder.

31

Bonds for Long-Term Investors?

Only six years out of business school, what would, over the next half-century, become a persistent questioning of investments in bonds was launched with this analysis back in 1970. The use of bonds beyond a liquidity reserve continues, in my view, to be dubious policy for long-term investors, particularly endowments and pension funds. Would that there were an easy way to show how much it costs long-term investors to invest in bonds—presumably to offset some of the notoriously uncomfortable short-term price fluctuations of common stocks. If the "opportunity cost" of accepting much lower returns over the long run were made clear as the true cost of reducing portfolio price fluctuations in the near term, would rational and objective long-term investors continue to accept large allocations to bonds? Not likely!

Since everyone knows that long-term bond yields are unusually attractive these days, at least in comparison of historical yields, this may be an interesting time to reconsider the merits of investing in bonds for the long term. After all, if bonds are satisfactory investments, why not pick up some good bargains now? And if they are not attractive now, will they ever be?

Should pension and endowment funds have long-term investment in bonds? This may seem at first to be a curious question to which the only answer is "Of course." Certainly, most major funds now have large bond holdings. But what persuasive, logical argument can be made in favor of sustained long-term investment in bonds that would explain satisfactorily why the custodians of almost every pension fund, endowment fund and large personal trust in the nation has owned, now holds, and plans to continue investing in long-term corporate and government bonds with a major portion of their assets? It seems appropriate to question the wisdom of this policy for long-term investors.

Proponents of long-term, continuous investment bonds in large portfolios argue four main propositions:

1. Preservation of principal is assured because at maturity the obligation must be repaid in full.
2. The yield on bonds is typically higher than common stock yields (and the extra income is often needed now). Moreover, interest income is assured as to amount and time of payment.
3. If the national economy should suffer a severe and prolonged depression, bonds would once again prove invaluable.
4. Trustees of pension funds, trusts and endowments are bound by the Prudent Man Rule of fiduciary obligation to invest in bonds to have a balanced portfolio.

Let's analyze these propositions carefully, taking them in reverse order, beginning with the Fourth. The Prudent Man Rule governing the duty of a Trustee in the Commonwealth of Massachusetts and now recognized quite widely states: "He is to observe how men of prudence, discretion and intelligence manage their own affairs, not in regard to speculation but in regard to the permanent disposition of their funds, considering the probable income as well as the probable safety of the capital to be invested."

Unfortunately, it seems that too many trustees of endowments and pensions have too fully adopted a position regarding bonds that may be well enough suited to personal estate problems, without carefully evaluating the important differences between the investment problems and responsibilities of estate planners versus those of managers of endowment funds, pension funds, and other long-term portfolios—including many personal fortunes that will remain invested for the long term.

Trusteed capital management is historically based on experience in managing the financial affairs of mortal women and men who unfortunately do not live very long. The investment manager of a personal trust that will not last forever and is subject to an uncertain date of termination may well emphasize conservation of capital for the individual's descendants while planning for an estate settlement and portfolio liqui-dation. In contrast, endowments, pension funds, mutual funds and insur-ance companies have one unique and distinguishing characteristic: they will continue for very long. virtually indefinite, periods. And there is no separation of interest between those who get current income ver-sus those who get capital later. For most institutional portfolios, money is fungible.

An endowment fund has an unusually long term financial role for at least a considerable portion of the activities of a presumably very long-lived organization or institution. A pension fund also has a long-term obligation to provide for the well-being of many workers during their retirement. Even most personal investments will be looked to for such long-term needs as education, retirement, and family security.

These investors cannot be bound by the rules of estate planning because those rules give no explicit attention to the growth of capital and income which any growing institution would naturally seek from its endowment, which any corporation would expect of pension-fund investments, and which any individual expects of his or her capital. Rules, particularly those formed for different times or purposes, must not be accepted blindly.

Let us analyze the more substantial propositions of the bond partisans. With regard to their third argument (i.e., the risk of economic depres-sion), a powerful case can be built to support the view that, excluding an externally caused calamity such as a major world war, this nation should suffer neither severe nor prolonged economic setbacks. Students of economic history can offer myriad statistics to show how different our economic position is today from the 1920s. High and widespread personal income provides stability, while research, technology and edu-cation provide growth. The high proportion of workers in services and white-collar jobs reduces cyclicality, while large investments in plant and equipment per worker support economic growth.

Meanwhile, political scientists will point to the important institu-tional changes that have so greatly changed our economic structure such as FHA and VA loans, FDIC deposit insurance, IMF reserves, unem-ployment compensation, Social Security, progressive taxation, enormous government spending at Federal, State, and local levels, the SEC, FPC, FCC, and other regulatory agencies, and the trend towards full funding of pensions. In particular, they will point to the Employment Act of 1946 which posits responsibility for economic growth, price stability, and low unemployment with the Federal Government, objectives which have been reinforced by the commitment of recent Presidents to fulfill this obligation. Ours is a greatly different economy from the economy of our fathers and grandfathers, and long-term investment policy should be commensurately different.

Perhaps the most favorable change over the past 40 years is that our economy is now a managed economy in which both Government and businessmen take part. Business managers have gained substantial control over the uncertainties which have in the past caused large fluctuations in inventories and capital spending which have in turn been the major progenitors of past business cycles. And the Federal Government has learned a great deal about the effective uses of fiscal and monetary policy to guide the economy away from inflation,[1] on the one hand, and away from accelerating declines, on the other hand. These managers of our economy are equipped with more voluminous, more accurate, and more timely data than could have been imagined in the 1920s. The development of computers and the advent of econometric model building have made forecasting, analysis, and evaluation increasingly rapid and reliable. We are steadily gaining understanding of the way a complex industrial service economy operates and how effective management can avoid serious imbalances and beneficially influence developments.

This is not intended to suggest that we live in a "new era" from which recessions are banned, but it does seem highly probable that we do not face the prospect of either prolonged or severe economic depression. Consequently, no major portion of long-term portfolios should sacrifice the opportunity to invest more positively in our dynamic economy merely to defend against the remote prospect of sustained economic adversity.

This positive outlook does not deny the possibility of unforeseen economic, business or investment adversities, and a contingency reserve may be desirable. On the other hand, it is hardly necessary to allocate 30, 40 or 60% of the fund to bonds to protect against a possible decline in investment income which may or may not develop and which is highly uncertain as to timing.

The degree of protection or insurance needed by most large and long-term portfolios can be accomplished in most cases with an expendable reserve of only 5 to 10% of the portfolio. On the other hand, a large bond portfolio incurs too great a long-term opportunity cost in investment profits foregone, as will be shown below, to warrant using large

---

[1]Note that the decade following publication of this article saw the worst ever ravages of inflation. President Lyndon Johnson, determined to hide the fiscal impact of his war in Vietnam, ignored the advice of his Council of Economic Advisors to raise taxes.

bond holdings as massive insurance against an unlikely and uncertain adversity.

The remaining pro-bond propositions—assurance of income at a high level and capital preservation—are the key investment considerations and can be tested by comparing bonds with a conservative portfolio of, say, utility common stocks as represented by Moody's Utility Average. In questioning the long-term financial validity of bond investments, we will use ten-year time periods as the basis for evaluating bonds and the equity alternative. This test period is only for analytical convenience, and the reader should keep in mind that ten years is actually a very short-term proxy for the long-term character of the funds with which we are concerned.

Turning now to the bond advocates' Proposition Two and comparing cash income from bond interest to cash income from utility common-stock dividends, the record presented in Table 31.1 shows that over each ten-year period since World War II, total cash income from utility commons purchased in the first year and held for ten years exceeded the income from long-term Aa utility bonds bought in that same first year. On average, over a ten-year span, Moody's utility dividends returned 6.4% on cost versus a peak yield of 4.6% for the bonds, or a minimum increase in income earned of 40% over the bond yield.

Over longer periods, the advantage of equities increases substantially. On a pure rate-of-return basis, a dividend yielding 4% currently and growing at 6% annually is equivalent in cash income over a 20-year period to a bond yielding 6.5%. And over even longer periods, the algebra is inexorable. What bond could compete for long with a utility

Table 31.1 Ten-Year Cash Income Per $1,000 Investment

Period	Interest on bonds ($)	Dividends on utility portfolio ($)
45–54	267	656
46–55	258	534
47–56	267	646
48–57	292	729
49–58	276	709
50–59	268	696
51–60	295	694
52–61	305	662
53–62	332	653
54–63	300	584
55–64	313	551
56–65	343	581

portfolio that currently yields 4% and is growing at 6%? This means the dividend will double every 12 years producing 8% on cost in 12 years, 16% yield on cost in 24 years, 32% in 36 years and, to carry the proposition to a century time span which will test our capacity to think in truly long terms, the dividend would yield 1,024% in the 96th year!

Granted utility dividends have yielded and are expected to yield more cash income than bonds over long periods, are not bond interest receipts more predictable? It is quite clear that the amount of common-stock dividend received over a period of several years cannot be forecast exactly. But the very probable rate of growth in earnings can be translated into a highly probable pattern of dividends, particularly for a portfolio of common stocks.

And although the pattern of dividend income will be less certain than the pattern of interest income received on a known, present portfolio of bonds, just the reverse will be true for a large, continuing, and therefore always changing, portfolio of bonds. While we know precisely what interest will be paid and on what date for each individual bond now owned, most issues in any present portfolio will have matured or been called in 20 years and will be replaced with other bonds at currently unknown future interest rates.

Viewed in this long-term perspective, we would expect a bond portfolio's income to be not more, but *less* certain than the income from a portfolio of conservative utility stocks because we do not usually know whether bond yields will trend higher or lower, whereas the utility portfolio dividend income will surely trend higher, only the rate of increase uncertain.

The essential conclusion is that while the yield of the present bond portfolio is highly certain, the yield of a *future* bond portfolio cannot be accurately predicted and is less predictable than the future yield on cost of a utility common stock portfolio. The evidence substantiates this view. While interest rates have declined nine times on a year-to-year basis, utility dividends for Moody's Average never once declined in the postwar period. Thus the utility portfolio actually provides both a higher and a more predictable level of income than a bond portfolio.

While this discussion of the very long-term advantages of common stocks over bonds has been based on a portfolio of electric utility common stocks, portfolio managers can and should consider a far broader list of equities. A review of total corporate earnings and dividends indicates quite dramatically that while aggregate dividends rise with increasing earnings, dividends generally do not fall when earnings drop in recessions. Thus, in the 20 years since World War II, aggregate dividends have declined on a year-to-year basis only once and even then, by only by a mere 2.3% in 1952. Yet, during that same 20-year period, dividends rose by nearly 400% or at an average annual rate of 7.2% compounded. On the record, bonds are inferior as a source of reliable income when compared to equities.

Regarding Proposition Four, preservation of capital, it is curious that advocates of bond investment appear so convinced that the contractual nature of a bond is always an advantage to the bond buyer. Granted that the contract protects the investor from receiving *less* than stipulated. it also prohibits the investor from receiving any *more*. This situation can be viewed as a source of risk when we consider inflation which erodes the future purchasing power of both income and capital. In fact, if inflation continued at the long-term historical rate of 2%, the assurance that a bond buyer will only recover at maturity the *nominal* dollars he puts up, is the assurance of an effective capital loss in real purchasing power terms.

Table 31.2 displays an historical comparison of bond and utility portfolios. During each decade, the market value of the utility common stocks rose significantly. The amount of increase ranged from 44% to 155% with an average appreciation of 115%. Eliminating the effect of changes in P/E, which did rise during this postwar period, appreciation due solely to earnings increases would have ranged from 46% to 77%. Not surprisingly, the utility portfolio produces an important capital advantage over bonds. The magnitude of this advantage is impressive. Using the earlier expectation for utilities of 6% growth in earnings, and assuming no change in Price/Earnings ratio, capital would increase

Table 31.2 Capital Appreciation of Moody's Utilities

Period	Investment	Original value	Tenth-year appreciation (%)
45–54	26.29	44.30	68.5
46–55	34.05	49.24	44.6
47–56	29.53	49.62	68.0
48–57	27.34	49.42	44.2
49–58	28.37	57.46	100
50–59	31.23	66.35	112
51–60	32.55	69.82	115
52–61	35.48	90.66	155
53–62	37.80	91.50	142

over a century—if we can contemplate such a long time period—to an amount 256 times its present size.

The remarkable result of this historical analysis is that a portfolio of conservative equities has been and is likely to continue to be greatly superior to a bond portfolio on all counts:

1. Equities produce much higher income.
2. Equities increase capital substantially.
3. Equity income is more predictable.
4. Capital is safer from inflation in equities than in bonds.

The evidence is impressively in favor of investment in conservative equities as the preferred means by which a conservative, long-term investment portfolio can achieve its goals. Yet, the question remains: Why do most pension funds, endowments, and other large funds continue to commit a large percentage of portfolio capital to long-term investments in bonds?

The explanation lies partly in the experience fiduciaries have had with terminal estate planning, and partly in the difficulty all investment managers face when asked to deal astutely with time periods in excess of five years (which for many investors is a working definition of infinity). For an investment manager faced with a heavy volume of daily business demanding immediate decisions, the really long term is a most awesome challenge to the imagination. Thus, the real problem is perhaps not whether bonds are a better source of income and capital values over the longer term, but rather how the investment manager and his fund trustees can shift to a strange and unfamiliar time dimension in which truly relevant long-term policy can be formulated.

If it is decided to change away from a policy of holding a large permanent portfolio of bonds toward a portfolio of conservative common stocks, how should the change in policy be implemented? At least two choices are available: (1) the change can be made in a single rapid program when conditions are deemed propitious; and (2) a program of dollar averaging can be used to make the transition from bonds to stocks over a period of years. The choice depends in part on the decision makers' confidence in their ability to time the transition from bonds to equities; in part on their confidence that the policy change is soundly conceived; and in part on the risk that if near-term market developments go against the long-term trend and expectation, a sound long-term policy decision may be interrupted or reversed for essentially short-term reasons.

In almost any situation, depending on the politics of policy formulation, a sound means can be chosen to achieve the end result of a policy of holding bonds only as needed for permanent defensive reserves. No other long-term bond investments should be held for the long-term investors.

32

What Role Should Bonds Play?

Investors who take a "wide angle" and long-term view of their investments are likely to invest less in bonds and more in stocks to earn higher long-term returns—and have much more to spend in retirement. This piece came 44 years later than the one preceding it (Chapter 31). The dour view of investing in bonds for the long term continues.

Global borrowing has soared since the financial crisis as central banks suppress interest rates to spur growth and corporations take advantage by raising capital at low cost. According to a recent report by the Bank of International Settlements, the amount of global debt passed an ignominious milestone last year, rising from $70 trillion in mid-2007 to over $100 trillion by the middle of 2013. This matters because yields on investment grade bonds are near all-time lows. The investment returns for those bonds over the next 10 years will almost certainly be lower than over the last 30 years.

"Don't fight the Fed!" is surely sensible advice as the Federal Reserve has skillfully, tenaciously, and properly focused on reflating the American economy in the five years since the financial crisis. Interest rates have been driven down to levels not seen for 60 years—since the 1952 end of the Accord between the U.S. Treasury and the Federal Reserve to hold down interest rates during World War II. The Federal Reserve has notoriously deep pockets—it prints its own money—and great staying power. The Board of Governors has very effectively combined this strength with increased "forward guidance" on its intentions.

Sooner or later, unemployment will be low enough and the risk of inflation high enough for the Board of Governors to let interest rates rise toward their natural market levels. Remember that when rates go up, bond prices go down. So today's Treasury bond investors are locking themselves into *low total returns*. And, if the Fed achieves its long-term objective of 2% inflation, owning US Treasury bonds at low yields will be even less attractive.

If you look back over time you find that investment returns on stocks have been significantly greater than the returns on bonds—particularly after both have been adjusted for inflation. In Jeremy Siegel's analysis of historical asset class returns (over the last two centuries!), he finds that stocks generated 6.6% annual real returns (i.e. after inflation) versus 3% annually for bonds.

At 6.6% average annual returns, you almost double your purchasing power every decade. At 3%, doubling takes 24 long years. To outpace inflation and meet your long-term goals, you need an equity-oriented portfolio and the main reason for owning bonds is diversification—to round out your portfolio and reduce the magnitude of stock market ups and downs so you can stay invested through market cycles.

In Econ 101, we learn that money is fungible, so we should always try to look at the whole picture: never artificially separating "vacation" money from "food" money or "home repair" money, since money is inter-changeable. So, as rational players, we should strive to have our marginal utility of each asset equal to our marginal utility in every other asset to maximize our total utility. The key message is clear: No asset is separate; each is part of the whole picture.

The same concept applies to investing. No investment is separate; each is part of the individual investor's whole financial picture. So don't compartmentalize and don't let conventional wisdom compartmentalize for you! Instead, always take a "whole picture" view of your investments.

To illustrate, a 40-year-old software engineer at a successful mid-sized private technology company earning $160,000 in salary might have $1,000,000 in vested company stock, and $200,000 invested in a 401(k) account with 20% of that invested in bonds. Her most important asset is her human knowledge capital that she effectively rents to her employer for $160,000 a year with a moderate upward slope due to annual raises. Capitalize that asset at 5% and she has $3,200,000 in a fixed-income equivalent. So, overall, she has almost 3/4 allocated to "fixed income" *not* just the 20% in bonds in her 401(k) portfolio.

If you are able to conceptualize the whole picture of your finances, including the fixed income from your knowledge capital, you will be more comfortable with most of your investment portfolio in stocks. Most components of your Whole Picture Portfolio do not fluctuate with the stock market. This recognition can help you tolerate the short-term ups and downs of the stock market much more easily.

Another important consideration is your investment horizon. Most investors will be investing over their entire working careers and into their retirement and for many years will have the opportunity to make regular investment contributions, so a typical 30-yea-old investor will be investing for over 50 years! You can help yourself be more realistic—*and* less emotional—about your investment portfolio if you can center your thinking on the long-term benefits of *time* diversification as well as your Whole Picture Portfolio. Your horizon is probably longer than you realize and you will have natural opportunities over your working years to contribute to your portfolio and dollar-cost average your investments. Thinking this way is equivalent to considering the overall climate in an area, instead of the daily weather.

When you consider the historical returns of stocks and bonds and in the context of today's bond market, it is clear that long-term investors should have equity-oriented portfolios comprised mostly of stocks. If you can think "whole picture" about your *overall capital*— financial capital *and* human intellectual capital— and that your investment portfolio today is just one part of your *total* lifetime portfolio, you will be more comfortable with the short-term ups and downs of your investments in stocks. Those who make sizable long-term commitments to bonds pay a high price in "opportunity costs" of not having more in stocks.

Source: *Wealthfront*, Spring, 2014.

33

Too Much Liquidity Will Cost You

Fifty years of personal investing experience and observing other investors, particularly those managing their own investments, have led me to conclude that too much liquidity has, in fact, done individual investors more harm than good. The benefits of liquidity are often overstated while the costs are all too often under-recognized.

When it comes to investing, the general belief is that liquidity is a good thing. But is liquidity always a positive? The answer is No.

Liquidity with a *specific purpose* in mind is usually positive. For example, there is a clear benefit to having ready access to cash in an emergency fund to cover unexpected medical costs or your expenses between jobs. Stock markets rise over the long term, and therefore getting out of the market is betting against this powerful upward trend. The record for market timing is clear: Nobody has been consistently right about when to get out of the market and when to get back in.

To reinforce this idea, let's look at some extreme, but illustrative, examples of how much it could have cost an investor to miss some key days of surging prices.

Let's take the 20 years from December 31, 1993 to December 31, 2013. The markets were open for more than 5,000 days. If an investor stayed invested through all those days, a $10,000 investment would have

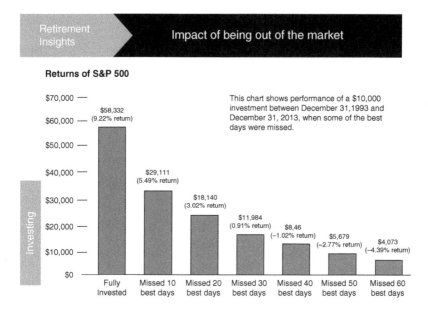

This chart is for illustrated purposes only and does not represent the performance of any investment or group investments.

Source: Prepared by J.P. Morgan Asset Management using data from Lipper. 20-year annualized returns are based on the S&P 500 Total Return Index, an unmanaged, capitalization-weighted index that measures the performance of 500 large capitalization domestic stocks representing all major industries. Past performance is not indicated of future returns. An individual cannot invest directly in an index. Data as if December 31, 2013.

Figure 33.1 Impact of Being Out of the Market

multiplied to $58,332. Now, take out just the best 10 days—less than 1/500 of the total time—and the total value of that portfolio drops to $29,111, wiping out almost exactly *half* of the returns over 20 long years. If an investor missed just 40 days, less than 1% of the 20-year time period, that 9.2% average annual gain would get converted into a *loss* of $854 (Figure 33.1). So patience and staying in for the long term are crucial for investment services. The same reality applies to individual stocks but even more forcefully.

For most individuals, excess liquidity means more time out of the market, which history has shown can be a costly mistake. *Cash drag* is another way of looking at the same issue. For example, if you have $10,000 more than you need in a money market account where returns are about 5% less than what you might earn from a long-term investment, then, on average, you lose $500 every year you keep it there!

A more subtle and serious problem with liquidity is the temptation of what's known as *easy action*. In other words, if you have the money sitting there and what may appear to be the *next big thing* comes along you are more likely to buy it—impulsively.

America's favorite investor, Warren Buffett, illustrates the discipline that can substantially improve your decisions on investments with a "decision ticket." Imagine you have a lifetime ticket that provides you with only 10 decisions to invest. Each time you make an investment decision, one of those 10 numbers gets punched. After 10 punches, you must turn in your card, and for you, it's game over! You can make no more investment decisions. So, you'd be particularly diligent and make each of your decisions with great care and self-discipline.

Source: *Wealthfront*, Summer, 2014.

34

Letter to My Grandkids: 12 Essential Investing Guidelines

All the important investment guidelines I wish my grandfather had been able to tell me years ago are provided here—for my grandchildren. If, as I fervently hope, they follow these guidelines, they will surely be successful long-term investors. The guidelines are well worth sharing with friends and family.

One of the great joys of my life is seeing my four young grandchildren growing up: learning to crawl and then walk, learning to talk and read stories, learning to ride bikes and play computer games—learning how to do all sorts of things.

Of course, they want to do all these things well: It's more fun and wins praise. It is way too early for my grandchildren, all now under 10, to learn what they'll need to know—and will want to know—about how to be successful at investing. But that time is surely coming and being successful in investing will inevitably be important.

After 50 fascinating years of working closely with nearly 100 investing organizations, knowing many of the world's most effective and successful investment managers, teaching the advanced investment courses at both Yale and Harvard, writing over a dozen books, and serving on many different investment committees, I've received a remarkable and treasured education in investing: theory and concepts, professional "best practices," and the realities of investing's history.

Having enjoyed this remarkable learning opportunity, I'd certainly like to share my understanding of investing with my adorable grandchildren. But, by the time they'll be really interested in learning about investing—in, say, 20 years—I may no longer be around. So what can I do?

I decided to write an investment letter to my grandchildren. I knew it should be brief so reading it would not be a chore. While "timeless" may sound a bit "highfalutin,'" my message certainly should not be dated or too tied to one specific time or era. It should be appropriate for my grandchildren to use at any time and in any economy or any stock and bond market.

Since my grandchildren will probably open my letter when they are in their twenties—when they will have another 60 or even 70 years yet to live and invest—the letter should focus on truly long-term investing. Finally, since the chances are high that they will not make their careers as professional investors, my letter should assume that my grandchildren will be consumers, not producers, of investment services.

Any grandmother or grandfather reading my letter will understand exactly how I chose my 12 investment guidelines, and they'd be right. The guidelines are what I most wish I'd been given when I started out 60 years ago. If I'd only known—and, of course, consistently used—these 12 guidelines, I'd have avoided some costly mistakes.

Since most people don't like getting advice unless they ask for it, each grandchild's letter is in an envelope with his or her name on it and this sentence: "Please open only if and when you have decided you'd like to get some ideas about your investing from your loving grandfather." Inside each envelope is my letter.

Dear Jade (or Morgan or Ray or Charles),

You decided to open this letter hoping to get some ideas about investing that you'll find useful and helpful. Naturally, in writing up these ideas for you, that's my hope too. So in writing this letter, my rule has been KISS—Keep It Short 'n' Simple—for your convenience.

You probably know that investing can be complicated, so this could have been a very long letter. (If you ever want a longer explanation of how to succeed in investing, you can always read my

Elements of Investing: Easy Lessons for Every Investor, or, if you want more, *Winning the Losers' Game*.)

Two suggestions: If, after reading the letter, you decide you're not yet all that interested in thinking seriously about saving and investing, put the letter back in the envelope and reopen it in about five years. If you're still not really interested, retain the valuable services of a professional investment adviser to guide you as you make decisions.

If you decide you are seriously interested in learning about investing, keep a diary of your investment decisions: what you expect of each investment when you make it and, later on, how the results compare to your original expectations. Like a videotape of you playing tennis or skiing, this objective feedback will help you learn both more and faster—how to do your best in investing. (As in driving, the secret to success is mostly *not* making big mistakes.)

12 Investment Guidelines

Here are 12 investment guidelines to consider. Naturally, I hope you'll find each of them useful.

1. Since you'll be investing for many years—you'll continue investing for at least 50 years—invest always for the very long term. Over the long term, the highest average returns are achieved with stocks. So, except for a modest "in case of emergencies" savings fund, concentrate your investing in stocks. (Before investing in bonds, give serious consideration to #11 below.)

2. Since nobody can know which companies and stocks will do "better" than expected, always diversify your investments widely. An important reality explains why: "Better" in investing really means better than expected by the full-time professional investors who have superb information and now dominate the stock market and set all the prices. (As I write this in 2013, professional investors do more than 90% of all NYSE trading, up extraordinarily from less than 10% 50 years ago.) As my friend Burt Malkiel so wisely says, "Diversification is the only free lunch in investing."

(*Continued*)

3. When observing the short-term behavior of the stock market, ignore the day-to-day and the week-to-week price gyrations and news reports. Concentrate instead on longer-term averages or norms. Just as when buying a home, you would ignore thunderstorms or a heatwave—the daily weather—but would think carefully about the area's overall climate, always take a long-term view.

   Remember that when stock prices go down that's actually good news for long-term investors, because you can buy more shares with the same dollars. Also remember that Mr. Market—a colorful, tricky rascal—is always trying to capture your attention and get you excited or upset so he can trick you into buying or selling by moving stock prices around. Don't let him ever interfere with your steady focus on the discipline and serious work of building long-term investment value.

4. Minimize trading to minimize costs and taxes. Never make an investment you don't expect to stay with for at least 10 years and hope to stay with for 25 years. If you invest this way, you'll not only save on taxes and trading costs, you'll teach yourself to make better investment decisions before you act. That's why Warren Buffett suggests we all limit our lifetime investment decisions to 10, so we'll oblige ourselves to make more careful, thoughtful, long-term choices whenever we do take action.

5. Carefully consider low-cost indexing. By reliably and consistently delivering the market rate of return with broad diversification and very low turnover (and so incurring low costs and taxes and fees), low funds outperform the great majority of "active" investors no matter what the chosen objectives (i.e., growth, value, small cap, international, etc.). Those who know the most about investing agree that low-cost index funds are best for most investors.

6. Beware of fees. They may look low, but they are actually very high when looked at realistically. Yes, most investors innocently describe mutual fund fees with one four-letter word and one number, but both word and number are wrong! Conventionally, we say mutual fund fees are "only" (the four-letter word) 1% (the number). But 1% of what? Your assets! Since you already have your assets, you are paying for something else: a return on your assets.

So, calculated as a percent of returns, that 1% of assets is closer to 15% of returns (if the consensus expectation of 7% returns holds). That 15% is a lot more than 1%—and nobody would say "only" 15%. But even 15% would be misleading.

As we all learned in Economics 101, every price should be compared to the price of every alternative good or service to reveal the incremental price of each alternative compared to its incremental value. (That's what smart shoppers do at the grocery store and what savvy diners do when studying a menu or a wine list.) When you do this, you'll quickly see that the incremental fees for active management are really high—on average, more than 100% of incremental returns!

7. While the past does not guarantee the future, understanding investment history is certainly the best way to understand how best to invest for the long term. So here are a few of the lessons of history:

   - Index funds achieve higher long-term returns than most actively managed funds, particularly after fees and taxes. (Over the past 15 years, 85% of mutual funds fell short of their chosen benchmarks—before taxes!)
   - Index fund fees are less than 1/10th as much as the fees of actively managed funds.
   - Index funds incur much lower taxes.
   - While index funds will never have "beat the market" results, they avoid the bane of active management: underperformance. And they do outperform most of the competition. "Top Quartile" performance is an unrealistic aspiration for active managers, but for indexers, that is the realistic *expectation*.
   - Unlike active managers, index funds reliably and consistently achieve their investment objective every day, every month, every year, and every decade.

   So please carefully consider indexing for all of your investments.

8. Active investment management is always "interesting," and in the short run, can be exciting—or painful. But be careful.

(*Continued*)

Many brilliant, imaginative, hard-working, extraordinarily well-informed, full-time professionals have flooded into investing institutions all over the world and are now competing with all the others all the time.

So it cannot be surprising that their collective best judgments—while necessarily imperfect—have become so good that, by the millennium, two major changes were evident to careful observers. It had become difficult for any active manager to beat the market after fees and operating costs over the longer term. Equally daunting, it had become virtually impossible to figure out in advance which individual active managers would be the lucky ones that would beat the market.

9. Fortunately for you, finding managers who would beat the market—which used to be many investors' goal when markets and investing were so different back in the 1960s and 1970s— is not nearly as important for your long-term investing success as knowing yourself.

What really matters most is figuring out—often best done with a professional investment adviser—the long-term investment program that is best suited to you: your financial resources, your spending objectives, your time-horizon, and your ability to stay the course.

Always remember that for long-term investment success, *you* are more important by far than the stock market. So take the time to "know thyself" financially. Once you have done this well, your other decisions will be much easier to make and your decisions will be better matched to your true objectives.

10. Most investors who do not succeed have made at least one— and sometimes all—of three "classic" mistakes. Please be sure you avoid all three.

- Trying to beat the market. Some folks do beat the market each year, but usually only because they got lucky. (While most patrons at gambling casinos lose, there are "lucky winners" every day, which keeps the gamblers coming.) Most investors who try to beat the market fail and, if honest with themselves, wish they had never tried. Besides, you'll have many much better things to do with your time than chasing after will-of-the-wisp "investment opportunities."

- Borrowing on margin to really beat the market—and then getting caught short. Leverage works both ways. So be careful.
- Buying after stocks have gone way up, particularly buying the stocks that are up the most, or selling at the bottom after stocks have gone way down and converting a temporary loss into a permanent loss.

11. Try always to see the whole picture when you make financial decisions. For example, your salary or earned income—with its predictable cash payments in exchange for your knowledge capital—will be similar to interest income from owning bonds: fairly predictable and low risk. What this means in a "whole picture" view of your financial situation can be surprisingly important. Social Security is another important part of your "whole picture." When you own a home, it will be part of your total portfolio. So you should be less concerned when the stock market goes up or down.

    If interest rates are 5%, the equivalent market value of your knowledge capital would be 20 *times* what you get paid in salary—multiplied by your future years of working and discounted back to its present value. So, if you are young and save each year just $10,000, that "knowledge capital" part of your whole picture financial portfolio would be a lot like the income from owning $2,000,000 in bonds.

    Recognizing this "whole portfolio" reality, you may decide that also holding substantial investments in bonds—often recommended for "portfolio balance"—does not make much sense when you are less than 50.

12. Saving is always the first step toward investing. Time is important too. In combination, time and saving—compounding—can be very powerful.

Sensible investing lets money make money for you. Here's an example. The amazing Rule of 72 tells you for any interest rate how many years it will take to double your money. At 8%, it takes nine years; at 10%, it takes 7.2 years; and at 3%, it takes 24 years to double—and the same number of years to double again, and so on.

(Continued)

So if you save $5 today and invest it at 6%, in 12 years, it will be $10; in 24 years, $20; and in 36 years, $40. So when you save $5 today, try to remember that those $5 want to be $40 that you can spend in the future (after, of course, adjusting for inflation).

In all his flying career, Admiral Koch never had an accident. I fly a lot too: 10 overseas trips a year and dozens of domestic flights. My record is perfect too: no accidents in over 60 years of flying. So, we both have been safe flyers.

But my flying is a lot like indexing: very deliberate, reliable, safe, no excitement (dull, really), no important skills required of me, and (on a cost per mile basis) low cost. All I need to do is decide where and when I want to go, make a reservation, get to the airport on time, check in, go to the right gate, sit in the right seat, and buckle the seatbelt. But I do need to decide whether I'm going to Hong Kong or London. So, as an investor, you will always want to be *active* on investment policy.

While the highly skilled and well-trained pilot and crew are doing all the work of actively managing the plane's operations, I've got better things to do with my time—like writing this letter to you with the hope that you'll find these ideas about investing useful to you as you decide how you will design and manage your investment program for success over the very long term.

Your loving grandfather, Charley

P.S.: My father-in-law was an expert U.S. Navy pilot. He was an Annapolis all-America athlete, commander of the *USS John F. Kennedy* when it was the world's most powerful warship, a two-star admiral and the world record-holder for one of the most dangerous actions in naval air: landing a fighter-bomber on a carrier. . .at sea. . .at night!

35

Miss Sally's Attic

Daydreaming, or "thought experiments"—as Albert Einstein described his extraordinary hypothetical reasoning—can take us away from our conventional habits of thought and action, perhaps with important benefits.

In the attic of my grandmother's home in the Delta region of Mississippi—where the Yalobusha flows into the Tallahatchie to form the Yazoo River and where we were living while Dad was in the Pacific during World War II—there were pieces of history and adventure for a boy with scabs on his knees, a crew cut, no need for shoes, and time on his hands.

My grandfather's full-dress Spanish-American War uniform bore witness to why he was known by all as "Cap'n"; a birding shotgun in the corner fit with the tale of my grandmother's taking 10 doves with 10 shots from horseback riding side-saddle; a peck basket of pottery shards and broken arrowheads was only part of the dig she ran for three 24-hour days barely before the highway builders bulldozed the burial mound at Belzoni; and it was almost certainly possible to see the stain where the peach brandy burst its cask on a hot summer day during Prohibition and leaked slowly but completely onto the big double bed reserved for a visiting revival preacher.

I loved that attic and the woman called "Miss Sally" by everyone except her husband, Cap'n, who preferred just "Sally." And I hope this brief piece will help readers pass some time with interest and pleasure.

Have you truly thought through and worked out the important components of your long-term investment program and established sound long-term investment policies? If you are a plan sponsor, do you have a sound set of investment objectives and appropriate policies by which to achieve them? If you are an investment manager, do you really have a clear and consistent investment concept or philosophy and a well-defined process by which to make investment decisions? Here's an easy and interesting way to find out for yourself.

Assume—partly for entertainment, but primarily for eventual clarity—that you have been summoned (with great respect, but on very short notice) to the White House, where you are meeting in the Oval Office with the President. As he confides to you his most important concerns, you agree (with some genuine surprise, since you had never anticipated such a situation) to accept his request to serve your country in a very special way.

You are going on an extraordinary secret mission. This particular mission has a remarkable requirement. You will be gone—and will remain completely incommunicado—for 10 consecutive years. Fortunately, there will be no risk of physical danger, and you are sure to return safely. Your income will be continued and your job protected for your return. The President assures you that your family and friends will know of your mission and will be both proud and grateful that you are engaged in the highest form of patriotic service. You will return a national hero at the end of a decade.

While there is no time to lose, the President has arranged for an hour's visit with your loved ones—they will join you in the Rose Garden—and is providing an additional hour before they will arrive, during which you can ensure the proper handling of all your investment responsibilities for the next 10 years. This is possible because the President has also arranged to have a very capable and reliable professional take over the day-to-day and year-to-year responsibilities of managing your investments.

While you will not be able to meet him (because he cannot get to the White House before it will be time for you to leave on your mission), this Competent Stranger is clearly able, willing, and determined to do exactly what you instruct him to do. While you await the arrival of your loved ones, the President invites you to sit at the large table in the adjacent Cabinet Room and write out your specific instructions for the Competent Stranger. You are secure in the knowledge that he will do just as you instruct—but nothing more and nothing less.

How well prepared are you to write out the requisite instructions for the Competent Stranger? Is there any reason to wait for the President's call to duty on a secret mission? Why not develop your program now—as if you were preparing to instruct the Competent Stranger—and then use it yourself?

Source: Charles D. Ellis (1988) Miss Sally's Attic, *Financial Analysts Journal*, 44:4, 13-16, copyright © CFA Institute reprinted by permission of Taylor & Francis Ltd, http://www.tandfonline.com on behalf of CFA Institute.

36

Ben Graham: Ideas as Mementos

Since Ben Graham was surely the most original and enduring thinker and writer about serious investing. It seems altogether fitting to end this section with a review article covering some of his many contributions. It concludes with an insight from Warren Buffett.

Ben Graham developed the idea of our profession just as surely as Sir Robert Peel created the idea of an effective London policeman, and just as certainly as the London constables are still called Bobbies in respect for Sir Robert's conceptualization of their mission and qualifications, those of us who serve in the profession as financial analysts are living out Ben's idea of what we might be able to do. We are, at least we aspire to be, adherents to the mission he originated.

My own acquaintance with Ben was all too brief: In his late seventies, he joined in a series of seminars I was leading for Donaldson, Lufkin & Jenrette, to which were invited, in groups of 20–25, the leading investment managers of the day. By common consent, Ben was the best informed, the most inquisitive, the most delighted with ideas and differences of view in the group. And, of course, he charmed us all by his grace, wit, and appreciation.

Sometimes, the incidental imperfection serves to illuminate the excellence of the man. For me, there is still special pleasure in the impossibility of sorting out one trivial misunderstanding. Ben was very pleased with Jacob Bronowski's television series on *The Ascent of Man*, watched every program, and was reading the book of the program's transcripts.

Ben was delighted with Bronowski's research and ideas: They were the twin dimensions of Ben's work. But Ben was even more enchanted by Bronowski's extraordinary ability, as Ben saw it, to "get every word in every sentence in every performance exactly right—exactly the way it was in the book!" It never occurred to Ben that the book was made *after* the television program, and that it was the book that was accurately repeating Bronowski. Twice I tried to help Ben "get the cart before the horse," to no avail. Then I realized he liked it the way he had it and would rather get on with the serious discussion of investment ideas.

Here, then, are a few excerpts from a dozen articles Ben wrote for *The Financial Analysts Journal* over 30 years.

The Campaign for Professionalism

Ben was an early advocate of what we now call Chartered Financial Analysts and the extensive examination and educational program conducted through the CFA Institute. His campaign for this professionalism was evident in a 1945 *FAJ* article where he posed the rhetorical question: "Should security analysts have a professional rating?" For a mind so quick, to isolate the central argument, the analysis was not difficult.

First, "The crux of the question is whether security analysis as a calling has enough of the professional attributes to justify the requirement that its practitioners present to the public evidence of fitness for their work."

Second, "The right of every individual to practice his chosen trade is subject to the higher right of society to impose standards of fitness where these are advisable."

Third, "It would seem to follow, almost as an axiom, that security analysts would welcome a rating of quasi-professional character and will work hard to develop this rating into a universally accepted warranty of good character and sound competence."

The elegance of Ben's thinking was complemented by a plain way with words and dress. He wore dark suits of a durable fabric that would last and last, and he described his work as "stock market operations." In a similar vein, his term for the recognized professional was simply Qualified Security Analyst.

In the course of a 1946 article, written as "Cogitator," Ben admonished his colleagues, saying that a professional analyst was "right" in recommending purchase of a security only when the stock appreciated in price for the reasons identified by the analyst. You should be right for the right reason—the one you identified when making your recommendation:

Recommendations to buy a stock for the main reason that next year's earnings are going to be higher are among the most common in Wall Street. They have the advantage of being subject to rather simple tests. Such a recommendation will be right if both (a) the earnings increase and (b) the price advances—say, at least 10 percent—within the next 12 months.

The objection to this type of recommendation is a practical one. It is naive to believe that in the typical case the market is unaware of the prospects for improved earnings next year. If this is so, the favorable factor is likely to be discounted, and the batting average of recommendations based on this simple approach can scarcely be very impressive.

Evident in this brief excerpt is Ben's respect for the other investors working in the market. In later years, after many more smart people had come into the market, he would doubt the ability of any large institutional investor to outperform the market and the competition.

Organized Knowledge

Ben enjoyed throughout his life that open-minded thirst for understanding and information that we admire in the term "childlike." At nearly 80, he was working out a new formulation *and* testing it against actual market results.

In 1946, at the time of the announcement of a new Awards Committee on Corporate Disclosure, Ben had addressed the need for organized knowledge in a profession:

It is amazing to reflect how little systematic knowledge Wall Street has to draw upon as regards the historical behavior of securities with defined characteristics. We do, of course, have charts showing the long-term price movements of stock groups and of individual stocks. But there is no real classification here, except by type of business. (An exception is *Barron's* index of Low-Priced Stocks.)

Where is the continuous ever-growing body of knowledge and technique handed down by the analysts of the past to those of the present and the future? When we contrast the annals of medicine with those of finance, the paucity of our recorded and digested experience becomes a reproach.

There are explanations and answers in rebuttal. Security analysis is a fledgling science; give it (and *The Financial Analysts Journal*) time to spread its wings. Contrariwise, many of us believe, perhaps unconsciously rather than consciously, that there is not enough permanence in the behavior of security patterns to justify a laborious accumulation of case histories. If physicians and research men keep on investigating cancer, they will probably end by understanding and controlling it because the nature of cancer does not change during the years it is being studied. But the factors underlying security values and the price behavior of given types of securities do suffer alteration through the years. By the time we have completed the cumbersome processes of inductive study, by the time our tentative conclusions have been checked and counterchecked through a succession of market cycles, the chances are that new economic factors will have supervened and thus our hard-won technique becomes obsolete before it is ever used.

That is what we may think, but how do we know whether, or to what extent, it is so? We lack the codified experience which will tell us whether such a codified experience is valuable or valueless. In the years to come, we analysts must go to school to the older established disciplines. We must study their ways of amassing and scrutinizing facts and from this study develop methods of research suited to the peculiarities of our own field of work.

Very little effort has been made to construct systematic inductive studies of our experience with various types of securities, or security situations. The experience we draw upon in forming our judgments is largely a matter of rule-of-thumb, of vague impressions or even prejudices, rather than the resultant of many recorded and carefully studied case histories.

Intrinsic Value

Ben was clearly identified in his investing with "intrinsic value" and not with "growth stocks." The reason for his preference was the confidence he could have in his own work when the analysis focused on present assets and liabilities rather than depending upon estimates of the future. Ben would have been comfortable, of course with Baron Rothschild's summary of a lifetime's learning: "Buy assets; sell earnings."

Here is Ben's logic from a 1957 article:

Of the various basic approaches to common stock valuation, the most widely accepted is that which estimates the average earnings and dividends for a period of years in the future and capitalizes these elements at an appropriate rate. This statement is reasonably definite in form, but its application permits of the widest range of techniques and assumptions, including plain guesswork. The analyst has first a broad choice as to the future period he will consider; then the earnings and dividends for the period must be estimated, and finally a capitalization rate selected in accordance with his judgment or his prejudices. We may observe here that since there is no a priori rule governing the number of years to which the valuer should look forward in the future, it is almost inevitable that in bull markets investors and analysts will tend to see far and hopefully ahead, whereas at other times they will not be so disposed to 'heed the rumble of a distant drum.' Hence arises a high degree of built-in instability in the market valuation of growth stocks, so much so that one might assert with some justice that the more dynamic the company, the more inherently speculative and fluctuating may be the market history of its shares. (On this point the philosophically inclined are referred to the recent article of David Durand on 'Growth Stocks and the Petersburg Paradox,' in the September 1957 issue of the *Journal of Finance*. His conclusion is 'that the growth-stock problem offers no great hope of a satisfactory solution.')

When it comes to estimating future earnings, few analysts are willing to venture forth, Columbus-like, on completely uncharted seas. They prefer to start with known quantities (e.g., current or past earnings) and process these in some fashion to reach an estimate for the future. As a consequence, in security analysis the past is always being thrown out of the window of theory and coming in again through the back door of practice. It would be a sorry joke on our profession if all the elaborate data on past operations, so industriously collected and so minutely analyzed, should prove in the end to be quite unrelated to the real determinants of the value—the earnings and dividends of the future.

Later in the same piece:

The market is, of course, fully justified in seeking to make this independent appraisal of the future, and for that reason any automatic rejection of the market's verdict because it differs from a formula valuation would be the height of folly. We cannot avoid the observation, however, that the independent appraisals made in the stock market are themselves far from infallible, as is shown in part by the rapid changes to which they are subject. It is possible, in fact, that they may be on the whole a no more dependable guide to what the future will produce than the 'values' reached by our mechanical processing of past data with all the latter's obvious shortcomings.

The Psychology of the Stock Market

In 1958, Ben was Visiting Professor of Finance at UCLA, and gave a long talk on what he perceived to be speculation in common stock:

Let me start with a summary of my thesis. In the past, the speculative elements of a common stock resided almost exclusively in the company itself; they were due to uncertainties or fluctuating elements or downright weaknesses in the industry or the corporation's individual set-up. These elements of speculation still exist, of course; but it may be said that they have been sensibly diminished by a number of long-term developments to which I shall refer. But in revenge, a new and major element of speculation has been introduced into the common stock arena from outside the companies. It comes from the attitude and viewpoint of the stock buying public and their advisers, chiefly we security analysts. This attitude may be described in a phrase: primary emphasis upon future expectations.

Ben developed his thesis, to the pleasure of his audience, with a bit of personal history:

In 1912, I had left college for a term to take charge of a research project for U.S. Express Co. We set out to find the effect on revenues of a proposed revolutionary new system of computing express rates. For this purpose we used the so-called Hollerith machines, leased out by the then Computing Tabulating Recording Co. They comprised card-punches, card-sorters, and tabulators—tools, then, almost unknown to businessmen and having their chief application in the Census Bureau. I entered Wall Street in 1914 and the next year the bonds and common stock of CTR Co. was listed on the New York Exchange. Well, I had a kind of sentimental interest in that enterprise, and besides, I considered myself a sort of technological expert on their products, being one of the few financial people who had seen and used them. So, early in 1916, I went to the head of my firm, known as Mr. A.N., and pointed out to him that CTR stock was selling in the middle 40s; that it had earnings of $6.50 in 1915; that its book value—including, to be sure, some non-segregated intangibles was $130; that it had started a $3 dividend; and that I thought rather highly of the company's products and prospects. Mr. A.N. looked at me pityingly. 'Ben,' said he, 'Do not mention that company to me again. I would not touch it with a ten-foot pole. (His favorite expression.) Its 6% bonds are selling in the low 80s and they are no good. So how can the stock be any good? Everybody knows there is nothing behind it but water.' (Glossary: In those days that was the ultimate condemnation. It meant that the asset account on the balance sheet was fictitious. Many industrial companies—notably U.S. Steel—despite their $100 par, represented nothing but water, concealed in a written-up plant account. Since they had 'nothing' to back them but earning power and future prospects, no self-respecting investor would give them a second thought.)

I returned to my statistician's cubbyhole, a chastened young man. Mr. A.N. was not only experienced and successful, but extremely shrewd as well. So much was I impressed by his sweeping condemnation of Computing Tabulating Recording that I never bought a share of it in my life, not even after its name was changed in 1926 to IBM.

Later on, another personal experience:

In my early years in the Street one of the favorite mystery stocks was Consolidated Gas of New York, now Consolidated Edison. It owned as a subsidiary of the profitable New York Edison Co., but it reported only dividends received from this source, not its full *earnings*. The unreported Edison earnings supplied the mystery and the 'hidden value.' To my surprise I discovered that these hush hush figures were actually on file each year with the Public Service Commission of the state. It was a simple matter to consult the records and to present the true earnings of Consolidated Gas in a magazine article. (Incidentally, the addition to profits was spectacular.) One of my older friends said to me then: 'Ben, you may think you are a great guy to supply those missing figures, but Wall Street is going to thank you for nothing. Consolidated Gas with the mystery is both more interesting and more valuable than ex-mystery. You youngsters who want to stick your noses into everything are going to ruin Wall Street.'

Always seeking lessons to be drawn from experiences, Ben summarized this lesson:

It seems a truism to say that the old-time common stock investor was not much interested in capital gains. He bought almost entirely for safety and income, and let the speculator concern himself with price appreciation. Today we are likely to say that the more experienced and shrewd the investor, the less attention he pays to dividend returns, and the more heavily his interest centers on long-term appreciation. Yet one might argue, perversely, that precisely because the old-time investor did not concentrate on future capital appreciation, he was virtually guaranteeing to himself that he would have it, at least in the field of industrial stocks. And, conversely, today's investor is so concerned with anticipating the future that he is already paying handsomely for it in advance. Thus what he has projected with so much study and care may actually happen and still not bring him any profit. If it should fail to materialize to the degree expected, he may in fact be faced with a serious temporary and perhaps even permanent loss.

On Price-Earnings Ratios

Observing how markets change and reverse apparent certainties, Ben gently admonished:

It casts some little doubt in my mind as to the complete dependability of the popular belief among analysts that prominent and promising companies will now always sell at high price-earnings ratios; that this is a fundamental fact of life for investors and they may as well accept and like it. I have no desire at all to be dogmatic on this point. All I can say is that it is not settled in my mind, and each of you must seek to settle it for yourself.

His conclusion draws upon his beloved classics:

When Phaethon insisted on driving the chariot of the Sun, his father, the experienced operator, gave the neophyte some advice which the latter failed to follow—to his cost. Ovid summed up Phoebus Apollo's counsel in three words:
    'Medius tutissimus ibis.'
    'You will go safest in the middle course.'
    I think this principle holds good for investors and their security analyst advisers.

Judgment and Efficient Markets

Despite his doubts about the ability of large institutions to beat the market regularly, Ben was confident that analysts could be "right" and that markets could be "wrong":

In its extreme form the hypothesis of the efficient market makes two declarations: 1) The price of nearly every stock at nearly all times reflects whatever is knowable about the company's affairs; hence no consistent profits can be made by seeking out and using additional information, including that held by 'insiders.' 2) Because the market has complete or at least adequate information about each issue, the prices it registers are therefore 'correct,' 'reasonable' or 'appropriate.' This would imply that it is fruitless, or at least insufficiently rewarding, for security analysts to look for discrepancies between price and value.

I have no particular quarrel with declaration one, though assuredly there are times when a researcher may unearth significant information about a stock, not generally known and reflected in the price. But I deny emphatically that because the market has all the information it needs to establish a correct price the prices it actually registers are in fact correct. Take as my example a fine company such as Avon Products. How can it make sense to say that its price of 140 was 'correct' in 1973 and that its price of 32 was also 'correct' in 1974? Could anything have happened—outside of stock market psychology—to reduce the value of that enterprise by 77 percent or nearly six billion dollars? The market may have had all the information it needed about Avon; what it has lacked is the right kind of judgment in evaluating its knowledge.

I can assure the reader that among the 500-odd NYSE issues selling below seven times earnings today, there are plenty to be found for which the prices are not 'correct' ones, in any meaningful sense of the term. They are clearly worth more than their current selling prices, and any security analyst worth his salt should be able to make up an attractive portfolio out of this 'universe.'

The pioneer of fundamental research in the 1930s, Ben felt the world of investors had changed and could say in 1976:

I am no longer an advocate of elaborate techniques of security analysis in order to find superior value opportunities. This was a rewarding activity, say, 40 years ago, when our textbook 'Graham and Dodd' was first published; but the situation has changed a good deal since then. In the old days, any well-trained security analyst could do a good professional job of selecting undervalued issues through detailed studies; but in the light of the enormous amount of research now being carried on, I doubt whether in most cases such extensive efforts will generate sufficiently superior selections to justify their cost. To that very limited extent I'm on the side of the 'efficient market' school of thought now generally accepted by the professors.

Later that year, Warren Buffett wrote in his FAJ tribute to Ben:

A remarkable aspect of Ben's dominance of his professional field was that he achieved it without that narrowness of mental activity that concentrates all effort on a single end. It was, rather, the incidental by-product of an intellect whose breadth almost exceeded definition. Virtually total recall, unending fascination with new knowledge and an ability to recast it in a form applicable to seemingly unrelated problems made exposure to his thinking in any field a delight. There was an absolutely open-ended, no-scores-kept generosity of ideas, time, and spirit. If clarity of thinking was required, there was no better place to go. And if encouragement or counsel was needed, Ben was there,

He still is for those who enjoyed even briefly the pleasure of his company.

Source: Charles D. Ellis (1982) Ben Graham: Ideas as Mementos, *Financial Analysts Journal*, 38:4, 41–48, copyright © CFA Institute reprinted by permission of Taylor & Francis Ltd, http://www. tandfonline.com on behalf of CFA Institute.

37

The Corporate Tax Cut

This piece has a sentimental place in my heart. It was my first published article investment subjects (and the first of many in the Financial Analysts Journal*). While tax rate redirection was getting all the attention for fast-growing corporations, accelerated payments resulted in a tax-paying increase, which few had recognized. This article analyzing JFK's Tax Cut went into specific detail no longer of interest to most readers, so they are not included. Still, the key concept was important: while tax rate reductions got all the attention and stimulated the economy, tax collections were accelerated so the government's tax income actually increased. Personally, only one year out of Harvard Business School, getting published in my new profession's most important journal was a thrill. This would, over the years, be the first of many.*

Reflecting the general belief that the reduction in corporate income tax rates would provide a major stimulating addition to the reductions in *individual* tax rates, President Kennedy told a national television audience, as he prepared to sign the Revenue Act of 1964 into law, "on larger corporations, the rate will drop from 52% to 48%. Companies can now pay more of their earnings to those who own their stock. And they can increase their investments which, in turn, will benefit the whole country . . . they will use much of this money to buy new machinery, for new construction, for goods of all kinds, and most importantly, for the creation of new jobs." In contrast to such optimism, this article shows that the revisions in corporate tax rates will not be so simply beneficial as the President and many investors seem to expect.

Many Will Benefit Less

Since some observers expect the corporate tax cut to benefit business generally, it may be well to begin by indicating some industries which will *not* benefit fully. First, any company currently paying a low rate of tax will not derive as great a *percentage* increase in net-after-tax income as would a company now paying at the full 52% rate. For example, many railroads have taken book losses on the disposal of obsolete or worn-out capital equipment (not depreciated during the 1930s) and have typically had effective income tax rates of between 30 and 35%. Reducing their tax rates by 4 percentage points in two years would increase after tax net income by only 6% rather than the "standard" 8% increase.

Many natural resource companies also do not pay full tax rates. An oil-producing company, such as Amerada, incurs little or no federal tax liability after deducting depletion, foreign taxes, and state taxes. On the other hand, an oil refiner and marketer, such as Sohio, typically does pay higher rates of tax and will benefit accordingly.

An American corporation with extensive foreign earnings will not enjoy the same benefits from the new tax rates as similar wholly domestic companies. Since foreign taxes paid on overseas earnings can be used as credit against U.S. taxes only on that portion of total earnings derived abroad, international companies paying taxes to foreign governments at rates higher than would be applied by the Internal Revenue Service will not benefit from a reduction in the U.S. tax rates. Since the cut will be only on U.S. tax levies, an "international" company will benefit relatively less than a "domestic" competitor.

Others Will Benefit More

On the other hand, some companies will benefit more than average. Corporations now paying a state income tax or filing consolidated tax returns, will derive a *higher* than normal percentage gain in net-after-tax income. Thus, elimination of the 2% surtax will add an extra 4% to Stanley-Warner's per share earnings. And, a company now paying Minnesota's income tax of 5% and the full Federal tax rate will enjoy a potential increase in net-after-all taxes from 43% of pretax income in 1963 to 47% in 1965, or a 9% increase in reported earnings over the two-year period (compared to 8% for a company subject only to the full federal income tax rate).

An interesting application of the tax cut will be made in the utility industry, where the rate of return on investment is regulated to within certain limits, usually 6–8% of the rate base. Those utilities now earning at maximum levels would have "surplus" earnings as a result of the tax cut and regulatory agencies might impose rate reductions to bring earnings back down to acceptable levels. At least one utility management has announced that it will pass the benefits of the tax cut on to its customers by voluntarily revising the present rate structure. Accordingly, it appears that the tax cut initially will tend to benefit the *customers* of the most profitable utilities; also, the *shareholders* of the utilities now earning less than the allowable rate of return on investment, since the latter are more apt to maintain present rate schedules and use tax reductions to increase net income.

Effect of Payments Acceleration

A relatively unheralded feature of the corporate tax reduction program has more general interest for financial analysts. To soften the impact of corporate tax reductions on the Federal budget, companies with annual tax liabilities in excess of $100,000 are required to advance their present tax-paying timetables. In recent years, corporations have paid taxes in four installments, due September 15 and December 15 of each year in which the income was earned, with "clean up" payments due in the following year on March 15 and June 15. The new law requires a gradual advance over a seven-year period so that by 1971, the quarterly payments will be due on the 15th of April, June, September, and December of the same year in which the income is earned and the tax liability incurred.

The net effect of the payments acceleration will be to postpone the effective reduction to a 50% rate until 1969 and delay the 48% level to 1971. In fact, *cash tax rates* actually rise above present rates and increase substantially for a company with a 20% compound growth rate!

Consequently, while rate reductions will result in higher *reported* earnings, the acceleration of payments will keep cash flow from rising, and dividends may not be increased proportionately. A *caveat* following from this possibility is that applying the present generous price-earnings multiples to higher reported earnings may be unjustified if higher dividends and retained earnings are not forthcoming to give support to stock prices—particularly for growth companies which have enjoyed lower effective tax rates by delaying current tax liabilities while earnings increase.

Source: Charles D. Ellis (1964) Implications for Financial Analysis: The Corporate Tax Cut, *Financial Analysts Journal*, 20:3, 53–55, copyright © CFA Institute reprinted by permission of Taylor & Francis Ltd, http://www.tandfonline.com on behalf of CFA Institute.

38

Repurchase Stock
to Revitalize Equity

Share repurchase by large public corporations is now done in substantial volumes, but when this article appeared in The Harvard Business Review *in 1965, most companies had never considered the idea. (Naturally, thrilled that the editors decided to publish such an unorthodox article, I was further delighted when Professor Alan Young proposed that we combine our efforts in the area to produce a book that Ronald Press agreed to publish and that opened the door for me to book writing.)*

The real winner was Goldman Sachs and its trading desk. Purchasing a few hundred copies of my book, Share Repurchase, *they sent the book to corporate Treasurers as validation of the share repurchase concept and offered to help. In days of 40¢ per share commissions, Goldman Sachs did brisk business in share repurchase, buying many millions of shares.*

An important new development is becoming increasingly apparent in the annual reports of a growing number of major industrial corporations: preferred stock is being retired, debt capital is being used less and less and, as retained earnings and cash flow rise rapidly, senior capital is being replaced with equity. The result is an unprecedented equity capital abundance. Is this a generous blessing or a curse in disguise? It all depends on your point of view.

While a plush financial condition allows management to do what it wants when it wants, without financial constraints and limitations,

plentiful liquid assets and/or limited debt usage usually mean an unnecessarily heavy reliance on stockholders' equity. The evidence may be
visible—large nonoperating assets or invisible—unused debt capacity
and redundant working capital. But in either case the result is a needless
waste of the potential strength and vitality of the investors' capital. This
waste creates a major new problem for the owners and their representatives, the board of directors.

Unless the trend toward increasing dependence on equity capital is
reversed, the problem just described will become more acute. The present situation calls for new methods of approach and action; the trends
toward the future demand a careful rethinking of that most basic of all
corporate money matters, the capitalization of the enterprise.

In this article I shall assume that the principal objective of capital
strategy, particularly the determination of the size and mix of capital,
is to maximize the owners' long-term interests as measured by wealth
(market value of shares) and income (dividends per share). I shall argue
that to accomplish this objective, financial planners should give careful
consideration to a flexible and potent, but often overlooked, procedure:
buying back common stock.

Bolder Role Needed

If a corporation is unnecessarily dependent on equity capital, it can
advance shareholders' interests significantly by what I like to call "reverse
dilution," or the concentration of equity by replacing unnecessary common shares with limited obligation capital, such as debt and preferred.
This can be seen with simple arithmetic. Suppose a company with
$20 million of earnings contracts the equity base from 10 million shares
to 9 million. The effect is as follows (Table 38.1) (assuming income taxes
at 50%, market value at 15 times earnings, and debt interest at 5% on the
purchase cost of $30 million):

The arithmetic (where applicable) poses a most important, but seldom specified challenge to the corporation with excess equity capital:
Can the board of directors justify a capital policy which tends to insulate
management from the rigors of financial discipline and obliges stockholders to leave unnecessary amounts of equity capital tied up in the
enterprise?

Stated as a challenge to present policy, the problem of redundant
equity is not limited to shareholders and the directors who represent
them, but extends to the management of the corporate entity, which

Table 38.1 The Benefits of Repurchase

	Before	After
Earnings from operations ($)	40,000,000	40,000,000
Interest on debt ($)	0	750,000
Earnings before taxes ($)	40,000,000	39,250,000
Net income ($)	20,000,000	19,625,000
Outstanding common shares	10,000,000	9,000,000
Earnings per share ($)	2.00	2.18
Dividends (60% of earnings) ($)	1.20	1.31
Market value of 100 shares ($)	3,000	3,270

would suffer a reduction in total net assets and income if equity were reduced and debt increased to develop reverse dilution. In a rapidly growing company, reverse dilution can be accomplished over a period of years by increasing the proportionate use of senior capital. But in most cases reverse dilution must be accomplished by both increasing the use of senior capital and actually reducing the amount of equity. The latter can only be done by repurchasing common shares.

Present Practice

Although no large corporation has as yet fully accepted the broad role of share repurchasing to be proposed in this study, neither has the procedure been wholly ignored. More and more companies are utilizing the repurchase technique.[1] Usually, however, repurchase has been viewed only as a defensive device to avoid dilution. Various reasons are given to justify expenditures on a reacquisition of shares. For instance, it is argued that repurchase will:

- Avoid diluting earnings per share when stock options are granted and exercised by management.
- Supply shares for employee stock-purchase programs.
- Obtain shares for common stock bonuses to employees.
- Provide shares for stock dividends.
- Avoid diluting earnings per share when convertible securities are changed into common stock.

---

[1]See Leo A. Guthart, "More Companies Are Buying Back Their Stock" (Thinking Ahead), *HBR*, March–April 1965, p. 40.

- Increase the per-share asset value of investment companies when shares sell at a discount in the market.
- Eliminate small odd-lot holdings, which are inordinately costly to service.
- Compensate for the dilution of earnings per share which is incurred in a merger through exchange of shares.
- Provide the means to acquire other companies. (It is ironic that many companies are proud of their policy of making acquisitions only with cash, "to avoid equity dilution." Yet, because of the federal tax on capital gains in a cash sale, sellers fare better with exchanges of stock than cash payments and will usually accept a proportionately lower purchase valuation when these taxes can be avoided. For example, assuming a 25% capital gains tax on a cash transaction, and assuming the stock alternative qualifies as nontaxable, $100 in stock may be worth $133 in cash to the seller. Consequently, the acquiring company's stockholders' equity would be far less "diluted" if payment were made in shares previously acquired for this purpose in the open market for only three-quarters of the money needed for a cash transaction.)

Repurchase programs which are undertaken for the foregoing reasons occasionally result in a sizable volume of trading. For instance, General Motors' repurchases in 1964 amounted to 1,136,457 shares—or 10.5% of the volume in this stock on the New York Stock Exchange. As a rule, however, such reacquisitions do not lead to significant changes in the number of outstanding shares because purchasing is done specifically for reissue. In a recent study, Barron's found only 100 companies (out of several thousand listed on the major stock exchanges) with more than nominal holdings of their own stock; even in this group most companies were found to hold less than 3% of their total stock and were simply anticipating employee stock options and other similar programs.[2] Although repurchasing is widely accepted for stock options and other minor uses, it is clearly not often used for substantial changes in the equity base.

Later in this article I hope to show that repurchasing should not be limited to the defensive role of avoiding dilution. I believe many managements should consider a more aggressive approach, using it as a step toward achieving a more rational corporate financial structure in which debt and preferred capital take the place of redundant equity funds. First, however, let us review the objections to repurchasing common stock.

---

[2] *Barron's*, August 17, 1964, p. 9.

Major Objections

There seem to be five main arguments against repurchase. To each of them there is, in my opinion, a good answer.

Management Defeatism?

For some, buying in common stock has an unfavorable connotation of defeatism and that any management not finding new ways to use surplus funds is inept and dull-witted. At present the suggestion that a company "invest in itself" often draws prompt criticism. The following statement is from the president of a medium-sized company with no debt and a portfolio of marketable securities equal to nearly 10% of the market value of the company's stock:

> We would never consider buying in our own stock. The task of this management is to invest funds; and if we can't do it, the directors should bring in a whole new ball team.

This attitude is not justified. Financial annals are replete with case histories of unsuccessful and unprofitable acquisitions and expansion programs. While some managements have avoided the pitfalls attendant to investing in or acquiring other companies, more and more annual reports show that millions of dollars of redundant cash and other liquid assets are being accumulated. It is doubtful that an effort to relinquish this corporate "padding" through repurchasing common stock can logically be considered "going soft" or defeatism.

Sign of Deterioration?

An unfavorable aura somehow surrounds repurchase of common stock in the writings of financial classicists. These writers generally recommend repurchase only as a means of gradually liquidating a deteriorating company or one with wasting assets—and then only when the total market valuation of the common stock is less than current assets.

In fairness to these traditionalists, the corporate laws of this country appear to be unique among the major capitalist nations in permitting corporations to reacquire their own shares. English law takes the delightful but archaic position that the repurchase of common stock is a constructive fraud against creditors. Canadian law is more moderate but still prohibits repurchase of stocks as an unauthorized reduction of capital.

Needless to say, it is facts, not legends, that we are interested in. The facts, I hope to demonstrate, favor repurchase.

Debt Taboo?

There seems to exist a general management preference for equity and retained earnings rather than debt and preferred capital. For instance, after refinancing a large preferred issue with debt, a large metals company reported with apparent satisfaction that it still had one of the lowest debt ratios in its industry. And executives of other companies advertise that their organizations have practically no debt. This antidebt policy apparently arises from the exercise of personal preference by financial managers. There are good reasons to believe that it often conflicts with the interests of stockholders.[3]

Abuse of Power?

In recent years there have been some abuses of the power of American corporations to repurchase common shares. To illustrate:

- One company bought out a single large stockholder without making a general tender offer, which would have allowed other shareholders to reduce or liquidate their holdings.
- Another company sought to increase the marketability of a large shareholder's secondary offering at the then prevailing market price by using $1 million of company funds to buy a rather large portion of the about-to be-offered stock for the corporate treasury. This move significantly reduced the number of outstanding shares, increased earnings per share, and lowered the price-earnings ratio to a level more in line with the capitalization rates of similar publicly held companies.

---

[3]See Gordon Donaldson, "Financial Goals: Management vs. Stockholders," *HBR*, May–June 1963, p. 126.

- Another firm incurred stockholder dismay and anger by acquiring shares on the open market, management's motive apparently being to maintain control over the firm for a particular group of stockholders.

Obviously, repurchases can be inappropriate and can discriminate unfairly among common shareholders. But such abuses can easily be avoided by corporations willing to make full disclosure of their plans so that all stockholders are treated equitably.

Unfair to Stockholders?

Finally, some have argued when a corporation repurchases its own common stock, either the sellers or remaining holders may be hurt, and that management should not engage in any activity that tends to help some stockholders at the expense of others. Three points should be made clear:

1. A full disclosure of repurchase objectives enables shareholders to reappraise and act accordingly.
2. When substantial amounts of stock are to be reacquired, a tender offer will give all shareholders equitable treatment. Such a tender offer should be priced sufficiently above current market levels to balance (a) the advantages the higher *present* price to those who may wish to sell with (b) the advantages of higher *future* per-share earnings and equity values to those hold their shares.
3. When relatively small amounts of stock are to be purchased on the stock exchanges, a regular buying program both increases the active demand for and decreases the available supply of corporation's shares, and consequently tends to increase the price at which the shares will trade to the satisfaction of both holders and sellers.

Possible Alternatives

Thus the standard objections to repurchasing lose their forcefulness when considered carefully, and repurchasing should not be rejected out of hand. Are there, however, alternatives that management should consider?

Distributing Surplus

When current and anticipated cash inflows exceed present and expected internal cash requirements, an increase in dividend payout is usually appropriate. Such an increase may, however, be an inadequate solution to the problem of surplus cash flows.

Since managers and investors both expect a given level of dividends to be maintained, dividend payments are relatively inflexible; and most managements have been unwilling to commit themselves to a payout rate much above 65% to 70% of reported earnings. But since net funds inflows are typically appreciably higher than reported earnings, capital can accumulate rather rapidly, even with a relatively high dividend rate.

Moreover, increasing dividends above a normal payout level implicitly assumes that stockholders prefer more current income to an increasing share of equity in a prosperous and progressive enterprise with the prospect of even higher dividends in the future. This assumption ignores the tax advantages of investing the funds in the corporation through share repurchase.

While higher dividends probably are the most attractive method for distributing a moderately and consistently increasing surplus of cash flow, they are not appropriate when the surplus arises in a sporadic pattern of large amounts. In other cases, when retained earnings have accumulated over a number of years and have become a sizable equity surplus, higher annual dividends would seldom be an acceptable means to most managers of substantially reducing total equity capital.

Investment Expansion

Surplus funds may also be applied toward expansion or modernization, cash acquisitions or investments, and retirement of senior securities. As examples:

- From 1956 to 1964, R. J. Reynolds Tobacco Company spent $160 million to expand and modernize facilities, increased working capital by $55 million, and reduced senior securities by $85 million. The total program more than doubled book values.
- Consolidation Coal Company recently bought 7.7% of the common stock of Chrysler Corporation for more than $55 million, The market value of this investment has risen since then to over $170 million.

Table 38.2 Companies with Substantial Holdings of Short-Term Securities

| | Nonoperating assets | Nonoperating assets | | |
| | Assets ($)* | As a percent of | | |
		Net assets	Value	Debt ($)
Eastman Kodak Company	310.3	33.8	5.6	—
Freeport Sulphur Company	39.2	18.1	11.5	—
International Nickel Company of Canada Ltd.	131.7	17.8	5.3	—
Libby-Owens-Ford Glass Company	121.7	43.5	16.5	—
Parke, Davis & Company	55.4	30.5	12.0	—
Phelps Dodge Corporation	145.4	15.2	20.5	—
General Motors Corporation	1,010.5	13.4	3.6	132.0
International Business Machines Corporation	724.0	31.4	5.0 3	70.4
Kennecott Copper Corporation	224.5	27.4	22.0	5.2
Minnesota Mining & Manufacturing Co.	57.9	10.2	2.0	8.5
Procter & Gamble Company	377.9	40.2	10.6	106.9

Assets and debt in millions of dollars.
* At year-end 1964, except for Procter & Gamble, whose assets are listed as of June 30, 1964.

While such investments have worked well for some companies, they often lack appeal for others. Modernization may not be called for. Expanding facilities and production may not be profitable if growth in market demand is limited. Cash acquisitions of attractive and compatible companies may be impracticable or prohibited by antitrust regulation. Investments in other corporations or marketable U.S. Treasury securities usually provide only a modest return on investment. Consequently, many firms find these methods of exploiting surplus capital neither satisfactory nor feasible. Moreover, these procedures may utilize only part of the redundant equity.

Because of the difficulties of profitably employing surplus capital in the company and/or distributing redundant equity funds to stockholders through dividends, a surprisingly large number of corporations have accumulated substantial holdings of marketable short-term securities to absorb redundant capital resources. The roster of such companies includes several having no long-term debt. Table 38.2 presents data for a few of these companies.

Reducing the Equity Base

Rather than accumulating liquid assets with only limited returns, financial managers may find that a better case can be made for repurchase- of a company's own common stock. For instance:

> Following the transfer of its computer division to Bunker-Ramo Corporation, a joint venture with Martin-Marietta, TRW Inc. (formerly Thompson Ramo Wooldridge Inc.) received $17.4 million, approximately 8% of the total market value of its outstanding common stock. The company then made a tender offer for 250,000 of its common with an expected cost of $14 million. According to Chairman J. D. Wright: "The company now has funds in excess of its operating requirements for the foreseeable future. After considering various alternatives for the use of these funds, we have concluded that the purchase of additional shares of common stock would be more beneficial to shareholders from the standpoint of earnings improvement per share."[4]

For many companies with existing or prospective holdings of low- and fixed-income securities, the repurchase alternative offers significant advantages to the common shareholder. But when managers or investors analyze the choice between expanding the company's operations and reducing its equity base, what standards should they use? I shall develop such a standard in the next section.

To begin, let us specify an ideal. A capital expenditure should:

- Be of significant size.
- Utilize the experience and skills of management without making undue demands on executive time and energy.
- Use existing channels of distribution and serve familiar markets.
- Require no substantially new technical or production skills.
- Be based on highly reliable projections of future business developments.
- Be limited to a specific capital expenditure.
- Return significant profits quickly.

These "impossible" requirements can often be met, I believe, with repurchase of common shares. To demonstrate this, I shall describe a method of assaying the value of capital expenditures by comparing the benefit to the stockholders of increasing productive assets with the benefit of reducing the equity base. This appraisal index will be called the "stockholder standard."

---

[4]*The Wall Street Journal*, March 3, 1964.

Deriving the Standard

Table 38.3 identifies the increase in per-share earnings which the management of a hypothetical company obtains by reducing the equity base by repurchasing common stock. It is assumed that $30 million is spent to buy 909,000 shares. For realism, the average cost of shares is assumed to be 110% of the prevailing market price. The gain in earnings per share for the present year (1965) is $0.20. To obtain an equal gain in earnings per share by spending the same $30 million on productive facilities would require an after-tax return of 6.7%. The calculation is made as follows:

$$\frac{\$0.20 \times 10,000,000 \text{ shares}}{\$30,000,000} = 6.7\%$$

Obviously, if the $30 million were spent for new productive new facilities, they could not be expected to return profits in the first year; it is highly doubtful that the facilities could even be completed in the first year. Over a period of years, however, an investment in plant and equipment would presumably be profitable; so the entire future stream of profits must be considered. This is done by present-value analysis.

Present-value analysis should also be used to identify the comparable benefits of reducing the equity by repurchasing shares. Unfortunately, profits in the distant future are not susceptible to easy or accurate prediction, and management will wisely avoid making tenuous estimates. However, we can use a reasonable, simple, and more reliable shortcut by estimating the improvement in earnings per share for the fifth year hence (or fourth or sixth year, if management finds a different time period more appropriate), and consider this one year's increase to be equal to the total stream of all future earnings-per-share increases discounted to their present value.

In Table 38.3 the fifth-year gain in earnings per share is $0.25, or the equivalent of an 8.3% after-tax return ($0.25 times 10 million shares, divided by $30 million investment). Alternative investments can then be appraised by discounting their future after-tax returns by this investment-return figure. In effect, 8.3% becomes what is often called an "opportunity cost." Its significance is this: if corporate funds spent on the repurchase of common stock return 8.3% after taxes, this is a more profitable outlay for shareholders than investments in productive facilities expected to yield a lower present-value return.

Table 38.3 Financial Effects of Buying Back Stock in a Hypothetical Case

Assumptions: 5% trend growth in earnings; market price is 15 times earnings; $30 million of available funds required to buy back 909,000 shares at 110% of market price.

	1965	1966	1967	1968	1969	1970
Earnings ($)	20,000,000	21,000,000	22,100,000	23,200,000	24,3000,000	25,500,000
Earnings per share:						
With 10,000,000 shares	2.0	2.10	2.21	2.32	2.43	2.55
With 9,091,000 shares	2.20	2.31	2.44	2.56	2.68	2.80
Dividends (60% of earnings)	12,000,000	12,600,000	13,300,000	13,900,000	14,600,00	15,300,000
Dividends per share:						
With 10,000,000 shares	1.20	1.26	1.33	1.39	1.48	1.53
With 9,091,000 shares	1.32	1.39	1.46	1.53	1.61	1.68
Increased produced by repurchase in:						
Earnings per share	0.20	0.21	0.23	0.23	0.25	0.25
Dividends per share	0.12	0.13	0.13	0.14	0.15	0.15

Table 38.4 Stockholder Standards for Various Growth Rates

Price/earnings	Growth rate (%)	Stockholder standards
30	10	5
27	9	5
24	8	6
21	7	6.85
18	6	7.25
15	5	8.25
13	4	9.25
11	3	10
10	2	11

The increase in earnings per share is the stockholder standard by which investment opportunities can be judged from the shareholders' point of view. Projects which improve on the stockholder standard should be undertaken when feasible; others should be rejected unless qualitative factors override the mathematical evaluation. When managers deviate from the standard, they should do so explicitly and intentionally.

In Table 38.4 the stockholder standard is calculated for a variety of possible growth rates and price-earnings ratios. While these combinations of rates and ratios obviously do not cover all possible circumstances in industry, they do suggest the range in standards for varying situations. Each company should calculate its own stockholder standard using the price-earnings ratio of its own stock and its own expected growth rates.

Use and Significance

A policy of repurchasing stock guided by the stockholder standard has all the advantages of the perfect capital expenditure described previously, but it does have important drawbacks for some managers. Repurchasing common shares reduces corporate net assets as well as incoming earnings and cash flow. Moreover, the stockholder standard is not based on management's principal guide to investment decisions: cash flow. However, if comparing the stockholder standard to present-value cash flow seems like comparing apples and oranges, this incompatibility can be overcome by generating a standard that relates to cash flow rather than to earnings by substituting the expected increase in cash flow per share for earnings per share in the scheme shown in Table 38.3.

While the stockholder standard can be a useful guide to managers striving to sustain an efficient use of corporate capital for the long-term benefit of the owners, more powerful measures appear to be warranted before many corporations will be using equity capital efficiently. These are measures that will change the capital structure in a desired way, develop "reverse dilution," and concentrate the power of equity capital by replacing redundant equity funds with fixed-cost capital. The next section will be focused on this question.

Rationalizing Capital

The most important use of common stock repurchases—and the most widely applicable—is the valuable flexibility provided to financial managers who are seeking ways to develop a rational capital structure which will meet the corporation's present and future requirements while optimizing the long-term wealth and income of the owners.

A rational capital structure may be described as one having the size and mix of capital that would be selected if the corporation were being fully recapitalized— if the slate were clean. Such a capital structure would have as its primary objective the long-range enhancement of stockholder wealth and income and would be based on the internal requirements of the firm after considering developments in the national or world economy, the industry with which the company is associated, and the markets to which it sells its goods and services.

The obvious and substantial differences in existing capital structures of large companies (see Table 38.5) are too great to be explained away as just differing opinions as to the optimum amount and composition of capital to enhance the stockholders' long-term interests while meeting the present and future requirements of the enterprise. Apparently, customs and traditions are going unchallenged. There seems to be too little awareness of the potentials of revised capital structures.

An example of a company that did see these potentials is Indian Head Mills: An unusual, but not unique, opportunity to exploit archaic capitalization was seen by the Indian Head Mills management. President James Robison was determined to create a rational capital structure in the equity-dependent textile industry and did so by substituting funded debt and preferred stock for the redundant equity capital in the firms he acquired. These were the exciting results: per-share earnings and dividends rose rapidly and with a higher price-earnings ratio, the market value of common equity zoomed ten-fold in less than four years!

Table 38.5 Variations in Debt–Equity Ratios in Various Industries

Industry	Company	(%)
Automobiles	American Motors)	0.0
	Chrysler	21.6
Chemicals	E. I.- du Pont de Nemours	0.0
	Air Products & Chemicals	48.0
Drugs	Parke, Davis	0.0
	Baxter Laboratories	48.0
Nonferrous Metals	International Nickel	0.0
	Cerro	15.0
Steel	Bethlehem Steel	8.8
	Wheeling Steel	32.1
Paper	International Paper	0.0
	Mead	23.0
Oil	Skelly Oil	0.1
	Sinclair Oil	29.0

The changes in capital that can be made by other companies in other industries may not be so dramatic, but nonetheless they can be eminently worthwhile. And effecting these changes does not require unwanted mergers.

Cost Analysis

How far is it profitable to go in buying back stock? Let us begin with a well-known concept in financial management. The traditional "weighted average" cost-of-capital analysis presupposes the existence of an optimum mix of debt, preferred stock, and common equity such that any change in the amount of one type of capital leads eventually to a proportionately equal change in all. This approach precludes the possibility that changing the capital mix can change the long-term cost of capital except in the special situation where the existing structure is substantially out of proportion to the optimum mix. In this "special" case, realigning the composition of capital can change the overall cost of capital.

The substantial decline in debt and preferred capital in recent years suggests that capital mix has been significantly skewed away from the optimum balance toward heavy equity usage, and that the special case in which rearranging the composition of capital will change the overall cost is actually becoming the general case today.

When a corporation has surplus equity capital, the true cost of this capital to the stockholders is the opportunity cost of not repurchasing common shares in the stockholder standard. A comparison of the stockholder standard to the cost of senior capital indicates the degree to which stockholder wealth and income can be advanced by reducing equity and increasing debt and preferred stock, that is, by moving the capital mix back toward the optimum through "reverse dilution." The point to stop borrowing is when the difference between debt cost and the return on repurchase becomes narrow and/or the level of future debt charges seems unwise in view of anticipated cash flows.

As we have seen, when the stockholder standard exceeds the after-tax cost of debt and/or preferred stock, equity should be reduced while debt and/or preferred stock are increased. What may startle most readers is this: even at a very high price-earnings ratio, the stockholder standard can be significantly higher than the cost of either debt or preferred would be. (The situations portrayed in Table 38.3 illustrate this.) Thus, even in an extreme case, reducing equity by repurchasing shares may well improve the position of the common stockholder.

Finding the Optimum

Identifying the optimum capital structure involves two basic steps:

1. Identifying and comparing relevant costs for debt, preferred, and common stock.
2. Using these costs as guides in determining the most desirable capital mix and the corporation's financial requirements.

While the economics of repurchasing common stock make a good case for maximum use of debt and preferred stock, determination of that maximum can only be made by consideration of the debt capacity of the corporation. Therefore, a rational capitalization will be consistent with management requirements (with debt not in excess of corporate capacity and with stockholder objectives with equity not in excess of corporate needs).

A management anticipates future changes in the company and its business position, the optimum or "target" capital structure will change over time. Every shift in either the company or its surroundings offers the possibility that adaptive, responsive adjustments ought to be made in the total amount or the mix of existing capital. Consequently, a regular review which will identify changing financial needs and capacities must be integrated with a continuing program of adaptation to change.

Role of Repurchasing

Repurchasing provides valuable flexibility to managers striving to develop an optimum capital structure. The number of outstanding common shares can be reduced in several ways:

1. *Tender offers*—For example, American Radiator Company acquired over 10% of its common shares through a tender offer in 1963, using a prime rate bank loan of $20 million to provide the necessary funds.[5]
2. *Block purchases*—In late 1964, General Fireproofing Company purchased 121,558 shares (17%) of its own common from Rockwell-Standard Corporation following approval by a special stockholders' meeting.[6]
3. *Regular purchases in the open market*—Amerada Petroleum Corporation had acquired over 2 million (15.5%) of its shares by the end of 1964.[7]
4. *Exchanging marketable securities*—During 1964, Emhart Manufacturing Co. exchanged 27,621 shares of its holding in Monsanto Chemical Company for 39,800 of its common shares held by a mutual fund.[8]
5. *Exchanging senior securities*—Early in 1964, Ling-Temco-Vought, Inc. offered to exchange a combination of $7.5 million and 500,000 shares of convertible preferred stock for 1.5 million shares of common.[9]

As the foregoing suggests, financial managers have a variety of methods available to them so equity capital can be reduced considerably and conveniently. It should not be treated as a fixed or inflexible portion of the corporation's capital structure.

Market Reaction

Before embarking on a repurchase program, each management should consider carefully the impact that both the procedure and the objectives

---

[5]*Moody's Industrials*, Section I, October 8, 1964.
[6]*The Wall Street Journal*, December 22, 1964.
[7]*Barron's*, August 17, 1964, p. 9.
[8]*Business Week*, November 21, 1964, p. 180.
[9]*The Wall Street Journal*, May 29, 1964.

of repurchasing are likely to have on the price-earnings ratio of the company's common stock. Although executives may conclude from a brief consideration of repurchasing that the price-earnings ratio will decline if per-share earnings growth derives in part from reducing shares rather than wholly from increasingly profitable operations, it seems more likely that if investors and their professional advisers clearly understand the reasons behind a repurchase program, they will look favorably on reacquiring shares either to restructure capitalization or to provide effective discipline for capital expenditures. In fact, the higher rate of earnings-per share growth resulting from a reduction of the equity base may well increase the market valuation of the company's shares.

Since only knowledgeable investors can react intelligently, management should accept responsibility for educating stockholders as to the objectives of capital policy and should inform them regularly of both the practices the company follows and the results achieved.

Prior to implementing a repurchase program, management should seek the advice of legal counsel on such matters as state laws, corporate powers, authorization, and disclosure to the Securities and Exchange Commission and to the stock exchanges. Investment bankers can provide helpful advice to management regarding details of the actual buying program like daily volume limits, pricing, and selection of brokers for continuing open-market purchase programs, or regarding the appropriate terms and procedures for tender offers.

Conclusion

In recent years, substantial cash flows have altered the capitalization of many corporations and produced an uneconomically high proportion of equity capital. Consequently, reorganizing corporate capital to regain an optimum capital mix will often mean buying back common stock. This may lead to important improvements in shareholder wealth and income. The stockholder standard described in this article can be a useful guide to appraising capital costs and capital budgeting from the investor's point of view.

Retiring common stock is not as simple or routine as retiring debt and preferred; the acquiring company is dealing with its owners rather than creditors, and equitable treatment must replace the philosophy of *caveat emptor*. However, the problems are usually not nearly so great as are the potential advantages to the stockholders.

It is widely known that industrial corporations have been "out of the market" for new equity capital for several years because capital requirements have been increasingly supplied by substantial retained earnings. The analysis of this article suggests strongly that many managements should now return to the equity markets, not as sellers but as buyers of their common stock, to eliminate excess equity, to rationalize capitalization, and to discipline capital budgeting. Using repurchasing, managers may be able to find new ways to act in the interest of the long-term common stock investor by revitalizing equity capital.

Source: *Harvard Business Review*, July–August, 1965.

39

Anti-Trust, Bank Mergers, and the PNB Decision

For this final piece, a bit of explanation seems called for, particularly since it has nothing to do with investing. One 1963 morning, I got a call in my dorm room at Harvard Business School from the assistant to my favorite teacher, Charles M. "Charlie" Williams, saying: "Professor Williams wants to see you in his office . . . this afternoon . . . to discuss your paper." My heart sank. Was it really so bad that he felt we had to discuss it in person?

When I arrived at the appointed time, I was told, "You can go right in. Professor Williams is expecting you." As I entered the office, he looked at me, held my paper above his head, smiled warmly and, in his West Virginia accent, said, "Pretty good!" What a relief! He went on, "Could get published!" and soon gave me a short list of trade journals, none of which I'd ever heard of, and advised me to send copies to all and hope for the best.

Three months later, I got a call from my father. This was unusual. Dad called because he wanted to congratulate me. His law partner, John Ferry, had just come to his office to ask, "Anyone in your family named Charles?"

"Yes, my son Charley. Why?"

"I've been reading a rather interesting article and checked to see who was the author, saw he was an Ellis, and thought there might be a connection. It's quite interesting, so if you have not seen it, I thought you might like to see

it—so I brought it along." Dad was more than interested. He was delighted and that's why Dad had called me.

A little background will explain. When Dad was at Yale, he was Managing Editor of the Yale Daily News. He had a great experience and hoped I would follow in his footsteps and have the satisfaction of seeing my work earn a byline. But, I had decided to join the student radio station instead, so there would be no byline. Now, at last, I did have a byline—even if only in a specialized journal. As anyone with a father would recognize, if Dad was pleased, I was delighted.

For me, the consequential result would be that this experience, thanks to Charlie Williams and John Ferry, launched me on a lifelong journey of writing, and as physicist Richard Feynman so aptly put it, "figuring it out." As I've learned, the discipline of writing for publication starts with thinking how to figure out an interesting question.

"**N**o one will be more surprised by this decision than the Department of Justice," wrote Associate Justice Harlan, commenting for the minority on the majority decision of the Supreme Court that the merger of the Philadelphia National Bank and the Girard Trust Corn Exchange Bank was in violation of Section 7 of the Clayton Act and therefore not lawful.

While the Justice Department probably was the *most* surprised by this decision, many official and private observers also were surprised. They included, among others, the Chairman of the Senate Banking and Commerce Committee, the Federal Judge about to try another bank merger case, the Comptroller of the Currency, the banking trade press, and two Associate Supreme Court justices.

Beside the initial expressions of surprise, this decision will have a profound influence on future bank mergers. The purpose of this article is to explain why informed observers were so surprised by the Supreme Court decision and to identify some of the implications of that decision for both economic and anti-trust policy.

Legislative History

The original laws governing corporate mergers and acquisitions were passed in response to the great merger movement at the turn of the century when major trusts were a recognized threat to the maintenance of a competitive business system. By 1914, the Sherman Act was believed inadequate to cope with most mergers because effective action could only be taken *after* a monopoly had been achieved.[1] The Clayton Act was passed to "arrest the creation of trusts, conspiracies, and monopolies in their incipiency and before consummation."[2] Section 7 of this Act prohibited the acquisition of the stock of one corporation by another: "where the effect of such acquisition may be to substantially lessen competition between the corporation whose stock is so acquired and the corporation making the acquisition, or to restrain such commerce in any section or community, or tend to create a monopoly of any line of commerce."[3]

While the provisions of the Act appeared effective at first, a series of restrictive court decisions left their application ineffective and the Justice Department sought "by regular efforts over a period of years"[4] to obtain stronger laws. Finally, in 1950, Section 7 of the Clayton Act was amended to prohibit any acquisition of *assets* which "might have the effect of substantially lessening competition or tending to create a monopoly in any line of commerce in any section of the country."[5] While this change gave the Justice Department the authority it had been seeking, the amendment applied only to corporations subject to the jurisdiction of the Federal Trade Commission and, therefore, did not include banking.[6] Thus, the Clayton Act applied only to bank mergers effected by stock acquisition, a method no longer used.

In virtually all post-war bank mergers, asset acquisition was the only method used,[7] and the Justice Department was powerless to contest any bank merger unless it resulted in a monopoly as defined in the Sherman Act. The difference between "monopoly" and "tends to lessen competition" made it much harder for the Department to demonstrate a violation of the Sherman Act than would have been the case with the Clayton Act, had it applied.

During the 1950s, an increasing number of bank mergers served to dramatize the Justice Department's campaign to obtain stronger and

---

[1] Report on Corporate Mergers and Acquisitions to the Committee on the Judiciary of the United States Senate, 1957.

[2] Ibid.

[3] 38 Stat. 730.

[4] See Note 1 above.

[5] See Note 1 above.

[6] Other industries were exempt from anti-trust when regulated by Federal agencies such as ICC, CAB, FPC, and the Maritime Commission.

[7] Hearings Before the Committee on Banking & Currency, USS 86th Cong. 1st Sess. on S.1062, a Bill to Amend the Federal Deposit Insurance Corporation Act, 1959.

broader authority over bank mergers. The President's Economic Report for 1956 called specifically for legislation in this area and Congress held initial hearings in the Spring. Representative Emmanuel Celler, who had proposed and supervised the 1960 amendment to Section 7 of the Clayton Act, sought to extend the same basic terms to cover banking. This Celler Bill would have given the Justice Department a veto over regulatory agency approvals and therein final authority on any bank merger.[8]

The three federal agencies charged with regulating banks and approving bank mergers[9] proposed an alternate bill which would sustain and formalize their authority to make the final decisions on bank merger applications. They expressed a willingness to consult with the Justice Department on anti-trust matters, but asked Congress to provide more liberal criteria for judging bank mergers than those which apply to industry generally.[10]

The terminology of the key phrases of these two bills differed in a significant manner. The Celler Bill provided that there should be no merger which would *substantially* lessen competition, while the Regulatory Agency Bill would have denied a merger only if it unduly lessened competition. The agencies contended that there could be a *substantial* lessening of competition that was not an *undue* lessening of competition.[11] In support of the agency contention that substantial need not mean undue, Senator Fulbright listed several situations in which a merger might substantially lessen competition and yet serve the public interest:

A. Reasonable probability of failure of bank to be acquired if it is not merged.
B. Inadequate, incompetent, or insufficient management.
C. Inadequate capital or unsound assets.
D. Uneconomic; too small to meet community needs.
E. Over-banking leading to unsound competition.[12]

---

[8]Hearings of the Subcommittee of the Senate Committee on Banking & Currency, USS 84th Cong. 2nd. Sess. on S.3911, a Bill to Provide Safeguards Against Mergers of Banks, etc.
[9]Responsibility for approving bank mergers is divided in this way: (a) Comptroller of the Currency if the result is a national bank, (b) Board of Governors of the Federal Reserve System if the result is a state member bank, and (c) FDIC if result is an insured non-member bank.
[10]See Note 8 above.
[11]See Note 8 above.
[12]Ibid.

While the Celler Bill had support from the Justice Department and the House Judiciary Committee, the Agency Bill was supported by its sponsors, by banking associations, and by the Senate Committee on Banking and Currency. In the end, those who advocated reliance on the bank supervisory agencies prevailed over those who favored the Justice Department. But it was not a quick and simple settlement. Before the final bill was enacted, three years had passed and both an attempt to exempt banks entirely from the anti-trust laws and an attempt to make banks explicitly subject to those laws had been proposed and turned down.[13]

The final compromise bill—an amendment to Section 6 of the Federal Deposit Insurance Corporation Act—enumerated the following criteria by which the regulatory agencies should evaluate a merger application:

A. Banking factors to consider:
  1. Financial history and condition
  2. Adequacy of capital structure
  3. Future earnings prospects
  4. Character of management
  5. Convenience and needs of community
B. Whether proposed merger may have the effect of lessening competition *unduly,* etc.[14]

Before passing on the merger's effect on competition, the regulatory agency was required to obtain an advisory letter from the Attorney General dealing with the competitive factors in the proposal. Thus, in the view of legislators, "the knowledge of the Anti-trust Division of the Department of Justice would be available to the banking agencies. However, we think it is wholly appropriate and necessary that the final decisions should be made by the respective bank supervisory agencies rather than the Department of Justice."[15]

The Senate Committee on Banking and Currency showed its determination to limit the authority of the Justice Department during the Committee's hearings when the representative of the Anti-trust Division was admonished at some length to restrict the advisory letters to the

---

[13] *George Washington Law Review,* Vol. 30.
[14] See Note 8 above.
[15] Ibid.

facts of the competition and not to become involved with considerations of public interest.[16]

Thus, the Congress ultimately passed an act which denied the Justice Department's petition for authority to control bank mergers, refused to extend the usual anti-trust regulations into banking, and specifically limited the Department's authority; and then provided a special means of controlling bank mergers and specified a novel set of criteria for judging the proprietary merger applications.

Even this brief review of legislative history makes Congressional intent quite clear and allows the reader to share with other observers the surprise of finding the Majority Opinion of the Supreme Court contend that there was real uncertainty regarding the scope of Section 7 and its applicability to bank mergers.

The key passage in the Majority Opinion argues that since Congress did not explicitly deny the applicability of the Sherman and Clayton Acts to bank mergers, it therefore could not have intended to make Section 7 inapplicable to bank mergers:

. . . our point is simply that since Congress passed the 1960 Bank Merger Act with no intention of displacing the enforcement of the Sherman Act against mergers—or even Section 7 against pure stock acquisitions by banks—continued application of Section 7 to bank mergers cannot be repugnant to the design of the 1960 Act.

It would be anomalous to conclude that Congress, while intending the Sherman Act to remain fully applicable to bank mergers and Section 7 of the Clayton Act to remain applicable to pure stock acquisitions by banks, nevertheless intended Section 7 to be completely inapplicable to bank mergers.

It was not Congress, but history that made the Clayton Act inapplicable. Bank merger "fashion" had changed and the new technique was not regulated by this Act. Recent bank mergers had been exclusively asset acquisitions and it was therefore solely to this merger method that the Congress felt obligated to direct its attention. Clearly, Congress intended something very different from a simple exercise in loophole plugging when it rejected the convenient plug offered by Representative Celler.

---

[16]See Note 7 above.

Special Experience of the Justice Department

Among those who would be surprised by the Supreme Court decision, Associate Justice Harlan singled out the Justice Department because this agency had been rebuffed not only by Congress, but also by the courts. Moreover, the Department seemed to have accepted defeat, at least for the present.

Prior to the Supreme Court decision, the Justice Department had failed on several occasions to win a courtroom reversal of a merger approved by a bank supervisory agency. The courts rejected the idea that anti-trust regulations should be applied with the same force and effect to a regulated industry as to one in the so-called "free enterprise" field. Moreover, the courts were disposed to rely on the bank supervisory agencies to which Congress had given authority and warned that the Attorney General must present substantial and convincing evidence to win a reversal of an agency approval.[17] Thus it appeared that the courts offered no hope of remedy for the Justice Department.

In its advisory letters, the Justice Department gave the appearance of the defeated contender withdrawing from the ring with nothing more than the hope of returning in the future for another, perhaps successful, bout. The advisory letters—which the new Act obliged the Justice Department to write to the bank supervisory agencies to advise on the effect of a proposed merger on competition—took a consistently negative position. While the banking agencies carefully discussed both pro and con, the Justice Department's comments were restricted to the disadvantages of a given merger. During the first year of the Bank Merger Act, the Department favored merger for only 3% of the applications which were eventually approved. The few mergers condoned by the Department were not only necessary to prevent a bank failure but were also cases in which the effect of the merger on any aspect of competition would be inconsequential.

In addition to taking such a persistently negative approach to these mergers that it was impossible to identify the Department's standard of acceptability, the Attorney General's letters also carefully avoided any mention of the banking business per se. By following this policy in the advisory letters, the Justice Department divorced itself from the eventual

---

[17]See particularly *U.S. v. Philadelphia National Bank* (E.D. Pa., 1962) 201 F. Supp. 348.

approval of the mergers and avoided both commitment to the decision-making process and acceptance of the special rules governing bank mergers.

Thus, prior to the Supreme Court's decision, the Justice Department had been explicitly limited to an advisory role by the Congress, had been rebuffed by federal courts, and had apparently refused to participate in an anti-trust process it could not control. It was the dramatic reversal of this history that led Justice Harlan to predict the Department's surprise.

It is an interesting matter of record that following the Supreme Court's decision, the Comptroller of the Currency received a letter from the Justice Department asking that two merger applicants "not be permitted to consummate their agreement until there has elapsed reasonable time to permit us to consider the significance and application the Supreme Court decision . . ."[18] Apparently, the Department had not anticipated and was not prepared for the surprise decision of the Majority Opinion. The writer is not an attorney and is therefore not qualified to pass judgment on the legal merits of the majority opinion. However, the decision bears significantly on the development of our national anti-trust policy and it seems appropriate to indicate the direction of recent developments. In a largely unnoticed sequence of decisions, the courts are developing a theory of anti-trust that protects small local business from abrupt intrusion by large and efficient competitors.[19] This theory is advocated by the Justice Department in a much broader application which tends to emphasize the number of competitors rather than the vigor of competition. Yet, the "public good" as represented by greater service at lower cost is not served by the number of competitors but by their ability and competitive determination to serve.

While preserving the motivation of competition is a traditional and fundamental objective of anti-trust policy, an overzealous campaign to preserve competition by preventing mergers and combinations may prevent firms from increasing their services and decreasing their costs. It was because determining the proper balance between protecting competition and promoting the expansion of bank services was a particularly difficult and highly specialized problem that the Congress refused to entrust the administration of bank mergers to the Justice Department.

---

[18] *The American Banker*, July 31, 1963.
[19] *Harvard Business Review*, May, 1963.

As the wise supervision of mergers becomes more dependent upon understanding the economics of a market area and the technical nature of a particular business, Congress may appropriately consider developing more sophisticated criteria for judging the proprietary of mergers than those now employed by the Department of Justice. A second effort to provide special treatment for bank mergers is appropriate now.

Index

Page numbers followed by *f* and *t* refer to figures and tables, respectively.

A

Abuse of power, share repurchase as, 300–301
Active "performance" investing. *See also* Loser's
  game of active investing
  academic research on, 16–20, 120–121, 164
  added value from, 164, 194
  alternatives to, 80–81
  and behavioral economics, 28–30
  beliefs about, xiv, 35–37
  defined, 94
  ETFs and indexing vs., 164–165
  fees in, 9–10, 30–34, 77–79, 199–201, 273
  future of, 71, 87
  historical returns from, 273
  history of, 5–14, 75–79, 114–116
  indicators of "progress" in, 93–97
  by institutional investors, 127–131, 174
  for institutional investors, 37–38, 45, 75,
    96–97, 115, 174
  investment guidelines on, 273–274
  justification of, 73–75, 84, 119–125
  for large funds, 94–97
  levels of decisions about, 64, 65, 161–162, 197
  liquidity in, 97
  manager selection policies for, 146
  market changes and, 20–28
  open operations in, 99–105
  portfolio diversification in, 167–170
  professional investors and end of, 111–117
  and profession vs. business of investment
    management, 77, 84–86
  rise and fall in popularity of, 73–87
  self-destruction of, 41–43, 93–97
  and social acceptance of innovation, 81–84
  successful investors in, 94–95
  as zero-sum game, 17, 81, 158

Added value, 65, 164, 194
Advertising of funds, 122
A.G. Becker & Co., 76, 184
Agent–principal conflict, 135
Alternative investments, 147, 153–155
Ambiguity effect, 28
Amerada Petroleum Corporation, 292, 311
American Funds, 174
American Radiator Company, 311
Analytic models, from other professions,
    181–185
Anti-trust policy, 315–323
  Bank Merger Act, 319–320
  Celler and Regulatory Agency Bills, 318–320
  history of, 316–320
  Justice Department's enforcement of, 317–323
  Sherman and Clayton Acts, 316–317
Appearance and reality, 191–197
  of beating the market, 194–195
  Dad's lessons on differentiating, 191–192
  and investment counseling, 195–197
  and investment program creation, 66–68
  and key propositions in investment
    management, 192–193
  of manager performance, 193–194
Armour, Tommy, 37, 39, 44, 65, 173–175
Assets, fees as percentage of, 30–31, 52, 78, 116,
    122–123, 199, 272
Asset gathering, 54
Asset growth, 186
Asset mix:
  changing, 70
  counseling clients on, 195–196
  level of decisions about, 63, 65, 161, 196, 197
  and long-term success, 192
  for retirement funds, 249
Avon Products, 289

B

Baker Weeks, 200
Balanced manager paradigm, 219
Banks, pension management by, 8–9,
    75–76, 200, 216
Bank mergers, 315–323
Bank Merger Act (1960), 319–321
Bank of International Settlements, 261
Barker, Robert, 144
Base rate fallacy, 28
Bear markets, 37, 152–153
Beating the market, 33–34, 36
    in active investing, 74, 76, 112, 115, 131
    appearance and reality of, 193–195
    changing beliefs about, xiv, 20, 22–23
    defining mission as, 49–53
    investment guidelines on, 273–274
    liquidity and, 265–266, 266f
    in loser's game, 43–44
    rise of professional investors and, 114, 159
Becker Securities, 38
Behavioral economics, 28–30, 68–69
Beliefs:
    about active investing, 35–37
    of investment committee members, 136
    in investment management field, xiv–xv
    resistance to changing, xv, 30, 35–36, 163, 245
Bell System, 239
Berkeley, George "Bishop," 121, 236
Berkshire Hathaway, 169, 174
Berra, Yogi, 187
Bismarck, Otto von, 234–235, 245
Black swan events, 155
Block transactions, 7, 8, 76, 105, 311
Blue-chip stocks, 75, 115
Board of Governors, Federal Reserve, 262, 318n9
Bonds:
    capital preservation with, 257–258
    changing beliefs about, xiv–xv
    converting, to conservative common
        stock, 258–259
    for institutional investors, 144, 251–259
    investment guidelines on, 275
    for long-term investors, 251–259, 261–263
    and Prudent Man Rule, 252–253
    retirement funds invested in, 249, 261–263
    and risk of economic depression, 253–255
    yield on equities vs., 255–257, 262
Boston Red Sox, 177
Bower, Marvin, 208
Broker research, 102–104
Bronowski, Jacob, 282
Bubbles, 186–187

Buffett, Warren, 79, 169, 174, 179, 197, 223, 225,
    237, 267, 272, 290
Bull markets, 41, 115, 239
Bunker-Ramo Corporation, 304
Business managers, performance of, 25–26, 208
Business of investment management:
    conflict between profession and, 119, 208
    ordering priorities for, 54–55
    performance investing and, 77, 84–86
    performance of, 159–160, 181
    success in, 213–214
Business strategy, 209–210

C

Capital gains, 288, 298
Capital preservation, 100, 257–258
Capital productivity, 100
Capital structure, 308–311
Cash drag, 158, 266
Cash flow, stockholder standard for, 307
Celler, Emmanuel, 318, 320
Celler Bill, 318–320
CFA Institute, xv, 282
Chamberlain, Neville, 235
Chartered Financial Analyst certification, 21–22,
    21f, 50, 99, 113, 282
Checking accounts, 61–62
China, 111
Choice-supportive bias, 28
Christie, Agatha, 127, 139
Chrysler Corporation, 302
Churchill, Winston, 114
Churchman, C.W., 204
Clausewitz, Carl von, 222–224
Clayton Antitrust Act, 317, 318, 320
Clients, at successful firms, 91, 213
Coca-Cola, 169
College savings, 61–62
Common stock. See also Share repurchases
    converting bond portfolios to, 258–259
    intrinsic value of, 284–285
    reducing outstanding shares of, 311
    retirement funds invested in, 249
    speculation in, 286–288
    yield on bonds vs., 255–257, 262
Communication, 103, 104, 142–143,
    210–211, 226
Compensation, 124, 212–213
Competent Stranger thought experiment,
    278–279
Competition:
    in active/performance investing, 97, 113–114
    as factor in antitrust decisions, 319–320, 322

and following optimal investment policy, 69–71
  for investment firms, 207
  manager performance relative to, 158, 159, 175
Compounding, 247–249, 275–276
Comptroller of the Currency, 316, 318n9, 322
"Computer People," culture of, 203–206
Computing Tabulating Recording Co., 286–287
Confirmation bias, 28, 68
Consolidated Gas of New York, 287
Consolidation Coal Company, 302
Cook, James, 183
Corporate tax cut, 291–293
Cost analysis, for share repurchase, 309–310
Creative excellence, 92
Credit card debt, 248–249
Culture, 24, 84, 203–206

D

Darwin, Charles, xv, 1, 2, 73, 81
Data overload, 210–211
Debt:
  credit card, 248–249
  share repurchase and, 300
Debt–equity ratio, 308–309, 309t
Decision making:
  about innovations, 82
  big decisions at investment firms, 92, 209–210
  Warren Buffett on, 169, 267, 272
  diary of, 271
  guidelines for, 275
  by investment committees, 101–102
  investment history as basis for, 273
  learning from past, 178–179
  levels of investor, 63–65, 161–162, 196–197
  managers' presentation of, 132
  J.P. Morgan on reasons for, 192
  pension funds' delegation of, 227–231, 228t, 229t
  and taking action, 174–175
  uncertainty in, 95
Defeatism, share repurchase as, 299
Defined-benefit pension plans, 57–58, 239, 240, 245–246
Defined-contribution pension plans, 57, 58, 239–242, 245–246
Depression, bonds and risk of, 253–255
Derivatives, 201
Diary of investment decisions, 271
Dickens, Charles, 68
Disney, 169
Distribution (12-b) fees, 31–32, 79

Diversification:
  guidelines on, 271–272
  with index funds, 16, 17
  for institutional investors, 58, 134, 146–148, 189
  for leaders of investment firms, 54–55
  for long-term investors, 262–263
  portfolio, 167–170, 189
Dividend income, 255–257, 302
DLJ (Donaldson, Lufkin & Jenrette), 200, 281
Dodd, David, 155
DOL (US Department of Labor), 239, 246
Donaldson, Lufkin & Jenrette (DLJ), 200, 281
Drucker, Peter, 89–92, 143, 160, 209
Durand, David, 285

E

Earnings per-share, 301, 305–308
"Easy action," 266–267
Economy, benefits of active investing for, 123–125
Efficient market hypothesis, 16. *See also* Market efficiency
80/20 Rule, 29–30, 84, 128
Einstein, Albert, 277
Emerson, Ralph Waldo, 130
Emhart Manufacturing Co., 311
Employee Retirement Income Security Act, *see* ERISA
Employer matching, in retirement plan, 247
Employer stock, 401(k) investments in, 240
Employment Act (1946), 253–254
Endowment funds:
  bond investments for, 251–259
  investment committees of, 137–138
  margin of safety for, 68
  Prudent Man Rule for trustees of, 252, 253
Endowment model, 153–155
Enron Corporation, 237, 240
Equity capital, excess, 295–297, 301–304
Equity mix, decisions about, 64, 161, 197
ERISA (Employee Retirement Income Security Act), 228, 239, 246
Errors:
  classic mistakes by investors, 274–275
  conformance to avoid, 185
  correcting investment professionals', 58–59
  in defining mission, 49–53
  diversification to protect against, 169
  in investment counseling, 55–58
  by investment professionals, 39, 47–59
  in ordering of priorities, 53–55

ETFs, *see* Exchange-traded funds
Evolution, theory of, 1, 73, 163, 164
Exchanges of securities, 311
Exchange-traded funds (ETFs):
   as alternative to active investing, 80
   fees and, 201–202
   growth of, 15, 15*f,* 85, 86*f*
   in winning strategy, 163–165
Expansion, 211, 302–303

F

Fairness, 212–213, 243–244
Fama, Eugene, 16–17, 19, 32, 81
Familiarity bias, 132
Fastow, Andrew, 237
Fat tails, probability curves with, 155
FDIC (Federal Deposit Insurance Corporation),
   318n9, 319–320
Federal Reserve, 261–262, 318n9
Federal Trade Commission, 317
Fees:
   in active/performance investing, 9–10, 30–34,
      77–79, 199–201, 273
   appearance vs. reality of, 191, 196–197
   attracting good clients with high, 91–92
   changing views of, xiv, 2, 30–34, 189, 199–202
   defense of, for active investing, 122–123
   institutional, 200–201
   and institutional underperformance, 130–131
   investment guidelines on, 272–273
   mutual fund, 31, 32*t,* 67
   real measurements of, 52, 78–79
   at successful firms, 209
   12b-1, 31–32, 79
   and value proposition for professional
      investors, 116
Ferris, Richard, 18
Ferry, John, 315–316
Feynman, Richard, xiii, 316
Fidelity, 75
Financial security, in retirement, *see*
   Retirement security
Fisher, Philip, 169
Followers, 3
Ford Foundation, 144
Foreign earnings, corporate tax and, 292
401(k) plans:
   borrowing from, 248–249
   impact of delaying retirement on, 236
   investment advice for individuals with,
      239–241, 246
   investment policy for individuals with, 66–67
   and multimarket multiproduct paradigm,
      218

Fundamental research, 289–290
Fund executives, underperformance caused
   by, 135–136

G

GEICO, 169
General Fireproofing Company, 311
General Motors, 8, 183, 216, 298
Germany, retirement age in, 233–235, 245
Girard Trust Corn Exchange Bank, 316, 322
Globalization, 50, 123–124
Global warming, 163–164
Goal conflict, 119, 208
Goldman Sachs, 295
Governance, by investment committees,
   139, 141–146
Graham, Ben, 6 7, 68, 155, 281–290
Grand Strategy, 221–226
Great Depression, 61–62, 93
Greenwich Associates, xv, 30, 89, 228–229
Growth, firm, 211
Growth liabilities, 228

H

Hanna, Mark, 187
Harlan, John Marshall, II, 316, 321, 322
Harrison, John, 183
Harvard Business School, xiii–xv, 269, 291, 315
Hedge funds, 13–14, 13*f,* 50
Heterophilous social systems, 4n5
Hinton, Longstreet, 183
Homophilous social systems, 4n5

I

IBM, 287
Illusion of skill, 24–26
Illusion of validity, 130
Incentives, for open operations, 105
Income, dividend, 255–257, 302
Income received, fees as percentage of, 9
Incremental returns, fees as percentage of, xiv,
   31–32, 52, 79, 116, 123, 200, 201, 273
Indexing and index funds:
   academic evidence supporting, 16–20, 120–121
   as alternative to active investing, 80, 81
   and behavioral economics, 28–30
   changing beliefs about, xiv, 4–5
   costs of active management vs., 78–79
   fees and, 30–34, 131, 202
   growth of, 14–15, 83–85, 86*f,* 115–117
   historical returns from, 273

for institutional investors, 151, 230
investment guidelines on, 272
investor decisions about, 64, 161, 197
loser's game of active management vs., 43–44
market changes favoring, 20–28
in winning strategy, 163–165
Index Participation Shares, 15n27
Index replication, by active managers, 121–122, 168, 189
Indian Head Mills, 308
Individual investors. *See also* Long-term investors; Professional investors
as amateurs, 158–159, 194
bond investments for, 261–263
classic mistakes of, 274–275
liquidity for, 265–267
successful, 94–95
views on fees of, 199–202
Individual retirement accounts (IRAs), 236
Industrial corporations, share repurchase for, 295–296, 313
Inflation, 254, 261–262
Influentials, 2–3, 164
Information:
access to/distribution of, 50, 74, 111, 113, 188, 207
Ben Graham on need for, 283–284
in open operations, 102–103
for performance investors, 94
Informationless trading, 159, 194
Innovation:
dynamics of, 2–5, 82f, 164
in portfolio management, 89–92
social acceptance of, 81–84
Innovators, 2–3, 164
Insight on investment:
from Tommy Armour, 173–175
and developing your own plan, 171–172
from Peter Drucker, 89–92
for future generations, 269–276
from Ben Graham, 281–290
from Joseph K. Klingenstein, 109–110
from Munich Marathon, 107–109
at successful firms, 213
from Ted Williams, 177–180
Institutional fees, 200–201
Institutional investors. *See also* Endowment funds; Pension funds
active investing for, 37–38, 45, 75, 96–97, 115, 174
bonds for, 144, 251–259
dependency in decision making by, 3n4
indexing by, 230
investment committees of (*see* Investment committees)

manager hiring/firing by, 129–130, 129f
market influence of, 41–42, 201
performance expectations of, 27, 80, 80f, 128
trading volume for, 113–114, 194
Institutional underperformance, 127–139, 141–142
evidence of, 128–131
fund executives as cause of, 135–136
investment committees as cause of, 136–139
investment consultants as cause of, 133–135
investment managers as cause of, 132–133
taking responsibility for, 139
Insurance companies, 8–9, 75
Intergenerational equity, 152
International investments, xiv, 112–113, 112t, 150
Intrinsic value, 284–286
Investments. *See also specific types*
performance of, as symptom of problem, 185–187
selection of specific, 179–180
time period for measuring performance of, 184–186
turnover in, 224–225, 272
Investment committees, 141–155
endowment model for, 153–155
in history of performance investing, 75
institutional underperformance caused by, 136–139
investing consultants and, 134–135
investment objectives of, 144–146
manager selection by, 51–52
mission of, 143–144
open operations vs. decisions from, 100–102
self-evaluation by, 146–151
spending rule for, 151–153
structure of, 142–143
Investment consultants:
on alternative investments, 154
committees' over-reliance on, 148–149
institutional underperformance caused by, 133–135
manager selection by, 10–11, 18–19, 133–135
in specialist manager paradigm, 217
Investment counseling:
and appearance vs. reality of investment management, 195–197
history of, 9
on investment policy selection, 70–71
and levels of investor decisions, 160–161
moving away from, 48–49, 52–53, 55–58
returning to, 189–190

Investment firms:
  big decisions at, 209–210
  communication at, 210–211
  compensation at, 212–213
  defining success for, 213–214
  good ideas and clients at, 213
  Grand Strategy for, 221–226
  growth and expansion for, 211
  in history of active investing, 76–77
  laws to improve performance of, 90–92
  professional and business goals of, 208
  professional development at, 210
  service-centric strategies of, 58–59
  strategic considerations for, 209
  structure of, 90, 212
  successful, 207–214
  turnover at, 212
Investment guidelines, 269–276
  on active management, 273–274
  and classic mistakes of investors, 274–275
  on diversification, 271–272
  on fees, 272–273
  on financial decision-making, 275
  on indexing, 272
  investment history, decisions based on, 273
  on investment programs, 274
  on long-term investing, 271
  on saving, 275
  stock prices, view of, 272
  on trading frequency, 272
Investment horizon, 263. See also Long-term
  investors
Investment management field. See also Business
  of investment management; Profession of
  investment management
  and analytic models for other professions,
    181–185
  appearance vs. reality in, 191–197
  behavioral economics and, 28–30
  changes in, xiv–xv, 1–34, 158
  cultures of Computer vs. Investment People
    in, 203–206
  and dynamics of innovation, 2–5
  early performance investing in, 5–14
  employment in, xiii–xiv
  fees in, 30–34
  growth of index funds in, 14–15
  investment performance as symptom
    in, 185–187
  key propositions in, 192–193
  levels of, 157–162
  market changes and, 20–28
  modern capital theory in, 229–231
  multimarket multiproduct paradigm
    in, 215–220

predicted future shortfalls in, 188–189
  research on active vs. passive investing, 16–20
  return to investment counseling in, 189–190
  signs of serious problems in, 181–190
  traditional vs. open operations in, 100–101
Investment managers (generally):
  changing, 70, 83, 129–130, 137
  firm tenure for, 212
  in history of active investing, 8–9, 76–77
  identifying first-rate, xiv, xv, 18–19, 27
  justification of active investing by, 73–75,
    84, 119–125
  number of, for institutional investors, 146–149
  open operations by, 99–105
  pension fund policy decisions by, 227–231,
    228t, 229t
  specialization for, 215–218
Investment manager performance:
  for active managers, 22–28, 33–35, 75, 77–79
  appearance vs. reality of, 193–194
  enhanced reporting of, 121
  expectations of, 80, 80f
  fees and, 201
  hiring/firing decisions based on,
    129–130, 129f
  institutional underperformance and, 132–133
  measures of, 167–168
  volatility and, 128
Investment manager selection:
  for active investing, 79
  informal system of, 5
  by investment consultants, 10–11,
    18–19, 133–135
  level of decisions about, 64, 161
  past performance as basis for, 51–52
  policies on, 145–146, 149
Investment objectives, 63, 67–68, 108–109,
  144–146
Investment philosophy drift, 187
Investment policy:
  committee's responsibilities for, 144, 145, 151
  creating, for clients, 63, 69–71
  pension funds' decisions about, 227–231
  staying committed to, 44, 160–161, 196
  thought experiment on setting, 277–279
Investment professionals. See also specific types
  culture of Computer People, 203–206
  errors made by, 47–59
  guidance from, for retirement security,
    237–242
  investment counseling by, 55–58
  mission of, 49–53
  values of, 48, 53–55
Investment program(s):
  competition and use of, 69–71

designing customized, 56–57, 61–71
developing your own, 171–172
and future of active management, 71
guidelines on, 274
helping clients design, 56–57
investors' self-knowledge in, 68–69
levels of investor decisions in, 63–65
market as distraction from, 66, 272
realities to integrate in, 66–68
winning triangle in, 63
Investor decisions, levels of, 63–65, 161–162, 196–197
IRAs (individual retirement accounts), 236

J

Jensen, Michael, 16
Johnson, Edwin C., 6
Justice, 243–244
Justice Department, 316, 317–323

K

Kahneman, Daniel, 24–26, 29, 84
Kelly, Walt, 70
Kennedy, John F., and administration, 291–293
Keynes, J. M., 5, 6
Klingenstein, Joseph K., 109–110
Kuhn, Thomas, 2, 4, 81, 83, 163

L

Large-cap funds, 17, 75, 94–97
Large-capitalization stocks, 74–75, 95–96, 117, 158
Law of small numbers, 114
Lay, Kenneth, 237
Leaders of investment firms, 54–55, 221–226
Learning, xv–xvi, 269–270
Leverage, 275
Lifecycle, of performance investing, 73–87, 95–96, 115–116
Life-cycle funds, 58
Life expectancy, 233–236, 247
Ling-Temco-Vought, Inc., 311
Liquidation, 299–300
Liquidity, 96, 97, 145, 265–267
Load funds, 32n55
Lodge, Henry Cabot, 225
Lombardi, Vincent, 40
Long-Term Capital Management, 155
Long-term investors, 69
bonds for, 251–259, 261–263
endowment model for, 155

guidelines for, 269–276
performance investors vs., 94
thought experiment on policy-setting for, 277–279
in traditional investment management, 100–101
Loser's games, winner's games vs., 37–41, 62–63
Loser's game of active investing, 33, 35–45, 50, 157
beliefs about, 35–37
future of, 71
and levels of investor decisions, 161–162
and self-destruction of winner's games, 41–43
strategies for winning, 44–45
Losses, 109–110, 124
Lucent Technologies, 240
Luck, 19, 25, 64, 79, 274

M

Mahan, Alfred Thayer, 225–226
Malkiel, Burt, 17, 30, 271
Managed economy, 254
Management, by investment committees, 142, 143
Mao Tse-tung, 225n3
Marginal cost of active management, 131
Margin of safety, 68, 155
Market(s):
average performance of, 249
Edwin C. Johnson on, 6
as distraction from investment program, 66, 272
fluctuations in, xv, 54, 67, 114, 145, 151, 251, 254
global integration of, 123–124
impact of Computer People on, 204
major changes in, 20–28, 188
portfolios constructed to withstand, 224
reaction of, to share repurchases, 311–312
and specialist manager paradigm, 217
Market efficiency:
Fama's hypothesis on, 16
Ben Graham on, 289–290
and history of active investing, 77, 79
increasing, 1, 50–51, 74
and returns for active management, 74, 165
as social good, 123–124
Market timing, xiv, 36, 70, 192, 265. *See also* Beating the market
Markowitz, Harry, 16
Martin-Marietta Inc., 304
Massachusetts, Prudent Man Rule in, 252
Massachusetts Investors Trust, 12
Maury, Matthew Fontaine, 183

Medicine, analytic model of, 182
Mencken, H.L., 168
Merrill Lynch, 76, 183
Micawber;s law, 68
Mies, van der Rohe, Ludwig, 44, 169
Minnesota, income tax in, 292
Mission:
　of investment committees, 138, 143–144
　of investment professionals, 49–53
Mitchell Hutchins, 200
Modern capital theory, 229–231
Money Game, see Active "performance" investing
Money market funds, 240, 249
Monsanto Chemical Company, 311
Moody's Utility Average, 255–257, 257t
Morgan, J.P., 131, 153, 192, 207
Morgan Bank, 200
Morgan Guaranty Trust, 183
Morningstar, 121
Morrison, Samuel Elliot, 37, 39, 44
Multimarket multiproduct paradigm, 215–220
Munich Marathon, 107–109
Mutual funds:
　demand for, 12–13
　fees for, 31, 32t, 67
　in history of active investing, 7–8, 75
　performance of, 11–13, 12f, 16, 81, 128
　switching, 160–161
　underperformance by, 23t, 24–28, 112–113,
　　112t, 157–158

N

National retirement security problem, 243–250
　addressing, with fairness and justice, 243–244
　and asset mix for retirement funds, 249
　current scope of, 244
　defined-benefit vs. defined-contribution
　　plans, 245–246
　five factors in retirement security, 247–248
　and retirement age, 245
　and Rule of 72 for compounding, 248–249
Natural resource companies, 292
Navigation, 183
Neff, John, 169
New York Edison Co., 287
New York Stock Exchange (NYSE):
　amateur investors in, 74, 158–159, 194–195
　"incorrect" prices on, 289
　institutional investors in, 188, 194
　professional traders in, 271
　share repurchases and trading volume, 298
　trading volume, 20–22, 21t, 50, 76, 112
Northwestern University, 61
NYSE, see New York Stock Exchange

O

Objectivity, 44–45
Ogilvy, David, 208
Open market transactions, repurchase, 311
Open operations by investment managers,
　　99–105
　incentives for, 105
　information for, 102–103
　investment committees vs., 101–102
　and staff analysts, 103–104
　and traders, 104–105
　traditional investment management
　　vs., 100–101
Operations research, 204
Opportunity costs, xiv–xv, 167–168,
　　251, 263, 305
Optimism bias, 29, 70
Optimum capital structure, 310–311
Organized knowledge, need for, 283–284
Ovid, 288

P

Pareto's Law (80/20 Rule), 29–30, 84, 128
Passive investing, 16–20, 122, 161. See also
　　Indexing and index funds
Past performance:
　enhanced reports of manager's, 132
　of investment strategies, 273
　manager selection based on, 51–52, 121
　predictive power of, 121, 193, 273
Past-purchase rationalization, 28
Patton, George S., 39
Payment acceleration, 293
Peel, Robert, 281
Pension Benefit Guaranty Corporation, 240
Pension funds:
　bond investments for, 251–259
　and fees, 200
　in history of active management, 8–10, 75–76
　investment committees of, 138
　policy decisions by, 227–231
　Prudent Man Rule for trustees of, 252, 253
　rate of return assumption for, 151
　and specialist manager paradigm, 216–217
Pension plans, defined-benefit vs.
　　defined-contribution, 239–242, 245–246
Performance-based investing, see Active
　　"performance" investing
Per-share earnings, from share repurchases,
　　305–308, 312
Peter Principle, 212
Philadelphia National Bank, 316, 322
Planning, strategy formation vs., 209–210

Polaroid Corporation, 240
Portfolio construction, for disruptive
    markets, 224
Portfolio diversification, 167–170
Portfolio management, 89–92, 101–102
Portfolio turnover rate, 42
Poverty, 124
Power law curve, 114
Price discovery, 74, 77–79, 84–85, 113–115, 122
Price-earnings ratios, 96–97, 257–258, 288
Princeton University, xv
Priorities, of investment professionals, 53–55
Private equity funds, 50
Professional development, 210
Professional investors, 111–117
    active investing by, 111–117
    difficulty of outperforming competition
        for, 113–114
    and history of active management, 19, 74,
        114–116, 119, 159, 165
    market changes due to increase in,
        20–28, 195, 271
    underperformance by, 112–113
    value proposition presented by, 116–117
Profession of investment management:
    conflict between business and, 119, 208
    Ben Graham on, 282–283
    performance investing and, 77, 84–86
    performance of, 159, 160, 181
    retirement security as problem for, 238–243
    success in, 214
Profitability, 25, 53, 100–105, 191–192
Prudent Man Rule, 252–253
Public policy, retirement security and, 240–244

Q

Qualified Security Analysts, 282–283

R

Railroad Retirement Act, 235
Ramo, Simon, 37–39, 44
Raskob, John J., 41
Rational capital structures, 308–311
Reality, appearance and, *see* Appearance
    and reality
Regulation Fair Disclosure (Regulation FD), 22,
    50, 74, 113
Regulatory Agency Bill, 318–320
Resistance to changing beliefs, xv, 30,
    35–36, 163, 245
Resources, identifying, 63, 67
Retirement age, 233–236, 245, 247

Retirement security:
    bond investments for, 261–263
    five factors in, 247–248
    guidance from investment professionals
        for, 237–242
    life expectancy, retirement age, and, 233–236
    as national problem, 243–250
    and need for investment counseling, 57–58
Returns, fees as percentage of, xiv, 31–32, 52,
    116, 123, 131, 199–200, 273
Revenue Act (1964), 291–293
Reverse dilution, 296–297, 297*t*, 310
Risk, underperformance and, 51
Risk-adjusted incremental returns, fees as
    percentage of, xiv, 31–32, 52, 79, 200
Risk management, 144, 145, 151, 188, 230
Risk tolerance, 69, 75, 168
R.J. Reynolds Tobacco Company, 302
Robison, James, 308
Rockwell-Standard Corporation, 311
Rogers, Everett, 3, 4, 82, 83
Roosevelt, Theodore, 225
Roth, Allen, 18
Rothschild, Baron, 284
Rule of 72, for compounding, 248–249,
    275–276
Russell 1000 Index, 120
Russell 2000 Index, 120
Ruth, Babe, 179

S

Sampling error, 186, 187
Samsonite Corporation, 14
Samuelson, Paul, 17–18
Saving, 247, 249, 275
Savings accounts, 62
Scudder, Stevens & Clark, 9, 77
SEC, *see* US Securities and Exchange
    Commission
Secular trends, identifying, 114
Securities. *See also* Bonds; Common stock
    exchanging of, 311
    short-term, corporate holdings in, 303, 303*t*
Security analysis, as profession, 282–283
Self-evaluation, investment committee, 146–151
Self-knowledge, 68–69, 178–179, 224, 274
Selling decisions, 44
Senate Committee on Banking and Currency,
    316, 319–320
Senior securities, exchanging, 311
Separate accounts, for fund executives,
    135–136
Servant leadership, 148
Service-centric investment firms, 58–59

Share repurchases, 295–313
    alternatives to, 301–304
    arguments against, 299–301
    benefits of reverse dilution, 296–297, 297t
    cost analysis for, 309–310
    market reaction to, 311–312
    and other methods of reducing shares, 311
    per-share earnings from, 305–308
    present practice, 297–298
    for rational capital structure, 308–311
Sharpe, Bill, 16
Sherman Antitrust Act, 316–317, 320
Short-term securities, corporate holdings
        in, 303, 303t
Shwed, Fred, 193–194
Siegel, Jeremy, 262
Signs, symptoms vs., 182
Silver, Nate, 11, 121
Skilling, Jeffrey, 237
Small-capitalization stocks, 120, 158
Small numbers, law of, 114
Smith, Adam, 5–7, 64
Snow, C.P., 203
Social Security benefits, xv, 234, 236, 249, 275
Society, benefits of active investing for,
        123–125
"Soft" decisions, 209
Sohio, 292
S&P 500 Index, 36–38, 43, 69, 157, 183–185
SPDRs (Standard + Poor's Depositary
        Receipts), 15n27
Specialist manager paradigm, 215–217
Speculation, 75, 189, 286–288
Spending, 151–153, 247–249
SPIVA (S&P Indices Versus Active) data, xiv
Staff analysts, 103–104
Standard Oil, 239
Standard + Poor's Depositary Receipts
        (SPDRs), 15n27
Standards, defining, 91
Stanley-Warner, 292
State Street Fund, 12
Stockholders, repurchase as unfair to, 301
Stockholder standard reappraisal index,
        304–308, 307t, 310
Stock prices:
    investor mistakes related to, 275
    long-term view of, 66, 272
    performance investing and, 96–97
    and rise of professional investors, 115
Strategy:
    investment firm, 209, 221–226
    investment program, 63
    phases of, 100
    planning vs. forming, 209–210

    tactics and, 222–225
    for winning at loser's game, 44–45
Stubbornness, 223–224
Subjective meaning, of numbers, 233–234
Sun Tzu, 224–225
Supreme Court, U.S., 316, 321–322
Surplus, distribution of, 302
Swensen, David, 68, 144, 225
Symptoms, signs vs., 182

T

Tactics, strategy and, 222–225
Target-date funds, 58
Taxes, 22n37, 291–293
Technology:
    for analysis, 182–184
    and culture of Computer People, 203–206
    taking advantage of, 225, 226
Tender offers, 311
Tenure, at successful firms, 212
Thomas, Lewis, 182
Tipping point, 3, 82
Tisch, Larry, 169
Tobin, James, 68, 152
Top Quartile results, xiv, 128, 149, 163
Total Financial Portfolio, xv, 263, 275
Traders, 94, 104–105
Trading frequency, 67, 189, 272
Trust, in professionals, 237–238
Trustees, Prudent Man Rule for, 252–253
TRW Inc., 304
Tsai, Gerry, 7
Turnover:
    investment, 224–225, 272
    and investment committee best practices,
        148–150
    investment manager, 149–150, 186, 212
    at successful firms, 212
12b-1 fees, 31–32, 79

U

UAW (United Auto Workers), 8, 216
UCLA (University of California, Los
        Angeles), 286
Uncertainty, 95, 222
Underperformance:
    and active investing, 43, 116–117
    for institutional investors, 127–139
    by investment firms, 207
    by investment managers, 186–189
    of mutual funds, 23t, 24–28, 112–113,
        112t, 157–158

by professional investors, 112–113
and risk, 51
United Auto Workers (UAW), 8, 216
US Department of Labor (DOL),
239, 246
US Securities and Exchange Commission
(SEC), 22, 74, 113, 238–239, 246, 312
US Treasury, 261, 262
University of California, Los Angeles
(UCLA), 286
U.S. Express Co., 286
U.S. Steel, 287
Utility function, 69
Utility industry, tax cuts in, 292

V

Values:
of investment firms, 210
of investment professionals, 48, 53–55
Value discovery, 85, 87
Value proposition, 77–78, 116–117, 131
Vanguard, 11–12, 14

W

Wall of money, 153
Washington Post Company, 169

Weighted average cost-of-capital analysis,
309–310
Wells Fargo, 14
West, Mae, 55, 160
Williams, Charles M. "Charlie," 315, 316
Williams, Serena and Venus, 62
Williams, Ted, 177–180
Winner's game(s):
achieving your objective in, 108–109
active investing as, 33–34, 41–42
correcting errors by investment
professionals in, 47–59
developing your own plan for, 171–172
indexing and ETFs in, 163–165
investment programs in, 61–71
loser's games vs., 37–41, 62–63
self-destruction of, 41–43
strategies for turning loser's game into, 44–45
Winning triangle, 63
Wolfe, Tom, 30
Woods, Tiger, 62
Wright, J. D., 304

Y

Yale University, xv, 68, 144, 183, 221, 269, 316
Yield, on bonds vs. equities, 255–257, 262
Young, Alan, 295